The Modest Ambition
of Andrew Marvell

The Modest Ambition of Andrew Marvell

A Study of Marvell and His Relation to
Lovelace, Fairfax, Cromwell, and Milton

Patsy Griffin

DELAWARE

Newark: University of Delaware Press
London: Associated University Presses

Associated University Presses
440 Forsgate Drive
Cranbury, NJ 08512

Associated University Presses
25 Sicilian Avenue
London WC1A 2QH, England

Associated University Presses
P.O. Box 338, Port Credit
Mississauga, Ontario
Canada L5G 4L8

PR3546
.G65
1995

The paper used in this publication meets the requirements
of the American National Standard for Permanence of Paper
for Printed Library Materials Z39.48-1984.

Library of Congress Cataloging-in-Publication Data

Griffin, Patsy, date
    The modest ambition of Andrew Marvell : a study of Marvell and his
relation to Lovelace, Fairfax, Cromwell, and Milton / Patsy Griffin.
        p.   cm.
    Includes bibliographical references and index.
    ISBN 0-87413-561-3 (alk. paper)
    1. Marvell, Andrew, 1621–1678.   2. Marvell, Andrew, 1621–1678—
Friends and associates.   3. Poets, English—Early modern,
1500–1700—Biography.   4. Lovelace, Richard, 1618–1658—Friends and
associates.   5. Cromwell, Oliver, 1599–1658—Friends and associates.
6. Milton, John, 1608–1674—Friends and associates.   I. Title.
PR3546.G65   1995
821'.4—dc20   95-733
                                                                            CIP

for
Eve and Patrick

Contents

Acknowledgments

Chapter 3 has appeared in part as an article, "'Twas No *Religious House* till now": Andrew Marvell's *Upon Appleton House*," which is reprinted by permission of *Studies in English Literature 1500–1900* 28, no. 1 (Winter 1988). Thanks are due as well to the University of Illinois Press for permission to use my article "Structural Allegory in Andrew Marvell's Poetry," *Journal of English and Germanic Philology* 91, 3 (July 1992). Acknowledgment is made to Routledge & Kegan Paul Inc. for permission to quote from *Archbishop William Laud* by Charles Carlton, copyright 1987.

I am grateful to Joseph H. Summers and Victoria Silver whose comments and suggestions were invaluable during this work's early stage as my dissertation at the University of Rochester.

The Modest Ambition
of Andrew Marvell

Introduction

WHAT Andrew Marvell's poetry reflects of his association with the poet Richard Lovelace, the retired Lord General Thomas Fairfax, the Protector Oliver Cromwell, and the poet John Milton constitutes the primary focus of this study. Involved in his ambition to "honor" these worthy men was a determination to portray them accurately and to present the situational truth as he saw it; yet he seems to have been determined as well to maintain his own integrity in that his evaluations of their works and days would ultimately measure most critically the integrity of their lives and their work.

Marvell's attraction to famous figures can hardly be ignored. What recommended him to them I take to be his wit and his intelligence. But we cannot know for certain; we know much more about the figures than we know about Marvell, who chose to be private. Aubrey's familiar comment that Marvell "loved wine [but] . . . he would never drinke hard in company, and was wont to say that, *he would not play the good-fellow in any man's company in whose hands he would not trust his life*"[1] describes a man who hesitates to be open, determines to be reticent. We do not have many statements of that sort; thus we resort to speculation and unquestioned assumptions. One such assumption has been that he had sufficient income to remain independent; in other words, his accepting tutorial positions and serving for twenty years as a Member of Parliament has rarely been regarded by literary critics as penurious necessity. Yet we speculate only on the reason for his deliberate reserve. Since he seems to have had to make his financial way through life in a way that never afflicted any of the famous figures with whom he associated, perhaps this had to do with his purposeful obscuring of himself. Perhaps. John Shawcross has discussed the "hidden self" of Marvell in explicating "The Definition of Love," which he sees as an expression of homosexuality.[2] Philip Larkin made the observation some time before about the same poem and commented that "many another" poem of Marvell "might bear such an interpretation."[3] Shawcross's conclusions present a coherence in a difficult poem, and help to explain why a poet so immersed in poetry as Marvell would keep his work under cover as he did. I think, however, that his keen intelligence and wit contribute in good part to what we perceive as his obscurity. In my desire to understand him better, I begin my study with the annals of Hull and what knowledge is available of his family life—not in itself unusual in a study of Marvell—but I see a similarity between what he early grew accustomed to and what he gravitated to in later life. His animosity to monarchs seems likely to have had its origin in his younger years, arising from Laud's repression of lecturers, a prohibition that jeopardized his father's position and his family's livelihood. Critics have assumed that his friendship with Lovelace was based on political agreement, an assumption not necessarily warranted by his poem addressed to Lovelace. Marvell surely surmised that his prefatory poem for the royalist Lovelace's poetry need not express his own political views, perhaps even required that he obscure his republicanism. The attraction to Lovelace may instead have sprung from Marvell's desire to be a poet; in support of this contention, I point out in my examination of "To His Noble Friend, Mr. Richard Lovelace, upon His Poems" that Marvell presents a definition of himself in the poem that holds true for his entire poetic career. His acquaintance with Lovelace's poetry may have encouraged Marvell to write "dark conceits" and allegory in some of his early poems.

Marvell's penchant for the "dark conceit" expressed itself in those poems that I categorize as containing allegories pertaining to Charles I. Marvell employs a poetic structure that reflects his equation of the fall of monarchy and the fall of man as providential events leading to change directed by an agent or circumstance sent by God, the consequences of which are advantageous for all mankind. The central accent that looks forward to triumph was not Marvell's invention, but he exploits its possibilities as he also pushes the previous boundaries of the lyric, the country-house poem, the epic, the *carpe diem* poem, whatever he turned his hand to. By way of finding a common thread between meaning and poetic development, I trace his usage of the allegorical structure.

His experience with Fairfax seems to have provided opportunity for poetic productivity more abundant than any other period of his life. The Mower poems may be seen to mirror turmoil pertinent to his poetic course, the resolution of which we see in "The Garden." He then continues in the direction he had set for himself in the poem to Lovelace, fulfilling his own "modest ambition" of praising a worthy man. Marvell also becomes a poetic character himself, a caricature of the Fairfax figure that throws into relief the retired Lord General's flaw without diminishing the poem as an encomium. Throughout these poems, his obscurant tendency functions, but he exhibits his own perspective (or so I identify it) in the allegorical structure and the caricature. I think that Marvell arrived at an understanding of the unattractive reality of the "retired" life as an evasion of responsibility rather than a return to Eden, that a true Edenic impulse could not be even a conception for mankind so far descended into the age of Cain as the English Civil War veterans were. He discovered for himself the paradox of the retired life: that while its apparent purpose was purity, arising from a sensitive conscience, its purpose was also evasion of virtuous responsibility for the active world. The passage describing England as former Eden in "Upon Appleton House," the Mower poems, and "The Nymph complaining for the death of her Faun" may be seen to form a psychological and philosophical progression.

Having said this, I nonetheless do not think Marvell so ungracious as to condemn the man Fairfax. Fairfax was a worthy, and Marvell fulfills his own "modest ambition" in "Upon Appleton House," that of conferring a true immortality upon Fairfax, one he could hardly have achieved otherwise. In the poem, Marvell illustrates that Fairfax fulfilled his providential role in creating a true religious house at Appleton. Marvell thus appeases Fairfax's nagging concerns that God had laid him aside, perhaps because he had offended God by his family's occupation of a former cloister. He portrays Fairfax as the epitome of the English gentleman with a war history that provides evidence that Providence guided his fate to the point at which he is presented as a Protestant saint in his own holy place, a shrine worthy of pilgrimage for all mankind.

Marvell's ambitions included the role that he thought to assume in the Fairfax poems: historiographer for the English Civil War's Lord General Fairfax. But because the great general had abandoned his country midway in its crisis and a greater man, Cromwell, assumed command, the poet/tutor easily enough saw who would perform the providentially decreed role of England's leader. Marvell may even have written "An Horatian Ode" while he was at Appleton, though the date hardly matters since his admiration for Cromwell and perception of him as providential agent must have been extant before his Appleton stint. With skill and incredible brilliance, Marvell had tailored his praise of Fairfax, but his encomia for Cromwell—though "The First Anniversary" and "The Death of O.C." are not so much admired as "Upon Appleton House"—seem to have had his whole heart. Marvell illustrates that Providence has chosen to exalt Cromwell and that the English stand as deterrent to God's will, thwarting God himself and the promised latter days. Marvell echoes Cromwell's speeches and letters—natural for this most echoing of poets—and indeed seems to have studied him in minute detail to create his poetic portrait. Though Marvell's poetry is often deliberately impenetrable, his portraits are rife with verifiable detail; this technique produces praise resonant with apparent truth. His propensity for truth in the poetic is of course present in the allegories, but there Marvell felt a necessity to overlay a story. He echoes material from all circumstance surrounding Cromwell so that the fabric of his poem presents simultaneously the history of the moment, quite consistent with what I perceive to be his self-prescribed role of historiographer—providential and profane. Little is omitted—the Levellers, the Fifth Monarchists, the Barebone's, the Presbyterians. We hear the clamor of their voices in the poem as surely as the raucous nightbirds "screeching" in delight over Cromwell's supposed death. Marvell has them echo—birds and sects—the *Eikon Basilike*, a resounding answer to those who wept for Charles I after the fact.

In his role as interpreter of God's will, Marvell may be said to have released Fairfax from his paranoia over his impropriation of church property and to go on to illustrate in "The First Anniversary" that Cromwell was "the man" chosen by God to lead England into the latter days. Amidst an atmosphere that should have made anyone paranoid and constrained by the mantle of his apparent heavy fate, Cromwell could well have needed Marvell's expression of certitude after the carriage accident. Marvell's allegorical pattern is evident in "The First Anniversary" as he adroitly turns the fall to advantage to refute the popular ridicule and interpretation of the event as God's displeasure with (even to casting down) His favorite. Marvell places the blame on Cromwell's new horses that are likened in their inexperience to the unseasoned English people. When he proved Fairfax to have sanctified Nunappleton rather than desecrating a holy place, Marvell manipulated the concept of space, illustrating that the nuns shut the world out so that they could lead lives of self-indulgent, hedonistic escapism and that the early Fairfax opened the cloister to active virtue. In "The First Anniversary," he uses essentially the same tactic in inverting rising and falling, asserting all the while that Cromwell cannot fall, that his only descent has been to accept leadership of England. The monarch-oriented English are portrayed as fated to sink, except that Cromwell prevent it. They fall when they resist him and would overturn England with their ignorance as the untried horses have Cromwell's carriage. If Cromwell dies (as he does hypothetically), he dies because God would punish the English for their failure by taking him from them.

Marvell's portraiture assumes a more personal quality in "The Death of O.C.," a quality that has been considered to flaw the poem. His assimilation of actual detail reveals more of the poet and his relationship with Cromwell than any other of his poems. He characterized Cromwell as he has before—providentially privileged and ever-sacrificing for England. The reality was that Cromwell's last days were a sad anticlimax to a dedicated life. Marvell will tell the "true" history of the worthy Cromwell and the unworthy, unruly English for whom he has given his life.

After Cromwell's death and Marvell's own rise in the political sphere to a member of Parliament, Milton alone remained of the hopeful Interregnum days. In writing a prefatory poem to the second edition of *Paradise Lost*, Marvell must have considered the opportunity as fraught with possibility for his own fall. What if he himself failed? The poem he wrote evinces that Marvell knew that *Paradise Lost* would be immortal; his own poetic immortality hung in the balance. Thus, in patterns now grown familiar, he displaces his fear for himself to transform it into fear for Milton's failure, uses that fear as vehicle to traverse *Paradise Lost* to the midpoint, then explodes his surmise to create exact and appropriate praise of Milton's triumphant accomplishment.

Milton died in 1674. I do not doubt that his memory in combination with other deeply disturbing events had to do with Marvell's publication of *An Account of the Growth of Popery.* Milton's doughty defense of Protestant government against Roman Catholicism/absolute monarchy in *Of True Religion* after thirteen years of silence—and in an atmosphere in which he was likely to be imprisoned for speaking out—expressed fears for England's government that Marvell saw materialize. *An Account of the Growth of Popery* presents the history of a Parliament that eagerly sacrificed its integrity to keep its place and a king who encouraged them to do so that he might better "gull" them of money. Marvell could hardly have avoided then the memory of Cromwell who summarily dissolved a Parliament in 1653 because they were unwilling to relinquish their seats. Thus Marvell *would* rise to "single [fight] forsaken Vertues cause."[4]

1

"Our times are much degenerate": Marvell's Early Life, his Friendship with Lovelace, and his Allegiances

THE poet Andrew Marvell sang of devouring time, of controlling time, of artful gardens, of wild gardens, of unfortunate lovers, of fortunate generals. The disparities in these topics lay for him in the manner in which his subject chose to live. This statement we are able to make, but we know little of how he lived. Most of what we know comes from his association with prominent figures: Lovelace, Fairfax, Cromwell, Milton—who were the subjects of his poetry as well as figures who influenced his life. His father was inevitably another strong influence, as were the circumstances of the pre–civil war period through which he traveled to adulthood, the civil wars, the Interregnum, and the Restoration. His intelligence and his sense of humor must have early set him apart. He does not seem to have been a bold person, though he rose boldly to occasions when he was moved; these emotional variances are sometimes referred to as his active and passive modes. For some years, he felt it desirable to disguise his political opinion, and thus he wrote enigmatic poetry. This has worked against his "definitive glory." Since little of his poetry was published during his life, and some of it censored in anthologies after its publication, we know nothing of what his poetic contemporaries thought of him. He did not circulate his poetry, yet to say this is erroneous in a sense. That is, he was not a courtier; to whom would he have shown his poems other than to Lovelace, Fairfax, Cromwell, and Milton? Apparently, he did, so that they were in some sense not only the subjects, but also the audience for his poetry. These associations and that with his father provide perspectives on his life and his poetry.

If he attended the Hull Grammar School—and there is little reason other than a lack of recorded attendance to suppose that he did not—and grew tall enough during his attendance time from 1629 to 1633, he looked out the window each day at the cemetery of Holy Trinity, the town's principal church where his father was lecturer. The chimes of Holy Trinity may have measured his school time, if they were accurate enough. Even if they were not accurate, they still sounded throughout the day, marking some kind of time, various though it may have been, and predictably degenerate in a sense. At this time, any clock's life was one of disorder; sundials would remain for a few more years the only timely time-tellers, and their time was that by which clocks were reset, often every day.[1]

Surely he played in the school garden, which was fairly large— some seven hundred square yards—and at least had glimpses of the even larger garden of the vicarage on the east side of the schoolhouse. With the many Dutch immigrants in Hull, one could expect that the vicarage garden would have been a particularly lovely one. Perhaps he played in the cemetery that, with the church, served as the center of village life. Philippe Aries tells us that, "well into the seventeenth century," the cemetery was as much a place for the activities of the living as a "space reserved for the dead."[2] According to Aries, the dual nature of the church and comotory "is explained by the privilege of the right of asylum or sanctuary, which had the same motives as burial *ad sanctos*. The patron saint granted a temporal protection to the living who honored him, just as he gave a spiritual guarantee to the dead who entrusted their bodies to his safekeeping. The territory in which the authority of the lay powers could be exercised stopped at the wall of the church and its atrium."[3] Thus, knowledge of sanctuary within enclosure was an early awareness for Marvell. Despite the town clock's sounding of hours, ubiquitous if irregular, so that time was ever present, the sense of sanctuary and sometimes even the solitude he treasured surely were a part, too, of his boyhood in the gardens of Hull.

This is not to say that his early life was quiet. The churchyard's many functions included military training; in a letter to the Hull Corporation, Marvell recalls seeing the young men of Hull "trained for" the militia.[4] What Marvell saw was probably Hull's adherence to the 1635 Council of State orders to the lord-lieutenants that militia be strengthened through recruitment and training, orders generated out of fear created by France's entry into the Thirty Years War and the increasing possibility of a Habsburg invasion. Along the coast, the requirements designed to ready defenses were strictly observed.[5] The church also served as a kind of clearinghouse for civic matters, and the pulpit for messages from the king.[6] Marvell's house itself was close to the river (fifty yards)[7] and the jumble of boats and sailors. Considering all this, Marvell would seem to have grown to adolescence in a relative hurly-burly.

His family life can hardly be separated from the community life. His lecturer father was central to the political, economic, and moral issues that the townspeople brought to the church; with his second marriage, his political involvement became somewhat stronger, for Lucy Alured came from a political family. She was the daughter of John Alured, M.P. for Hull in the 1580s; her brother's sons were "intransigent" republicans: Matthew Alured was a parliamentary colonel and John Alured a member of the Long Parliament and a regicide. The relationship for the younger Marvell doubled with the marriage of Mary Alured, the daughter of Matthew, to Marvell's beloved nephew William Popple, son of Marvell's sister Mary.[8] Finally, of course, Marvell senior's religion became political. His leaning was to Puritanism since his college was Emmanuel, founded as Calvinist by Sir Walter Mildmay, great-grandfather of Mildmay Fane, who was brother-in-law to General Fairfax.[9] Laurence Chaderton, a "sponsor of puritan trends," was master from 1584 through 1622[10] when he would have been there. To be a Puritan and an Anglican clergyman was not quite ordinary. The percentage of Puritans in the clergy at the time has been estimated as low as 4 percent, no greater than 17 percent.[11] This would seem to identify the more rigorous Puritans though. As to whether he was rigid or moderate, we have his son's description of him: "he was . . . a Conformist to the established Rites of the Church of England, though I confess none of the most over-running or eager in them."[12] Hilton Kelliher includes the item that he was disciplined by the Archbishop of York in 1639 and instructed "to read more of the Prayer Book."[13] We may be confident that he was not a Laudian. Lecturers were not within the control of the Anglican hierarchy since they were hired by the parishes themselves. Charles Carlton gives a valuable definition of the position:

> Money would be raised to support a minister chosen for his preaching ability to give extra sermons, particularly on Wednesdays or market days. Since merchants could usually afford them, lecturers tended to be concentrated in towns: 90 per cent of London's parishes had them, for instance. While most lecturers were orthodox men, intent on reviving the faith—a goal that Laud shared—they had a

degree of independence from episcopal authority, a licence that he abhorred.

Since they were not under his control, Laud set about to redirect the circumstance; he had King Charles "issue" injunctions in 1629, and reissue them in 1631 and 1634 (when his goal was accomplished) "that lectures be given only by beneficed clergy, subject to the discipline of their bishop, who could deprive them of their livings. . . . Laud did not bother to try and seek a mutually agreeable solution."[14]

As lecturer, Marvell was devoted to his congregation. When, for example, the unusually tenacious plague of 1637–38 that raged through two years rather than one[15] visited Hull, and took at least "one person in every ten in the town,"[16] he stayed with his parishioners throughout the time.[17] In Marvell's first published poem (1637) celebrating Charles and Henrietta Maria's fifth child and his "first Horatian Ode," he refers to the plague,[18] which would seem to be the same plague. Though he was at Trinity, Marvell would have known of the tumultuous circumstances occuring at home.

Military training ordinarily ceased when the plague marched, but Hull, the East Riding, and all of Yorkshire had such an important role in the king's wars that it probably did not. The governor of Hull and sheriff of Yorkshire Sir John Hotham was a faithful king's man who had been assiduous in collecting ship-money. When in 1639, the governing of Hull was taken from him and given to another, he turned against the king and would no longer pay ship-money. When asked to muster again for the king in that year, Hotham objected that his county (Yorkshire) had suffered £40,000 in military expense in the year before and could pay no more.[19] By 1642, Hotham was a Parliament man, and expecting his support, the House instructed him "to secure" Hull with Yorkshire soldiers and to withhold the king's arsenal, earlier amassed in Hull for the Scottish war. Captain Hotham, Sir John's son, was an eager warrior and accomplished the security of Hull for his father, who then took over to refuse admittance to the king. The House and Charles were immediately drawn into a constitutional battle over whether Sir John's act was treasonous.[20] G. P. Gooch and H. J. Laski connect Hull's resistance to the king's rejection of the House's "demand for the control of the Militia";[21] Christopher Hill, however, cites Bishop Hacket as having considered the lecturers responsible for Hull's resistance.[22] If the elder Marvell still functioned as lecturer when he died in 1640/41, it was likely because Hull held his service to them in greater regard than Laud's or the king's.

Marvell's earliest impressions almost certainly would center on his father, and I think we may safely assume that the son's faith closely resembled the father's. The families, the Popples and Blaydes, into which his sisters married in Hull seem to have been of the same religious tenor as the lecturer Marvell. Michael Craze rejects the story of Marvell's being briefly seduced by the Jesuits and his father's "rescuing" him since the story did not emerge until Cooke told it in 1726; Cooke dated the occurrence "soon after 1633."[23] I consider the story probable in the light of Marvell's interest in and ability to see issues from more than one perspective. Another motivation is possible. John Dixon Hunt considers the incident happened "probably in 1639,"[24] which makes sense to me, if the other circumstance that I think a possibility transpired. Marvell's mother died in April of 1638 when he had just turned seventeen and was away at Cambridge. Before the year was out, his father had remarried. Our lack of involvement may cause the marriage not to seem "o'erhasty"; from the young Marvell's perspective, it may have been no less than treason. If his becoming Roman Catholic took place at this time, then the incident seems a logical rebellious act and likely to have occurred. His father's diligence in searching him out and the young Marvell's awareness of his own act's import should have healed the breach. His father's death would have resolved all differences. Despite an act that may be interpreted as aimed at his father, Marvell's loyalty before and after 1639 must have been strong for his father and his position, denied legitimacy by Laud and the government, but apparently honored by those who knew him best, his parishioners. The elder Marvell's situation may be compared to that eventually encountered by Cromwell, whose position as Protector was continually challenged. In addition, Marvell's father's daily, even hourly, reception of townsfolk needing his settlement of their affairs, along with the other activities taking place in the church and churchyard, must have created an atmosphere something like a minor Whitehall.

Empson proposes that Marvell went abroad by means of his brother-in-law Popple's shipping firm, perhaps as a kind of "relief-man only, not looking for a settled job, often reporting possibilities or taking letters from one port to another. He came back as soon as the war was over because he was then released from doing this emergency work. The emergency had clearly left him enough time to learn four languages and acquire a lot of information."[25] Empson's plausible speculation answers the mystery of Marvell's near-silence about his travels as well as of the "good service" to Hull, the basis of his recommendation to the Hull Corporation to be made a freeman, the step before his being elected M.P. What Empson's explanation does not fully account for is "Fleckno, an English Priest at Rome," which Marvell is thought to have written in March of 1646. But after Naseby, 14 June 1645, the war was virtually over. Perhaps Marvell had earned enough in his brother-in-law's service to provide himself a year abroad. This is having it both ways, but not impossible. On 12 November 1647, Marvell sold some property in Meldreth, Cambridgeshire, bequeathed to him by his grandfather who had his own reasons for disliking monarchy (he died at Hull in 1628, "having left his native county rather than pay an enforced loan to the King").[26] We do not know what Marvell's financial circumstances were. His composition of the Hastings poem, the commendation for Lovelace's *Lucasta*, and even "An Horatian Ode" may have been written in hopes of a position as recompense. We don't know that his first determination was to be a poet, though he had a definite (and traditional) opinion about a poet's role, which he tells us in the prefatory poem to *Lucasta* was "to honour . . . worthy men" (10). I think it likely that his father's having been included among Thomas Fuller's *Worthies of England* had some part in this ambition.

London may not have seemed alien to Marvell after his youth spent amidst the continuous activity of his father's church, yet he must have longed at times for the occasional quiet that was previously integral to his life. Though the city itself presented no difficult adjustment, England's atmosphere was everywhere far different from that before the war. Marvell tells us first in "To His Noble Friend, Mr. Richard Lovelace, Upon His Poems," that the "times are much degenerate" (1). And from some perspectives they were, and were to become even more for Lovelace, so that Marvell's poem, which he wrote late in 1647,[27] seems prophetic. Manfred Weidhorn writes that in April of 1648 "Lovelace's world fell apart." Searching Lovelace's house for his brother Francis, Fairfax's troops "seized a cabinet of jewels"; when Lovelace objected, he was imprisoned "on the pretext that his papers were not in order."[28] While Lovelace was in prison, King Charles was executed. When he was released in April of 1649, the Interregnum had begun. Nothing certain is known of the rest of his life.

Lovelace's enrollment at Cambridge did not happen until 4 Oc-

tober 1637, over a year beyond the time that he—only eighteen
and at Oxford a mere two years—had been so remarkably honored by having the Master of Arts degree conferred on him. In
the assembly were Charles I, William Laud, and Prince Rupert,
who seems to have received the degree at the same time. If the
just mentioned event were as unusual as it seems, then Lovelace's
fame must have preceded him at Cambridge and his friendship
would have been greatly sought. Whether he and Marvell were
actually friends, we do not know, though they may have been.
They shared the friendship or acquaintance of the musicians
William[29] and Henry Lawes and an admiration for the painter
Peter Lely. Perhaps Marvell and Lovelace met as former Cambridge acquaintances while they were abroad. In such an acquaintance, the younger, as-yet-unhonored Marvell's role would
have been that of the learner; that he did learn is illustrated in
the influence of *Lucasta* on his poetry. In the *Politics of Mirth*,
Leah Marcus observes that "a common poetic motif of the late
Civil War and Interregnum period is the discovery of cryptic
vestiges of the lost court and its ritualism in the midst of a country landscape," and continues with an illustration of how Marvell's prefatory poem to Lovelace's *Lucasta* "displays an early
version of Marvell's ambivalent ways with royalist symbology
. . . based on a deliberate disjunction."[30] Marcus writes that the
"candid age" that Marvell's poem claims as the time of Lovelace's
poetry is presented as if it were long ago, but that "in actuality,
as Marvell well knew, much or most of Lovelace's poetry had
been written during wartime. . . . But Marvell's commendation
of Lovelace writes him out of the contemporary political
scene. . . . [by a kind of apotheosis raising him until he] becomes
an apolitical icon, encapsulated, suspended in air, separated
from his 'cause' so that his virtues can be reevaluated and admired independently of their political significance for the parti-
sans of Charles I." She sees that as an undermining of Lovelace's
political affiliation "even as it praises the verse."[31] Admiring her
thesis, I find that only here must I disagree with Marcus; it is,
however, central to my own theory that Marvell did not compromise his own integrity by praising what he could not praise in
truth, certainly not in a poem in which he exalts integrity.

What Marvell does not do is praise the verse; he will not tell
us that Richard Lovelace is an excellent poet. The focus on the
fallen times that have caused poets to destroy with their art
rather than to build the fame of those who are deserving serves

a dual function in that the absence of praise for Lovelace's poetry itself is rarely noticed:

> Sir,
>> Our times are much degenerate from those
>> Which your sweet Muse which your fair Fortune chose,
>> And as complexions alter with the Climes,
>> Our wits have drawne th'infection of our times.
>> That candid Age no other way could tell
>> To be ingenious, but by speaking well.
>> Who best could prayse, had then the greatest prayse,
>> 'Twas more esteemd to give, then weare the Bayes:
>> Modest ambition studi'd only then,
>> To honour not her selfe, but worthy men.
>> These vertues now are banisht out of Towne,
>> Our Civill Wars have lost the Civicke crowne.
>> He highest builds, who with most Art destroys,
>> And against others Fame his owne employs.
>> I see the envious Caterpillar sit
>> On the Faire blossome of each growing wit.
>
>   (1–16)

Marvell establishes his own voice as one that honors "worthy men" by defending Lovelace's integrity, asserting that Lovelace "shall for faultlesse be accus'd" (26). (Marvell's incorporation of "the beauteous Ladies" sets a witty limit to Lovelace's purity, which exists only in regard to accusations and jealous barbs.) Delegating the judgment of Lovelace's work to others (a technique he will employ with a different motive in "The First Anniversary") is appropriate, for his point is that ultimately the "barbed Censurers" (21) must accede to public demand: "But he secure of glory and of time / Above their envy, or mine aid doth clime. / Him, valianst men, and fairest Nymphs approve, / His Booke in them finds Judgement, with you Love" (47–50). *Clime* in this portion of the poem adds a dimension to the *climes* of line 3: Marvell contrasts Lovelace's "climb" to glory, to the rise of the "infected" aspirants who employ their art destructively—like the "envious Caterpillar." Marvell's own well-spoken tribute in both the poem and the offer to die in defense of the appealing and "undressed" admirer of Lovelace or in Lovelace's cause can be considered an affirmation of the still-living state of at least one who is spiritually tied to "That candid Age [that] no other way could tell / To be ingenious, but by speaking well" (5–6).

Lovelace's *Lucasta* made a deep impression on Marvell.[32] The impress of Lovelace's imprisonment on Marvell's imagination also may be in part responsible for the abundance of confinement imagery in his poetry. Marcus sees his "installation" of Lovelace "in the secure but isolated Elysium" as "imitating a characteristic strategy of the collection to which his poem was affixed—doing little more than Lovelace had already done through the creation of protective enclosures."[33] R. I. V. Hodge sees evidence of "Aramantha" as particularly influential in "Upon Appleton House."[34] Interestingly, Christine Rees writes that Lovelace's "On Sanazar's being honoured . . . by the Clarissimi of Venice" was influenced by Marvell's "Tom May's Death."[35] Manfred Weidhorn finds "Tom May's Death" "reminiscent of Lovelace's 'On Sannazar.'"[36]

Dates for most Marvell poems are tentative; L. N. Wall has called attention to a 1647 Thomason collection tract entitled A Parliament of Ladies: with their Lawes newly enacted that possibly has some connection with "Daphnis and Chloe"[37]; thus dating "Daphnis and Chloe" in 1647 might seem reasonable—except that the connection seems tenuous. The lady Chloe doesn't seem to know the "laws," but rather behaves in a human way; the crafty Daphnis knows the laws. Chloe does not admit her love for Daphnis until she discovers he intends to leave off wooing her. When she does love Daphnis—"Love in her Language breath'd / Words she never spake before" (25–26)—he rejects her, saying that he will not to his "Departure owe / What [his] Presence could not win" (59–60), for she has not obeyed the laws. Therefore, the association of laws and the Parliament of Ladies tract seems to me to possess interest, but not much validity. The connection of Charles I and Daphnis because of lines 97–100 seems more valid—"At these words away he broke; / As who long has praying ly'n, / To his Heads-man makes the Sign, / And receives the parting stroke." These lines are sufficiently obtrusive to warrant interpretation as a signal in themselves that the poem has a specific referent. A date of 1649 seems more justifiable than 1647; "The Unfortunate Lover" is also dated 1649 on the basis of internal evidence (the echo of Dialogue—Lucasta, Alexis, [ll.15–16]). Moreover, both display obscurity remarkable even for Marvell, which may be construed as evidence of their having been written at or near the same time. Obscurity in 1649 is to the point. Earl Miner has described the appropriateness and popularity of "dark conceits" for the times.[38] In Censorship and Interpretation, Annabel Patterson has analyzed the role of the period's censorship in creating literature. Lois Potter's Se-

cret rites and secret writing Royalist literature, 1641–1660 sub-
stantiates the popularity of writing with encoded meaning that
reached a kind of zenith in Charles I's letters to Henrietta Maria.
Potter's discussion includes John Wilkins's *Mercury, or the Secret and Swift Messenger* (1641), a book on how to conceal meaning in a text. The book's apparent popularity evinces the general
interest in concealing one's true meaning. Potter condenses Wilkins's concept of "the relation between ornament and secrecy":

> Secrecy, he argues, may be an added ornament to rhetoric if, as with
> the parable of the vineyard which Nathan told David by way of up-
> braiding him with his treatment of Uriah,it enables a moral point to
> be made more effectively under the guise of a story. Where the moral
> is too effectively concealed, however, a story can appear merely gro-
> tesque (pp. 15–17). Wilkins attributes the obscurity in the works of
> ancient writers to their imitation of the ways of God, who had con-
> cealed so many of the secrets of nature. The hierarchy implied by
> this theory is one in which not only literal meaning but more subtle
> matters like the sense of tone and aesthetic evaluation will be acces-
> sible to readers in proportion to their worthiness. The analogy is no
> longer simply that of the cipher, with its one-to-one corres-
> pondences, but with the art of translation, where the 'best' meaning
> may sometimes be the least literal.[39]

Marvell's desire to conceal would account for the depth of the
enigma of "Daphnis and Chloe," the moral of which seems effectively enough concealed that it borders on what Wilkins termed
"the grotesque," as does "The Unfortunate Lover," both of which
may be said to mask political statements.

But another perspective must needs arise because "Daphnis
and Chloe" is one of a number of Marvell's poems that may be
seen as possessing shifting meaning. These poems must mean
something, but agreement on what they mean is rare. Thomas
Clayton's brilliant essay, "'It is Marvel he outdwells his hour':
Some Perspectives on Marvell's Medium," explores this characteristic perspectival ambiguity. Clayton describes what Marvell
creates in "Upon Appleton House" as "verbal architecture and
the projection of the mind into several frames of space," comparing the technique to "dimorphic representation, with a human
head as one expression and a landscape or any combination objects as another, as in paintings by Guiseppe Arcimboldo, Frans
Floris, Athansius Kircher, and De Momper" (49). According to
Clayton, "The Ode" exhibits "perspective and attitudinal ambiguity entailed by lexical and syntactical ambiguities" (58), and

is the "epitome" of those poems that share "a complex verbal vision of a kind that shifts its 'faces,' its effects, its dimensions, its meanings, and its significances, depending upon how it is looked at—and I am talking not about the fancifully subjective propensities of the reader—but the craftily designed and finely cut facets of Marvell's own making." He includes "Daphnis and Chloe" among them. Clayton comments on the fascination of graphic artists with "systematic distortions of perspective . . . as a means of reconstituting reality and revealing aspects and modalities ordinarily concealed." He does not attempt a "proof" that Marvell wrote "under the influence of such paintings, but his writings and the paintings are artistic manifestations of the same complex and penetrating sensibility."[40] In his illustration of the ambiguities of "Mourning," Clayton writes of the poem as "ashimmer" with meanings that come forward and recede as the poem progresses. . . . [It is] a complex perspective poem . . . [that] continues to look different as its elements rearrange themselves in our perception, even as those in a painting do when we look at it now one way, now another, and now both ways at another time retrospectively." Clayton is also sensitive to Marvell's aural ambiguities that are not often noticed by Marvell critics: "like 'Mo[u]rning . . . seen by the eye they can be better understood, but they must almost always be heard, too."[41]

Of Marvell's thirty-three poems most familiar to readers, Clayton considers twelve "especially interesting for their perspective epistemology."[42] Clayton's theory is more attractive and interesting than perceiving Marvell as having written in such as way as to hide his true feelings, which in a sense is to accuse him of being motivated by paranoia. What had he to fear since his poems, with a few exceptions, were not published nor widely circulated that we can tell? When he decided to be published, as in "The First Anniversary," the Painter poems, and *The Rehearsal Transpros'd*, the works possess little equivocation. Creating a surface beneath which another glimmers and emerges irresistibly at times reflects more truly the nature of the mind than a firm resolution at all times. Milton gave Satan and the fallen deities some of his favorite positions and even allowed that "Evil into the mind of God or Man / May come and go, so unapprov'd, and leave / No spot or blame" (*Paradise Lost* V 117–19). Of course, Milton's is a definite two-value orientation in this passage; however, Satan stands "stupidly good" (*Paradise Lost* IX 465) at the sight of Eve's "graceful Innocence" (459). The greatest of literary works possess this ambiguity: Hamlet is both

insane and not insane; Don Quixote, too, and always more sane
in his insanity than those with whom he interacts, whose natures
are more insane in their sanity than he. The court masques presented Charles I as a "lover of his people," a view that he sub-
scribed to publicly and perhaps even privately. And to that
perspective his actions were directed, according to his perception and that of those around him. Yet other perceived his acts
as duplicitous, finally as treasonous.

To fix Marvell firmly to one interpretation, either the surface
or the one lying just below it, which may be called the allegorical
meaning, is reductive. Marvell provides signals to prevent this,
either obtrusive images or the allegorical structure that I will
discuss in a later chapter.

In "Daphnis and Chloe," the grotesque imagery of the poem's
latter part points to political reference. The surface meaning involves what would seem to be the consequence for Chloe of ig-
noring the lover's *carpe diem* plea; she has failed to seize the
day—her sense of timing has been quite faulty. Marvell's initial
presentation of Daphnis is of the lover whose pursuit of Chloe
has been his prime motivation:

> *Daphnis* must from *Chloe* part.
> Now is come the dismal Hour
> That must all his Hopes devour,
> All his Labour, all his Art.
>
> Nature, her own Sexes foe,
> Long had taught her to be coy:
> But she neither knew t'enjoy,
> Nor yet let her Lover go.
>
> (1–8)

Chloe behaves as "nature" has "taught" her, and she has not been
artful enough to unlearn what her "foe" has schooled her in.[43]
Daphnis, however, seems to have artifice by heart—"well read in
all the wayes / By which men their Siege maintain"(17–8)—with
none of the lessons that Nature might have imparted to him: that
the male animal conquers through aggression, not hopes, labor,
and art.

But Marvell examines more than Daphnis's apparent lack of
wisdom in love. Daphnis's determination to suffer is not to be
thwarted by Chloe's acquiescence. In fact, he is "so full possest" (21) that he no longer has any interest in the possession of

Chloe. His behavior exploits the histrionic possibilities of his situation:

> At that *Why,* that *Stay my Dear,*
> His disorder'd Locks he tare;
> And with rouling Eyes did glare,
> And his cruel Fate forswear.
> As the Soul of one scarce dead,
> With the shrieks of Friends aghast,
> Looks distracted back in hast,
> And then streight again is fled.
>
> (33–40)

When his dramatic antics are over and he speaks, it is to castigate Chloe severely for the love she has finally "breath'd," which he will regard only as a bequeathal:

> Are my Hell and Heaven Joyn'd
> More to torture him that dies?
> Could departure not suffice,
> But that you must then grow kind?
>
> Ah my *Chloe* how have I
> Such a wretched minute found,
> When thy Favours should me wound
> More than all thy Cruelty?
>
> (45–52)

Time is of the essence: Daphnis arrived at the "dismal hour," which was past the last minute of the time allotted to his living as a lover of Chloe ("For, Alas, the time was spent"(29)), to find that "wretched minute" when she would stop the course of events on which he has embarked by changing her mind! This is not to be endured: "Rather I away will pine / In a manly stubborness / Than be fatted up express / For the Canibal to dine" (69–72). The cannibal devours his own kind, and since Daphnis considers himself already dead, a "Lovers Ghost," whatever she could add now would only be feeding Death, the great "Canibal." The intricate intellectual play of the following stanza has a ghoulish fascination: "Whilst this grief does thee disarm, / All th'Enjoyment of our Love / But the ravishment would prove / Of a Body dead while warm" (73–76). The image of frustration projected by the next stanza—that of the "Gourmand Hebrew," who desired delicacies, yet receiving, died at the moment he would enjoy them—is seemingly reiterated by the next passage, but the meaning emerges somewhat altered: "Or the Witch that midnight wakes / For the Fern, whose magick Weed / In one minute casts the Seed, / And invisible him makes" (81–84). The sexual implications remind the reader if not Daphnis that all his hopes, labor, and art are directed to a pursuit that ends only in a physical act, a magic "nothing" of a minute's time and which, in Daphnis's perspective, can change in a minute (*minute* is repeated too often in the poem to escape the emphasis on brevity). Yet this sophistical reduction perhaps arises only when love becomes a ritualized quest. And Marvell is not finished with his spoof: "Gentler times for Love are ment. / Who for parting pleasure strain / Gather Roses in the rain, / Wet themselves and spoil their Sent" (85–88).

Marvell presents myriad motivation here, akin to the manner in which a liar overexplains himself. Phrased differently, Daphnis's motivation may be interpreted several ways, and the language changes the action, as art alters the natural emotion, love. This stanza, conveying the notion that those who try to snatch a moment destroy the beauty of what they seek to hold, is more to our liking, and it is the best of Daphnis's battery of artful excuses for his intention. His refusal in the next stanza to "pollute" (92) his "Grief" ends his explanations, but the emotionally wrought language continues through his dramatic exit lines: "Fate I come, as dark, as sad, / As thy Malice could desire" (93–94). The wit of his double entendre in the next two lines—"Yet bring with me all the Fire / That Love in his Torches had" (95–96)—gains force with the last two stanzas' "true" explanation in which we discover "Last night he with Phlogis slept, / This night for Dorinda kept; / And but rid to take the Air" (102–4). Any guilt he might feel for this duplicity is dispelled by his remembrance that Chloe did not abide by the "Lawes" (107).

This strange poem with the lover justifying his duplicity by blaming the true partner's lack of observation of the "laws" provokes the reader to discover a covert meaning. Stanza XXV then points to a political allegory: "At these words away he broke; / As who long has praying ly'n, / To his Heads-man makes the Sign, / And receives the parting stroke" (97–100). Marvell was said to have helped Milton write his *Eikonoklastes*. His mention in this poem of long praying and then acceptance of "the parting stroke,"[44] can hardly fail to suggest Charles I, the figure everyone associated with long praying since *Eikon Basilike* and with beheading since the event of the century. Marvell manipulates time in the poem; Daphnis seems to have played the lover's role for some long time with Chloe; when she acquiesces at his imminent departure, suddenly there seems no more time: "Alas, the time was spent, / Now the latest minut's run" (29–30). Time becomes only "a wretched minute" (50). This may reasonably be equated with the king's long protestations of love for England and the country's patient credulence that ended in so startling a manner. Even the royalist journalists did not expect the beheading.[45] The reversal of expectation that the poem presents in the apparently ardent and artful lover who achieves his goal at the moment he thinks to relinquish it and refuses to accept or value its winning because it does not fit with convention becomes the poet's comment on the political circumstance that one might tentatively date 1640 with the purge of the king's ministers, but continuation of his rule. Despite the populace's desire for "root and branch" abolition of episcopacy, in October of 1641, King Charles appointed seven bishops. His refusal to relinquish his conception of his divine and exclusive right to rule continued; in January of 1642 came his abortive attempt to arrest in Commons the five most prominent of his opposition. His obduracy created the impass of 1642, and it was he who made the decisive move toward war, seeing in it a "simple solution to the complex dilemma that faced him and his realm."[46] The discovery of the coded letters between the king and queen dispelled any conviction that he kept faith with his people, and ultimately led to the execution. Marvell creates an erotic situation that parallels a political one. The encoded and very true letters of Charles to his French Catholic queen, who was in France, revealed the falsehood of Charles's stance as lover of England. Decoded versions were published in 1645 as *The King's Cabinet Opened*, though singly others were published earlier, and the originals were displayed in Westminster for anyone to see. Potter writes of the publication in March 1643 of one

> which revealed the double game that the king was playing in his response to Parliament's articles of cessation. . . . Their contents were all that any parliamentary supporter could have hoped. Not only did they make plain that Charles had been saying different things to different opponents throughout the war, but he was shown not even to like or trust many of his own supporters: he had complained to the queen of the dull company at his Oxford court (9 April 1645). . . . Here was all the deviousness and 'kingcraft' of which his father before him had been accused. Most damning of all was his

willingness to promise concessions to the Roman Catholics in England and Ireland, in exchange for their support.[47]

In the last two stanzas of the poem, Marvell injects a reversal of expectation that makes the first reversal—Daphnis's refusal of Chloe—more comprehensible. His artful portrayal of the devoted lover is a ruse only fully revealed by his last scene as a frivolous lover. The king had only been "acting" the role of devoted lover of England; had he been willing to compromise, he should likely have kept his role both as king and devoted lover. John Morrill writes that the civil war "had solved none of the problems which brought about the war, but had created immense new problems. They still had to treat with a king utterly insincere, utterly unchastened (except by the belief that his concessions of 1640–42 constituted a breach of his sacred trust and that the scourge of civil war was the consequence of his failures in those years) and deluded into imagining that he could divide and rule his enemies."[48] His intransigence never wavered: presented a treaty by the Presbyterian parliament late in 1648, he appeared to consider it, but he planned to use it only to regain his freedom and resume his efforts to conquer his adversaries. Stoutly maintaining that his love and faith resided solely with the English people, he was privately writing to the Marquis of Ormonde in Ireland, assuring him that at a favorable time he would negate any concessions or treaties that he might make and that the Marquis's efforts must go forward to accomplish that time. Charles's faith resided only in his own sovereign authority; any government other than by his will was blasphemous. Like Daphnis, he was convinced that those with whom he was in negotiation were at fault and not he for the treaty's failure. Daphnis "excuses" his actions by recourse to "the Lawes" (107), which become his "Cause" (106). And in historical fact, King Charles had brought the war along with more speed than was necessary by his insistence on focusing on laws and constitutional matters. Daphnis sees the fault entirely as Chloe's, though the reader finds his attitude autocratic: "Why did *Chloe* once refuse?" (108). Thus, love, we find, was not his cause, but the maintenance of tradition. Moreover, he himself takes license with the laws in his traffic with Phlogis and Dorinda, thus subverting his own justification.

What Marvell does in "Daphnis and Chloe" is slightly different from what he later does: that is, in a lyric, he masks historical circumstance as an ideal corrupted. In "Upon Appleton House" and to a greater extent in "The First Anniversary" and "The

Death of O.C.," he presents actual corrupt circumstance in the midst of which an ideal arises. Charles's statement from the scaffold that his journey was to be "from a corruptible to an incorruptible crown, where no disturbance can be" may have possessed an irony for Marvell that inspired the poems that explode corrupt traditions to expose their exploitations. The *Eikon Basilike* continued the play on a people's wish to believe that their king had been devoted to them, an ideal that could hardly be supported by any evidence when Charles lived. Its publication created a far greater stir than Lovelace's *Lucasta*, and I see evidence that "Daphnis and Chloe" and "The Unfortunate Lover" were replies that revealed the hypocrisy of the king and the *Eikon* to the enlightened reader. The culmination of the thought process that produced these sketches might be said to be "An Horatian Ode" in which the *"Royal Actor"* (51), an actor of roles on "The *Tragick Scaffold"* (52), is cast opposite the true man of action Cromwell, the active star "That does both act and know" (76) and break (or keep) "the antient Rights" (38) with his "greater spirit." Juxtaposing "The Unfortunate Lover" and "An Horatian Ode" illustrates the relation between the two poems and the connection to "Daphnis and Chloe."

The accepted date of "The Unfortunate Lover" is 1648–49,[49] and my interpretation requires the 1649 date. Annabel Patterson identifies "The Unfortunate Lover" with Charles I, and she sees the poem as possessing "connotative possibility";[50] that is, as she says in speaking of "The Unfortunate Lover" and "The Nymph complaining for the death of her Faun," "In neither poem is there any attempt to provide equivalencies of meaning in which one set of signifiers requires exegesis in terms of the other; but in each the quality and quantity of emotion involved seems somehow more appropriate if a political context is recognized."[51] Patterson sees "unmistakable political connections in the last stanza" in the "famous heraldic image on which the poem ends [that] was in fact taken directly from a satire [1647] by John Cleveland on the Westminster Assembly" concerning what Cleveland thought of as 'unnatural alliances,' those "between different Puritan sects,"[52] all of which he ridiculed. She also comments on the associational quality that the fire and storm imagery had taken on, "thanks to the *Eikon Basilike*."[53] Margarita Stocker perceives "The Unfortunate Lover" as belonging with the "Horatian Ode" and "The First Anniversary" among "the poems which actively engage with the process of history," and sees it, as I do, "as a parabolic expression of his reaction to the fall and regicide of Charles I"[54] and response to *Eikon Basilike*. In Stocker's view, the "Un-fortunate lover is fortune's victim."[55]

In addition to Stocker's, the term *unfortunate lover* possesses other definitions. An unfortunate lover may be one who loves but is not loved in return. In this sense, an unfortunate lover has at least the pleasure of loving, painful though it may seem; that is, he does not long to be free of his love. Or an unfortunate lover may be defined as one who feigns love, yet is loved in return; that is, he is unfortunate because none of the joy that comes in loving can be his. Marvell's unfortunate lover possesses little joy, though he did when his love was young:

> Alas, how pleasant are their dayes
> With whom the Infant Love yet playes!
> Sorted by pairs, they still are seen
> By Fountains cool, and Shadows green.
> But soon these Flames do lose their light,
> Like Meteors of a Summers night:
> Nor can they to that Region climb,
> To make impression upon Time.
>
> (1–8)

Identifying the unfortunate lover with Charles I and his love affair with England, the state to whom he is married in the traditional Renaissance hierarchy, we are told that their love soon cools; that is, the "Flames" that represent their love are like shooting stars—"Meteors of a Summers night." Together, they hardly can make "impression upon Time."[56]

Meteors fall; however, in "An Horatian Ode," Cromwell's star is rising, for he has "Urged his active Star" (12), until it burns "through the Air" (21). In "The Unfortunate Lover," the lover is passive for most of the poem:

> The Sea him lent these bitter Tears
> Which at his Eyes he alwaies bears.
> And from the Winds the Sighs he bore,
> Which through his surging Breast do roar.
> No Day he saw but that which breaks,
> Through frighted Clouds in forked streaks.
> While round the ratling Thunder hurl'd,
> As at the Fun'ral of the World.
>
> (17–24)

This passivity in Charles showed itself in his dependence on Buckingham until his death in 1628, on Henrietta Maria's counsel afterward, on Laud until the unpopularity of Laud made his removal politically expedient, and Strafford until circumstances persuaded Charles that an exchange with Parliáment for Strafford's life would be advantageous, and abundantly in the *Eikon Basilike*, in which he is presented as the innocent victim. Like the unfortunate lover who early played "By Fountains cool, and Shadows green" (4), Cromwell has lived in a garden, but he left it through love for England. He is the true lover; hence, the fortunate lover, and his leaving-taking of the garden has indeed made an impression on time:

> 'Tis Madness to resist or blame
> The force of angry Heavens flame:
> And, if we would speak true,
> Much to the Man is due.
> Who, from his private Gardens, where
> He liv'd reserved and austere,
> As if his highest plot
> To plant the Bergamot,
> Could by industrious Valour climbe
> To ruine the great Work of Time,
> And cast the Kingdome old
> Into another Mold.

(25–36)

The "angry Heaven" controls the circumstances of both poems. In "The Unfortunate Lover," it not only "breaks, / Through frighted Clouds in forked streaks" (21–22), it is the demanding "Flame," imagery identical to "An Horatian Ode" in the "force of angry Heavens flame." That Marvell deems it "madness to resist or blame" in "An Horatian Ode" presents a strong judgment against the king. The traditional quality of the imagery speaks to the poem's political intent: the equation of a shipwreck with the destruction of the ship of state in a sea of trouble, a storm. It has been noticed, and Stocker makes comment that "In *Eikon Basilike*, the frontispiece showed the martyrdom of Charles I against a background of stormclouds and a turbulent sea, and there too that background signifies the rebellion of the Civil War."[57]

Only when "angry Heaven" becomes ready for change—"when angry Heaven wou'd / Behold a spectacle of Blood" (41–42)— does the unfortunate lover turn into a warrior, but he's hardly fit, despite his desperate effort. Cromwell, too, was not a warrior, "liv'd reserved and austere" (30); however, he *was* fit, a quality that Marvell will again emphasize in "The First Anniversary." "The force of angry Heavens flame" supports him; he is the trusted servant through whom Providence will work the divine will, for he is "fit for highest Trust . . . fit he is to sway / That can so well obey" (80–84).

The poem presents then the history of the lover:

'Twas in a Shipwrack, when the Seas
Rul'd, and the Winds did what they please,
That my poor Lover floting lay,
And, e're brought forth, was cast away:
Till at the last the master-Wave
Upon the Rock his Mother drave;
And there she split against the Stone,
In a *Cesarian Section.*

(9–16)

Charles's fate was hardly in his hands in his early life; he had expected his brother to be king, but found himself married to England and its church. The "Seas" in the poem would seem to signify Providence working through the general populace; the "Winds" that do as they please, the factions; the "master-Wave" that brings about the shipwreck, God whose will it was that the division occur. Charles has been "born" of Roman Catholicism and Scottish Presbyterianism; now he is driven against the "Rock" that seems here to be the Anglican Church with the adamantine Laudian rule. He, too, has been a rock in a sense in his absolutism that wished to retain the rigor that had been associated with Laud. The king's retreat into docility—acting the role of the "unfortunate and abject" (30) king—in 1640 lost him powers that he later refused to acknowledge having lost. John Morrill writes that the civil war "came about because Charles I made a series of disastrous mistakes and miscalculations that drove into reluctant warmongering those who had continued until the last minute to hope for and to expect a peaceful resolution of their differences with him."[58] In the frontispiece to *Eikon Basilike,* the rock is portrayed in the midst of the stormy sea. Marvell thus contrasts the emblematic associations with the reality of inflexibility. In *Secret rites and secret writing,* Lois Potter cites a prefatory letter written by royalist wit John Berkenhead to a travel book published in 1648 in which he uses storm and shipwreck imagery to describe England's condition: "'you'l see *Great*

Brittaine a Floating Island, and the most vertuous *Monarch* under Heaven cast into a small Isle as on some plank in a great Ship-wrack."[59] These are not unusual images, but Marvell may well have seen the volume since it was a narrative of an Italian journey, which would have interest for him, having so recently been in Italy.

The birth brings about more storm, more contention from the "Winds," while he is taken into the "cruel Care" of "A num'rous fleet of Corm'rants black" (27–29), representing—in probably the most obvious correspondence in the poem—the bishops, whom nearly everyone blamed for Charles's poor rule. Marvell apparently shared Milton's view that they were greedy and uninvolved with religion. The middle stanzas, as Maren-Sofie Rostvig has observed, speak in their repetition of significant nouns to the importance of the cormorants.[60] They would seem central to the fall of King Charles. Almost no one wished to condemn the king; almost everyone was willing to condemn the bishops. This peculiarity serves to explain why so many—including Marvell—are perceived as having changed their loyalty before, during, and after the civil war. Charles Carlton presents a cogent discussion of this phenomenon in *Archbishop William Laud.*[61] He observes that

> Anti-clericalism had long been a force in English history. It was rather like a chronic infection that remains dormant in the body politic until some accident, a broken limb or concussed pate, causes it to flare up. . . . Perhaps it is inherent in Christian doctrine. Very few priests can completely practise what the Bible tells them to preach, and if the church grows rich and they become ostentatiously powerful, this intellectual gap becomes a chasm of hypocrisy[;] . . . . at the end of the personal rule complaints about clerics centred on bishops, who were seen as epitomising all that was wrong with the church. . . . During what a group of Huntingdonshire clergy described to Laud as "these anti-episcopal and unsettled times", bishops made first-rate villains. The scriptural basis for their authority was debatable, particularly in a period of intense scriptural debates. They had popish connections. . . . They had unpopular secular functions, backed up by church courts, High Commission and Star Chamber. They were associated with failed royal policies. And they were new men, selected for their academic qualifications in a society that normally allotted power and promotion on the basis of birth, connection, estates and kin.

In this midsection of the poem, two cormorants of the "fleet" (27) control the lover—"and as one corm'rant fed him, still /

Another on his Heart did bill" (35–36)—and the specific association would be Archbishop Laud and Bishop John Williams. Carlton writes that "Because out of the whole villainous tribe of
bishops the archbishop was the obvious arch-villain, in the over-
heated popular imaginations he—and his co-conspirator, Strafford, made scapegoats *par excellence*."[62] But Marvell would not
indict Strafford in this context and perhaps not at all. Bishop
John Williams, however, the archenemy of Archbishop Laud and
the possessor of Cawood Castle, on which the "sight" is focused
from Fairfax's "*Bastions*" (361) in "Upon Appleton House," is
the obvious candidate for the other cormorant. Williams was released from his Laud-induced Tower imprisonment as Commons
began to accept petitions against Laud at their convening in November of 1640, and he regained the king's ear and trust at
Charles's personal dismissal of Laud simultaneous with Laud's
going to the Tower. The king knew well that the furor was over
religion. Carlton observes that "though legal and constitutional
arguments became more significant in 1642 than they had been
in 1641, they were never as powerful as the religious motif."[63] In
no manner did the king exert himself to save Laud nor his other
ministers that the Long Parliament purged in 1640; again, his
passivity reflects that of Marvell's lover. "Orphaned," so to speak,
through the imprisonment or exile of his leading ministers, the
king turned again to a strong alliance with his queen and her
group, all Catholic. He did not consider acceding to the reform
that Commons desired, but rather held stubbornly to his accustomed attitude. Carlton writes:

> The king's intransigence combined with pressure from outside par-
> liament, particularly from the Scots, to destroy any chance of moder-
> ate episcopal reform. With his usual lack of tact Charles had a royal
> chaplain preach at court that Presbyterianism was a faith "fit only
> for Tradesmen and Beggars". Soon afterwards the king told parlia-
> ment that he was utterly committed to bishops. Williams, who be-
> lieved that regulating episcopacy was tantamount to demolishing
> it, chaired a Lords committee to examine the possibility of a weak
> Presbyterian system in which bishops were answerable to diocesan
> committees of laymen and clerics. The proposal was defeated, be-
> cause the pressures for total abolition were mounting so fast.[64]

Marvell's lover is the cormorants' victim, which in a real sense
was true. Even Williams's moderate attitude was more politically
beneficial to the clergy than to the king, and very likely had
much to do with his hatred of Laud. Almost everyone hated

Laud, with the exception of Buckingham (He and Laud enjoyed discussing astrology.) and Strafford. The king needed him, accepted his guidance, but never made him his confessor, though Laud was vicar to the royal family. Carlton states that "Charles and Laud shared a common sense of place, hierarch and order; both felt that as a king and a bishop respectively they were ultimately answerable to God, and must support each other."[65] Laud and Williams, the king's chaplain Bishop Wren whom he allowed without complaint to be sent to the Tower in 1640, and the other bishops, would form the "num'rous fleet of Corm'rants black, / That sail'd insulting o're the Wrack," (27–28). To their own advantage, they have instructed him in what he as king should expect from the people. To his disadvantage, he has entrusted his care, his country, "into their cruel Care" (29):

> They fed him up with Hopes and Air,
> Which soon digested to Despair.
> And as one Corm'rant fed him, still
> Another on his Heart did bill.
> Thus while they famish him, and feast,
> He both consumed, and increast:
> And languished with doubtful Breath,
> The *Amphibium* of Life and Death.
>
> (33–40)

Their manipulation ends for him in despair; he lives in perpetual fear, subject to "Angry Heaven," who calls him out to fight against his now "Tyrant Love," England, whose "Flames" of love have turned their artillery against him:

> And now, when angry Heaven wou'd
> Behold a spectacle of Blood,
> Fortune and He are call'd to play
> At sharp before it all the day:
> And Tyrant Love his brest does ply
> With all his wing'd Artillery.
> Whilst he, betwixt the Flames and Waves,
> Like *Ajax*, the mad Tempest braves.
>
> (41–48)

Poor lover, all are against him—Providence, the stubborn Rock of the English church; he is now "Torn into Flames" (54), truly the "Orphan of the *Hurricane*" (32). His have been "Malignant Starrs" by which he has been "Forced to live in Storms and

Warrs" (59–60). Have the stars alone caused all this? Marvell
limns the Petrarchan lover, full of tears and sighs (17–20), "unfortunate and abject" (30), using the conventional militaristic language, all of which reveal as well as hide his subject. "Angry
Heaven" has deemed that Fortune be his adversary; in "An Horatian Ode," Cromwell is "Fortunes Son" (113). His great spirit
achieves his victories:

> Though Justice against Fate complain,
> And plead the antient Rights in vain:
> But those do hold or break
> As Men are strong or weak.
> Nature that hateth emptiness,
> Allows of penetration less;
>   And therefore must make room
>   Where greater Spirits come.
> What Field of all the Civil Wars,
> Where his were not the deepest Scars?
>
> (37–46)

He not only "acts," which the unfortunate lover does not, he also
"knows," in comparison to the lover who "languishes" "with
doubtful Breath" (39). The *Eikon Basilike—The Pourtraicture of
His Sacred Majestie in His Solitudes and Sufferings* presents
itself as Charles's meditations and prayers performed in solitude
with loving concern for England. The "self"-portrait that emerges
is of a prince of high principles, deeply religious whose enemies,
identified only as "they," are determined to destroy both state
and church,[66] but he, forgiving all malice will go to his "violent
death with [his] Saviour, [for] it is but mortality crowned with
martyrdom."[67] The unfortunate lover faces the storm, saying only,
and they are his only words: "a Lover drest / In his own Blood
does relish best" (56). His audience to whom he speaks likes its
lovers suffering, bleeding, dying,[68] reminiscent of "An Horatian
Ode" in which "the armed Bands / Did clap their bloody hands"
(55–56) and "The Death of O.C." in which the people do not
"deem" Cromwell's death noble because it was not "horrid,"
bloody.

The "story" in which the "lover" rules is the *Eikon Basilike*,
but it is a fabrication, as "story" indicates. Interpreted thus, Marvell's reputed vacillating allegiance appears fabrication as well.

2

"I have a Garden of my own": Marvell's Poetic Direction

ALLEGORICAL interpretations of Andrew Marvell's poetry are sometimes hard to understand or difficult to accept, sometimes even grotesque. Yet literal explication can only partially satisfy with Marvell, as we have seen. His often hypothetical verse seems to assume the shifting quality of the circumstances he presents, and the critic who does not read his verse on a provisional basis risks absurdity. As I have observed earlier, Marvell somewhat predictably signals his reader through obtrusive imagery or allegorical structure. Moreover, Alastair Fowler has shown Marvell's poetry to yield without equivocation to certain numerological analysis. In *Triumphal Forms: Structural Patterns in Elizabethan Poetry*, Fowler points out Marvell's use of the "central accent" in which he presents at the center of a poem a figure, a particular moment, or an emotion such as love that "looks. . . . forward . . . to triumph." He illustrates Marvell's 'finesses' of the "convention of central accent"[1] in "The Picture of little T.C. in a Prospect of Flowers," in "An Horatian Ode," in "The First Anniversary," and notes the instance of it also in "Upon the Death of the Lord Hastings."[2]

That Marvell uses the sovereign position, however, so consistently for a fall and that the fall is so frequently followed by an ascent (which, of course, is the triumph) suggests that he planned the structure to allegorize the "fortunate fall." Generally, the structure allegorically speaks for his advocacy of what may be called a destined progression and, whatever the theme, is consistent with his evident faith in the providential nature of occurrences. (Or as John Wallace has so elegantly shown us to do, we may vary Marvell's own phrase and say in his use of this structural allegory, he opts for destiny as his choice when he chooses sides on gardens and political parties.) For example, the structure functions eloquently in "An Horatian Ode" as a reflection

of Marvell's attitude on Charles I's loss of his divine right as the
first man and Cromwell's position as the one whom God had
shown by events to possess the divine right. In some of the lyrics,
Marvell's central accent may present a fall—in the Mower poems,
for example—that does not paradoxically turn upon itself to become an ascent nor look forward in any way to a triumph. In
this usage, the structure may reflect despair about his own future.
There are poems, of course, that do not contain the central accent. The distinction perhaps hinges on the time they were written. The poems of this discussion are almost certainly, with the
exception of "Mr. Milton's 'Paradise Lost,'" the products of the
Interregnum years, the years of greatest choice in Marvell's life.

Out of an analysis of this structural allegory emerges an anat-
omy of Marvell's perception of his role as providential historiographer and poet, as well as his resolution of a poetic crisis. These
would seem to be very nearly if not the same decisions, and
perhaps with another poet they would be. But Marvell in the
Mower poems seems to grapple with a poetic crisis, whereas in
the poems that are considered "public" he defines himself in
roles that can only be seen as active. "The Garden" suggests a
resolution of his despondency in the proposition that art can
create a respite from temporality, but only a respite.

The midpoint accent is present in Marvell's earliest poetry.
"To his Noble Friend Mr. Richard Lovelace upon his Poems"
(1647/48) contains a fall—"You shall for being faultlesse be accus'd" (25)—that by its nature will ultimately be a triumph. Only
in such "degenerate" (1) times could this happen. But since
Lovelace's guilt is nonexistent, he will remain "faultlesse" and
achieve "glory" (47) when time has been fulfilled. By extension,
Marvell's well-spoken tribute is also faultless in the sense that
his wit obviously has not "drawne th' infection" (4) of his time,
but remains true to the spirit of the Golden Age when "Modest
ambition studi'd only . . . To honour not her selfe, but worthy
men" (9–10).[3]

In another early poem, "Upon the Death of Lord Hastings,"
Marvell presents the fall in the entire first half which mourns
the too-early death of the young man, and then gives the center
or sovereign position to the metaphor of the Prince who saves
"his neerest and most lov'd *Ally*" (28). Hastings' earthly fall
makes possible his ascent, for his "thought" will go with him:
"So he, not banisht hence, but there confin'd, / There better recre-
ates his active Minde" (31–32). I believe this is odd consolation
and more applicable perhaps to Marvell whose sensibilities at

the time of the poem (Hastings died on 24 June 1649) may have still been shocked by the political turmoil. He himself may have longed for solitude in which to think, to recreate his own "active Minde," his own "neerest and most lov'd *Ally.*" His parents both dead, his connections apparently few, he seems to have been in London for less than two years at this time. What he did there, we do not know, but he had sold the last of his grandfather's property in 1647, perhaps to go to London or to stay if he had already determined on living there after his return from abroad. We can surmise that he went to London to seek patronage for his poetry if we see statement of poetic intent in the Lovelace poem. As for the desire for solitude in which to think, we recall his pleasure in "The Garden" and in "Upon Appleton House," as well as the mower's frustration in his "Song" with what Juliana "does to my Thoughts" (6).

In the next two years (1650–52), Marvell wrote two of his finest poems in praise of worthy men of the civil war, presenting in one of them a fair account of the king. As fittingly graceful and dignified as Marvell's portrait of Charles is, the king loses his head in the sovereign position of the poem. Fowler, commenting on Marvell's central placement of the beheading, observes that the "positioning of the king's execution evidently focuses a complex range of ideas and feelings about Cromwell's triumph."[4] True. But what is unequivocal is the moment: "that memorable Hour / Which first assured the forced Pow'r" (69). And that "forced Pow'r," working through Cromwell—"so fit he is to sway / That can so well obey" (83–84)—will effect the state's foreseen "happy Fate" (72).

As apologist in "An Horatian Ode," Marvell had found his metier. In the composition of "Tom May's Death," he discovered an additional facet compatible with his perception of how to serve the new state—historiographer of particular events as they mirrored the whole. He may be seen to fulfill Sidney's dictum that poetry should 'couple' "the general notion with the particular example." Moreover, his moral condemnation of May and pronouncement of appropriate behavior indicate that he hoped to function as Sidney defines the "peerless poet," as both historian and moral philosopher.[5]

In "Tom May's Death," Marvell has Ben Jonson address May as "Malignant Poet and Historian" (42) and gibe at May for his wrongheaded comparisons of Rome and England; he refuses May admittance to the poets' company for purposefully misusing history to satisfy a personal vendetta: "But the[e] nor Ignorance nor

seeming good / Misled, but malice fixt and understood" (55–56).
John Coolidge has admirably elucidated Marvell's probable motivation in writing "Tom May's Death." The central accent of the
poem is contained in the passage crucial to Coolidge's argument
that Marvell condemns May for his use of "historical simili-
tudes" that imply Charles "is like one or another tyrannical Roman emperor":[6]

> Foul Architect that hadst not Eye to see
> How ill the measures of these States agree.
> And who by Romes example England lay,
> Those but to Lucan do continue May.

> (51–54)

May's fall is one from which there should be no ascent. He has
exploited the change, not only out of spite at not having been
chosen poet laureate, but also for his personal gain. His manipulation of opinion through invalid analogy can only weaken the
English by seducing them into incorrect estimates of what has
actually happened; thus, he is a "Foul Architect" who would
undermine rather than build the new state. May's burial in Westminster Abbey would seem to assure him earthly triumph; but
for his prostitution of knowledge, Marvell condemns him to a
hellish punishment: "Thou rivited until Ixion's Wheel / Shalt
break, and the perpetual Vulture feel. / 'Tis just what Torments
Poets ere did feign, / Thou first Historically shouldst sustain"
(93–96). Marvell thus exposes May, and in his dicta of what the
poet should do in troubled times illustrates his own suitability
for the role of moral philosopher.

Though Marvell proved his own worthiness to be state historian, he seems to have been the only one who knew of his quali-
fications. To be Maria Fairfax's tutor could have struck him as
providential opportunity, for at Appleton he could draw at close
range a most accurate portrait of the great General Fairfax. Retired for a number of reasons, Fairfax maintained that he was
always opposed to the regicide; I think that his opposition did
not alter Marvell's opinion.

Several poems likely to have been written during the Appleton
period exhibit political allegory that favors the path that destiny
apparently has dictated. My guess is that "The Mower Against
Gardens" arose out of his decision to create a pastoral figure
appropriate to the time.[7] (The other Mower poems, extensions of
this, possess more complex meanings.) In this poem, Marvell

makes sport of the sovereign position and allots it "To Man, that sov'raign thing and proud" (20), probably because he makes sport of the single-minded, cantankerous figure who looks at a created garden and can think only of mankind's pride. Yet it is the Mower's own pride that causes his anguish. He is indignant that his meadow where he ruled over life and death is no longer the world's measure of order and beauty. His reign has been supplanted by the artful gardener who nurtures his subjects rather than merely determining whether they will live or die. In this interpretation, the mower, the monarch of the meadow, allegorically represents the king; Marvell's choice of mower rather than shepherd for his pastoral figure takes on a gruesome significance, but one not beyond Marvell's sometimes deadfall wit. The Mower as stoutly maintains that the gods favor him as Charles had been strong for divine right. Yet he neglects to remember, as the king did, that he himself possesses no actual divinity. Rather he is fallen, responsible for the death of sweet fields, and in fact a part of man's alteration of nature that has led to the artifice of the garden, the new measure, as the king was responsible for the necessity of the new order. Moreover, the gods whose favor he claims to possess have not acted to halt the change, as Providence had failed to act for Charles. The mower remains fallen, but at his own insistence; those he rails against seem to have found renewal and redemption in the new gardens. Of course, one may take the perspective of the mower.[8]

At Appleton, Marvell seems likely to have embarked immediately on the writing of the two poems addressed to Fairfax. Both "Upon the Hill and Grove at Bill-borow" and the fine "Upon Appleton House" praise Fairfax for his humility. The fortunate fall pattern would have been unthinkable in a poem such as "Upon the Hill and Grove," but Marvell incorporates it in "Upon Appleton House" in which the midpoint descent is into the meadow, that surreality where the reader reels with the allegorical possibilities, all of which may be seen to possess reference to the civil war in some way or another. The descent is from the Fairfax Eden, where the family lives what Marvell presents in this poem as a providentially guided life, into the abyss of shifting perspective and "unfathomable" (370) bottom. The descent for the poet is paradoxically fortuitous. In the scorn he experiences in the meadow, he is designated prophet; in the wood where he escapes the flood, he becomes priest—the "great Prelate of the Grove" (592). Thus translated, he ends his spiritual ascent in a reentry into the Fairfax garden. For the role of provi-

dential historiographer, higher than that to which he aspired in
"Tom May's Death," he has proved himself qualified to assume
through the justification he has provided for Fairfax, illustrating how his retirement has been the natural and God-guided
response of a conscience such as his and elucidating how Appleton House became a religious house only at the Fairfaxes'
assumption.

But having arrived at what must be termed an exalted destiny,
albeit self-appointed, where was the poet then? Still at Appleton
House and still tutor to a young girl. Marvell may well have
experienced at this time an episode of what has sometimes been
called his passive mode, though I think that the definition falls
short of accuracy. Action he perhaps thought impossible for him
until another position beckoned. If he stayed at Appleton House,
poetry and only poetry would seem to be his destiny. No more
thought of a chosen role in the parliamentarian regime. But what
kind of poetry could one write at Appleton? A kind of mutant
pastoral. He had finished (or so I surmise) his encomia of Fairfax.
I believe he then began a kind of exploration and the results were
the other Mower poems and "The Nymph complaining for the
death of her Faun," for they exhibit a similar distressed attitude.
In each, the lamenting figures are alone in a landscape that does
not respond to their sorrow.

Whoever or whatever Juliana is, Damon describes her as destructive. I suppose Marvell could have fallen in love while he
was at Appleton House, but there's not much that's real about
Juliana as a woman. Moreover, he uses some of the same description for her that he uses for Maria Fairfax,[9] and I don't believe
that anyone has ever thought that he was in love with her. These
poems do seem to have been written over a summer, for a passage
of time exists. "The Mower's Song" may precede "Damon the
Mower" and "The Mower to the Glo-Worms," and since it seems
more fraught with despair than the others, I will consider it
first.[10] Damon's attitude toward his work has changed; that is,
before Juliana, his work was his joy. Now there is the sense of
imminent death. He is angry that the meadows can grow happily
on without his corresponding growth, that they can ignore what
he has thought a symbiotic relationship while he lies "trodden
under feet" (16). This line is the central accent. "Under feet"
makes clear the fall and there is obviously no ascent in this
poem. As revenge for nature's desertion, he will bring ruin to
all: "Flow'rs, and Grass, and I and all" (22).

In "The Mower to the Glo-Worms," the nightingale can compose "Her matchless Songs" (4) by the "dear light" of the glo-worms, but he cannot. Useful these glo-worms may be to nightin-gales and wandering mowers, but not for him. The customary midpoint "fall" position is honored in the word *fall* (8). The mower looks forward to nothing, for he has "in the Night . . . lost" his "aim" (11), astray in the wake of "foolish Fires" (12).

The alienation continues in "Damon the Mower"; Damon's thoughts have been torn from his world, and in the unnatural atmosphere created by Juliana, he becomes as separate from that world as the grass he severs from the earth. Damon's fall is Juli-ana. He complains throughout the first half, then attempts to rise through his reminders to himself of who he is: "I am the Mower Damon, known / Through all the meadows I have mown" (41–42). He also attends to his wealth and appearance: "Yet am I richer far in Hay. / Nor am I so deform'd to sight, / If in my sithe I looked right" (56–58). But how can he look "right" mirrored in a scythe, curved and distorting, symbolic of the unnatural shape of his mind and warped vision? He speaks with satisfac-tion of his dances with the "deathless Fairyes" (61):

> The deathless Fairyes take me oft
> To lead them in their Danses soft;
> And, when I tune my self to sing,
> About me they contract their Ring.
>
> (61–64)

His "Fairyes" may be the surviving spirits, "genii"[11] of the Golden Age; when he "tunes" himself "to sing," he has the bar-rier of "their Ring" to stay the power of Juliana. (This is some-thing like the solace available from the "active Minde," the "neerest and most lov'd *Ally*" of "Upon the Death of Lord Has-tings.") Now, however, he "all the day" (58) complains. While some escape may be possible, no compromise is for Damon: though he can rise from his self-inflicted wound, he says he cannot from Juliana's.

Had it not been for Juliana, he might have mowed on happily. But where did she come from and who is she? She is neither a shepherdess nor a milkmaid.[12] In their way, the Mower poems are as enigmatic and almost as perfect as "The Nymph complain-ing for the death of her Faun," and none looks forward to tri-umph. The Nymph interrupts her path to death—her response to her loss—only to "bespeak" the Faun's "grave" (110). If these poems were the result of a poetic crisis for Marvell, then the conclusion one draws from the allegorical structure is that to fall without rising from the fall is to die spiritually.[13] "The Garden" seems to reflect a resolution of his dilemma. He finds in the garden that which he foresaw for Hastings, a re-creation of "his active Minde." Although the garden is a sanctuary, there is nothing passive about the atmosphere. In the "Fair quiet" and "Innocence" (9–10) of "this delicious Solitude" (16), one can think. He meditates on the ambitions of men for military glory and poetic fame and laughs at their frenzied activity. He contemplates also what other poets have conventionally thought of in gardens—of mistresses—and of their poetry in praise of those mistresses: "When we have run our Passions heat, / Love hither makes his best retreat!" (25–26). Warren Chernaik has commented on both the resemblance and difference in Marvell's and Waller's use of Apollo and Daphne, concluding that the difference is greater than the resemblance since "Marvell uses the myth . . . as one of a string of related conceits to support his case for asexual retirement and solitude.[14] The specific lines in Waller are those in which he reveals that his poetry for Sacharissa has itself brought him sufficient reward without her:

> What he sung in his immortal strain,
> Though unsuccessful, was not sung in vain.
> All, but the nymph that should redress his wrong,
> Attend his passion, and approve his song.
> Like Phoebus thus, acquiring unsought praise,
> He catched at love, and filled his arms with bays.
>
> (15–20)

But Marvell reiterates, perhaps as a comment on Waller, that love poetry is written more for fame's sake than love's. The poem starts on this note; then he proposes in the passage that Chernaik discusses that Apollo's and Pan's pursuits were quite as mundane as those of poets. Has Marvell become a poet as worldly as Waller? Did Juliana exist or was she merely a fabrication on which to practice poetry? Or is this the completely recovered lover who denigrates his former love-longings? Whatever. The poet has apparently recovered his active self; there is the midpoint fall, but he falls in the bounty that the garden lavishes on him. He is no ungrateful lover. The fall, rather than constraining him, leads him to a depth of thought and creativity that transcends all other experience. Empson has drawn our attention to melon as Greek for apple,[15] and rightly so, it seems to me, for this *is* a fall in the garden, that comes about through the self-indulgence or indolence that the garden's seductive pleasures encourage. In this garden, the indolence appears vital to the creative mind:

> Mean while the Mind, from pleasure less,
> Withdraws into its happiness:
> The Mind, that Ocean where each kind
> Does streight its own resemblance find;
> Yet it creates, transcending these,
> Far other Worlds, and other Seas;
> Annihilating all that's made
> To a green Thought in a green Shade.
>
> (41–48)

This transcendence traditionally suggests growth. Whereas the single state in the garden provides bliss uninterrupted by concerns extraneous to its enjoyment, Marvell reminds us in the same bantering mood that "'twas beyond a mortal's share / To wander solitary there" (64), however paradisal it may be. Marvell is not simply advocating the "happy Garden-state . . . without a Mate" (57–58). The garden is a retreat, but one cannot live there. Even nature has its work: "as it works, th'industrious Bee / Computes its time as well as we" (69–70). This is a created garden, the kind of garden the Mower rails against in "The Mower Against Gardens"; it is not the first Eden, but an artful re-creation for which there should be no need if man had never fallen and the original still existed. Thus art may be considered a result of the fall. Within its power is the ability to create a new Eden, however briefly, that can evoke Edenic feelings, which should be its purpose rather than "To win the Palm, the Oke, or Bayes" (2). A part of Marvell's resolution of his anguish was the self-knowledge that he desired "longer flight" (55). As nourishing as the "Fair quiet" of Appleton is in "The Garden," there have also been the sharp sorrow and withered hopes we hear of in the Mower poems.

Two other poems that I suspect he wrote during this time seem beyond his self-defining period in that they are like development from rather than part of a psychic process. Though "The Nymph complaining for the death of her Faun" does not look forward to a triumph, it does present what I see as a resolution in a different though relevant way to "The Garden." The nymph has a garden that is not an artful paradise. Hers is "so with Roses over grown, / And Lillies, that you would it guess / To be a little Wilderness" (72–74). She is "very well" (30) content with it, and the faun

flourishes there: "all its chief delight was still / On Roses thus
its self to fill" (87–88). They are two creatures fit for an Edenic
garden tainted only in that it has grown wild. An artful garden
would be alien to them. The faun, once a wild creature, reversed
its nature to grow tame with the nymph, as Sylvio, the giver of
the faun, changed places with it to grow "wild" (34). The man
and the beast have exchanged roles. The nymph is satisfied with
the exchange:

> Thenceforth I set my self to play
> My solitary time away,
> With this: and very well content,
> Could so mine idle Life have spent.
>
> (37–40)

She could tolerate the loss of Sylvio who took away "his Heart"
(36), but she cannot abide the death of her faun. She will join it
in death. Perfidy was a sin with which she could live out her
ordinary mortality, but wanton cruelty destroys her will to live.
Yet wantonness prevails in the poem. The troopers are wanton,
Sylvio is wanton, but the nymph is not. The nature of gardens
is to grow wild, and the nature of men has imitated it, a descent
for mankind beyond the first fall. The wild beast, because of its
willingness, can rise above its bestiality, can grow tame, civilized,
loving of the nymph who is entirely faithful to it. Unlike Sylvio
for whom the garden is an entrapment from which he wishes to
escape, the faun loves to live in the captivity of the garden. And
the nymph loves living there with it:

> For it was full of sport; and light
> Of foot, and heart; and did invite,
> Me to its game: it seem'd to bless
> Its self in me. How could I less
> Than love it?
>
> (41–44)

She cannot be "unkind , t' a Beast that loveth me" (44–45); that
is, she has not descended to the levels of Sylvio and the troopers.
Though a creature of the first fall and mortal in that she can die,
the nymph has escaped the second fall. She remains innocent of
blood lust; her monosyllabic diction reflects her simplicity and
guilelessness. The faun is an intelligent, loving beast. These two
creatures are not like any mortals or beasts that we have known.
Significantly, they are unnamed other than by species, faun and

nymph, and who has known a nymph or a faun? Only Sylvio has a name—that is, only Sylvio of the three is a creature such as we might know. To be named is to be known.[16] The wanton troopers are known by their category; their species is man, but descended to a state so base that they exploit the mortality of man and beast. They do not enter the nymph's garden; "The wanton Troopers riding by / Have shot my Faun and it will dye" (1–2), the Nymph cries. She in her innocence is certain that there will be retribution, that "They cannot thrive / To kill" (3–4). We are so certain that there will not be retribution that we hardly give cognizance to the statement, but rather absorb it as part of her innocence. Marvell extends her expression of indignation and faith in justice through the first twenty-four lines. God will surely make the "wanton" soldiers answer:

> Heavens King
> Keeps register of every thing:
> And nothing may we use in vain.
> Ev'n Beasts must be with justice slain.
>
> (13–16)

Marvell emphasizes the waste of life not simply in the death of the faun, but in Sylvio's unfaithfulness, as well as in the cumulative grief to the nymph so that her life in the garden has been destroyed by the wanton and wild natures of men. Sylvio had his moments of love for the nymph, but he is an ordinary, inconstant mortal, enjoying the paradise for awhile, but ready to move out of what is essentially only occasionally necessary to his nature. So fallen is mankind's nature that living in Eden would soon cause him to grow as restless as Sylvio.

The midpoint accent looks forward to a fall; the faun's fall that occurs in the first two lines of the poem is only its death; the incident itself reflects the sin of Cain in the wanton murder of a creature that "neer didst alive / Them any harm: alas nor could / Thy death yet do them any good" (4–6). Marvell mounts a portrait of the faun in its beauty while honoring the position in praising its feet:

> And oft
> I blusht to see its foot more soft,
> And white, (shall I say then my hand?)
> NAY any Ladies of the Land.

> It is a wond'rous thing, how fleet
> 'Twas on those little silver feet.

> (59–64)

There is no ascent; mankind has fallen too far from Eden to return or even to want to return. The Nymph will die; the faun will lie at her feet. Though no one will grieve for them, she will grieve for her loss through eternity:

> For I so truly thee bemoane,
> That I shall weep though I be Stone:
> Until my Tears, still dropping, wear
> My breast, themselves engraving there.
> There at my feet shalt thou be laid,
> Of purest Alabaster made:
> For I would have thine Image be
> White as I can, though not as Thee.

> (115–22)

The ultimate witchery Marvell performs in this poem, however, is to create a work of art so perfect, so satisfying that it is itself like an Edenic garden, and I suppose I must say our fallen nature forces us to look for the "meaning," not content to be merely aesthetically nourished by it.

The serpent, instrument for the fall, occupies the midpoint position in "The Coronet," and the poem looks forward to a fall that is paradoxically an ascent. Here, Marvell executes a finesse of his favored tactic of centering the fall or honoring it in the mention of feet; he ends his poem with a fall, the fall of Satan, though it may be the fall of his art as well. That is, that Christ will destroy the serpent's power in his art, though it destroy the art, is the ultimate triumph. Thus, he hopes that his "curious frame" will crown Christ's feet:

> When for the Thorns with which I long, too long,
>   With many a piercing wound,
>   My Saviours head have crown'd,
> I seek with Garlands to redress that Wrong:
>   Through every Garden, every Mead,
>
> I gather flow'rs (my fruits are only flow'rs)
>   Dismantling all the fragrant Towers
> That once adorn'd my Shepherdesses head.
> And now when I have summ'd up all my store,
>   Thinking (so I my self deceive)
>   So rich a Chaplet thence to weave

As never yet the king of Glory wore:
  Alas I find the Serpent old
  That, twining in his speckled breast,
  About the flow'rs disguis'd does fold,
  With wreaths of Fame and Interest.
Ah, foolish Man, that would'st debase with them,
And mortal Glory, Heavens Diadem!
But thou who only could'st the Serpent tame,
Either his slipp'ry knots at once untie,
And disintangle all his winding Snare:
Or shatter too with him my curious frame:
And let these wither, so that he may die,
Though set with Skill and chosen out with Care.
That they, while Thou on both their Spoils dost tread,
May crown thy Feet, that could not crown thy Head.

This poem may be seen as marking Marvell's awareness that religious poetry was not his metier. Donald Friedman terms it palinode and draws the comparison to Herbert's "Jordan" poems.[17] Though disagreeing that it is a palinode, Margaret Carpenter makes a striking case for Marvell and Herbert's thematic resemblance in "the notion of man's central concern as the effort to live in some kind of creative relation to God's own providential creativity."[18] Almost everyone has noticed that "The Coronet" resembles Herbert's "A Wreath," the structure of which creates a wreath. A circular pattern as well is discernible in Marvell's poem, albeit imperfectly formed, which would seem to be the point. Marvell's opening with "When" suggests the sonnet form, and resounds, for example, Milton's "When I consider how my life is spent" and Shakespeare's frequent "when-when-then" pattern. And the rhyme scheme of abba, cddc, effe presents the familiar Shakespearean sonnet. Had Marvell not interposed the line between "Alas I find the Serpent old" (13) and "About the flow'rs disguis'd does fold" (15), we should have a very neat sonnet. I surmise that Marvell expected his reader to recognize the sonnet form *and* surely the midpoint accent that "Alas I find the Serpent old" marks and to understand the descent from perfect form caused by the serpent. The suspension of meaning through the first four lines is reminiscent too of Milton. Milton uses the talent parable; Marvell, albeit obliquely, uses the first fruits metaphor—"Through every Garden, every Mead, / I gather flow'rs (my fruits are only flow'rs) / Dismantling all the fragrant Towers / That once adorn'd my Shepherdesses head" (5–8)—which incorporates as much as Milton's sonnet the theme of one's return to

God. Marvell, however, may be interpreted as seeing his poetry as inchoate in the sense that his "fruits are only flow'rs." (With Marvell of course many meanings will be played upon, so that his lines are a 'posey' in the figurative sense, as well as flowery praise of the nature that one might pay to one's "Shepherdesses.") This is consistent with the perfect sonnet that becomes imperfect because the fall—the serpent—interrupted.

Though "The Coronet" is a remarkable poem by the highest standards, religious poetry per se was not to be Marvell's poetic direction; he would continue on the path he had originally chosen—to honor great men.

3

"'Twas no *Religious House* till now":
Marvell and the Retired Life with Fairfax

MARVELL'S first major panegyric, "Upon Appleton House," has
been considered flawed, however, by the twenty-five stanza historical section—thrown off balance by the William Fairfax–
Isabel Thwaites-nuns' story.[1] Yet as Marvell presents it, the
history is essential to his purpose in the poem, which is to recon-
stitute the chronicle of Nunappleton House, representing the
Fairfax possession as providential. In this beautifully crafted
poem, Marvell guides us through a landscape, explicitly and covertly controlling the vista to cast the story of the Fairfaxes in
its true mold. Rather than praise General Fairfax, he eulogizes
the traditions and ideals embodied in his family.

In 1650, Fairfax, Commander-in-Chief of all the Commonwealth of England forces, resigned in opposition to the Council
of State's decision to invade Scotland. He would defend England,
but the staunchly Presbyterian Fairfax maintained that he would
not act as the aggressor against Scotland with whom England
was joined in the National League and Covenant. For Fairfax,
Presbyterian against Presbyterian was a corruption of their
united effort against episcopacy. The commonwealth itself and
the great estates ambitious Parliament men were gathering for
themselves were opposite to his principles and signaled to Fairfax the additional degeneration of Civil War goals.[2] Marvell's
strategy is to make his poem an indirect witness and tribute to
the integrity of Fairfax's conscience. He also reflects the religious
dichotomy in opposing Nunappleton to Cawood Castle, the seat
of the Archbishop of York. Thus Marvell will suggest that Fairfax's civil war participation was directed solely to the abolition
of episcopacy and its abuses. Cawood Castle and the "Ambition
of its Prelate great" (366) symbolize the ecclesiastical regime and
its most secularized representative, Archbishop John Williams.[3]
They represent an analogous situation to that presented in the

estate's history of the cloister and the nuns' corrupt spirituality
that Marvell shows as the reason for their dispossession by William Fairfax, whose "Religion taught him Right, / And dazled
not but clear'd his sight" (227–28).

But Marvell's reshaping the nuns' story answers another issue—the possession of Nunappleton House itself. To live in a
former monastery or build on the site of one was widely regarded
as sacrilege. Marvell's reconstruction of the Fairfax legend suggests an effort to relieve Fairfax's fears that Providence was acting
against him or would do so because he assumed and retained
the Nunappleton property. Nunappleton had been a Cistercian
priory until 1542 when it was given to the sons of Isabel
Thwaites and William Fairfax, and the first residence there was
built from materials of the nunnery (whether actual sections of
the nunnery were retained and expanded is not known). Nor is
it certain that the General and his family were living in the new
Appleton House. The consideration that John Newman has given
the question[4] makes it easy to believe that they lived in the original house constructed out of the priory, which would encourage
Fairfax's anxiety and Marvell's focus on the landscape.

Divine retaliation for such sacrilege might come suddenly or
it might be worked out in time (usually three generations). In
his excellent *Religion and the Decline of Magic*, Keith Thomas
identifies Sir Henry Spelman as the popular disseminator of the
belief that the impropriation of church lands was sacrilege. Spelman's work grew into a catalogue "of the punishments which
God had bestowed for sacrilege from the time of the Old Testa-
ment onwards, but the most influential part related to the fate
of the purchasers of the monastic lands in England."[5] According
to Spelman, the former monasteries brought only misfortune to
their new owners; families withered in them, producing a pau-
city of male heirs who seemed inordinately prone to "grievous
accidents and misfortunes." The cloisters "flung out" their in-
habitants. "It hath not happened that any of them, to my knowledge, or any other in all this country, hath been the permanent
habitation of any family of note." Spelman also observed that
"no man almost" dared "to build or dwell" on the former monastery sites, and lists the experiences of many who had and the
dreadful "infelicity"[6] that pursued them.

General Fairfax held other properties that were formerly
Church holdings, and unlike many others, he was punctilious
in returning their tithes to the clergy. While this expresses some
personal integrity, it may also be construed as an effort to ward

off the curse.[7] If the Fairfaxes were indeed living in the house built with material from the nunnery, and constructing another house on the site, both sacrilegious acts, and if Fairfax had the strong seventeenth-century respect for divine retribution, then it is possible to see that Marvell's impulse in the historical reconstitution may rest in part on the desire to allay Fairfax's fears and convince his fastidious conscience that his ownership of Nunappleton fit a higher design in God's scheme than the nuns' possession did. As a maneuver to disguise this propaganda, Marvell puts history into the whole of the landscape, thus expanding the traditional "walkabout" of the estate poem into a journey. Marvell introduces in stanza 5 the pilgrimage theme, and the trip itself begins at stanza 10, just before the account of the nuns, and ends only with his invitation at the end to reenter the house itself. The multiplicity of sights suggests also a pilgrimage—its goal the shrine of order and beauty that is Maria Fairfax in the garden of Nunappleton. Marvell, in a sense, makes destiny his choice by creating a poem to illustrate that Providence took a hand in placing the Fairfaxes at Nunappleton, and that General Fairfax's conscientious stewardship (in the best tradition) provides a pattern for England.

Thus in "Upon Appleton House," Marvell contends that the religious purposes of the house are "likely better thus fulfill'd" (276) by the seat's going to the Fairfaxes, for "'Twas no *Religious House* till now" (280). Much of his description emphasizes Nunappleton House's religious character: the first line of the poem introduces it as a "sober frame," not extravagant or excessive, and *sober* is repeated in the fourth stanza to establish the relationship between the house and England's Golden Age:

> But all things are composed here
> Like Nature, orderly and near:
> In which we the Dimensions find
> Of that more sober Age and Mind,
> When larger-sized Men did stoop
> To enter at a narrow loop;
> As practising, in doors so strait,
> To strain themselves through *Heavens Gate.*

(25–32)

This is a house "composed" to an earlier English tradition that was more God-fearing, when men practiced humility and shunned ostentation in such things as houses and doorways for a moderate, pious expression of themselves. It also seems possi-

ble that Marvell intends to erase the meaning of the tiny doorways still existing from the cloister and transform the narrow
openings into the familiar image from Erasmus's *Paraphrases* of
the "eye of the needle" through which a camel can more easily
pass than the "covetous rich" can enter the gate of Heaven.[8] The
following stanza persuades the reader that the Fairfaxes belong
to that "more sober Age"—those who could enter "*Heavens
Gate*"—by projecting the "after Age" (33) pilgrims' wonder
that the Fairfax magnitude could pass through such low and
straight doors.

Moreover, Marvell presents Fairfax as illustrating his virtue
through his employment of his wealth; he displays more than
the customary noblesse oblige. The "Stately *Frontispice of Poor
. . .* [that] Adorns without the open Door" (65–66) has the feel
of a gracious almshouse, but when "*Furniture of Friends*" (68)
is added to it, the house becomes something more than ordinary.
In these two phrases, Marvell transforms the inanimate into the
animate and the house takes on a vital quality. The last four lines
of the stanza reinforce this effect. Nunappleton had not been
built to impress anyone, but "built upon the Place / Only as for
a *Mark of Grace*" (69–70), that is, a mark of the family's grace
(and favor) for the estate. It was to provide entertainment and
occasional shelter for its lord, his friends, and the surrounding
poor, and was never intended for continual occupancy.

But Marvell's parabolic language imparts a religious purpose
to the Fairfaxes' building. As he begins the story of Nunappleton,
he guides his audience out of the house into the landscape, ef-
fecting the transition by directing our eyes—"While with slow
Eyes we these survey" (81)—to the landscape before us: "fragrant
Gardens, shaddy Woods, / Deep Meadows, and transparent
Floods" (79–80). The rich vocabulary of sight and the repetition
of *eye* and *eyes* are too present to be unaware that Marvell creates
this particular perspective. He also directs our pace—"on each
pleasant footstep stay" (82)—and thus constructs the ideal setting for telling us the "Progress of this Houses Fate" (84). In
keeping with the vitality of the house assumed earlier, we now
find that it had a mother, a virgin mother who was violated, and
thus "brought forth" the house: "all the Neighbour-Ruine shows /
The Quarries whence this dwelling rose" (87–88). That is, the
house was constructed of the ruins of the cloister.

The next stanza describes the nuns' seduction of Isabel
Thwaites. Marvell creates the "suttle" speaking nun as a "distorted image" of his own role as "authority,"[9] a parallel that par-

odies. She, too, directs the eye of her audience: "'Within this holy leisure we / Live innocently as you see'" (97–98). In reality, the nuns may have been innocent of all that Marvell accuses: the abbess was Isabel Thwaites's guardian, Lady Anna Langton, and she served as the head of the nunnery until the dissolution. Isabel Thwaites might often have been at the nunnery with her guardian, and Lady Langton possibly shut her up to keep her from William Fairfax, not to make a religious of her. Or perhaps William Fairfax seduced her from the nuns rather than the other way round. Whatever the actual circumstance, Marvell is charmingly slanderous, providing a justification for the Fairfax impropriation: he creates a dichotomy between false and true religious houses premised on the Protestant standard of personal faith and integrity of conscience. Marvell makes the nuns rivals to William Fairfax, perhaps to Christ, and also to his own role; the nun's inadvertent exposure of the order's hypocrisy—"'And, if our Rule seem strictly pend, / The Rule it self to you shall bend'" (155–56)—makes Fairfax himself appear more righteous in a dubious action, just as the nun's suasion makes Marvell as poet and guide appear guileless in his manipulating of the reader.

"The Nuns smooth Tongue" (200) 'sucks' Isabel into the convent, and William Fairfax must go to the court to gain "the lawful Form; / Which licens'd either Peace or Force, / To hinder the unjust Divorce" (234–36). Marvell effects a neat inversion here, for Isabel cannot be Christ's bride when she is William Fairfax's: Marvell assumes as a postulate her previous betrothal to William Fairfax; thus, the seduction amounts to an "unjust Divorce." In Fairfax's remonstration with Isabel, Marvell allots him a diatribe against the building itself. Whereas Spelman documented cases of the monastic buildings avenging themselves by throwing their walls or stones on those who tried to put them to secular use,[10] Marvell upends this superstition and directs it at the nuns in the form of a humorous surmise:

> 'Were there but, when this House was made,
> 'One Stone that a just Hand had laid,
> 'It must have fall'n upon her Head
> 'Who first Thee from thy Faith misled.

(209–12)

He makes it part of a larger strategy to subvert the belief that those given monastic property came to disorder and dispossession; so Marvell's first Fairfax asserts that the buildings them-

selves came to grief because they were "Founded by Folly, kept
by Wrong" (218). Thus the orders, rather than Henry VIII, were
responsible for their own misfortune, nullifying any possibility
of sacrilege by the Fairfax family. Certainly William Fairfax has
no desire to commit sacrilege:

> What should he do? He would respect
> Religion, but not Right neglect:
> For first Religion taught him Right,
> And dazled not but clear'd his sight.
> Sometimes resolv'd his Sword he draws,
> But reverenceth then the Laws:
> For Justice still that Courage led;
> First from a Judge, then Souldier bred.
>
> (225–32)

Donald Friedman has observed that "The indecision is resolved,
strangely enough, by the poet's reminder that William Fairfax is
'he whose Offspring fierce / Shall fight through all the *Universe*'
(241–42)."[11] But it is not really strange that the reminder of the
prophecy resolves William Fairfax to action ("Till one, as long
since prophecy'd, / His Horse through conquer'd *Britain* ride"
(245–46)): Marvell is putting forth the higher fate of the house
as young Fairfax's spur to action.[12] Without the compunction
that Fairfax has shown, "the *Nuns* his Right debar'd" (237) with
their "holy Guard," which consists of "Their *Wooden Saints*,"
"their old *Holy-Water Brush*," and "The gingling Chain-shot of
. . . [the Abbess's] Beads"; "their lowd'st Cannon were their
Lungs; / And sharpest Weapons were their Tongues" (250–56).
Fairfax, however, has the true holy guard of Providence, and
"through the Wall does rise" (258). Whether the "Wall" through
which Fairfax rises is that which the nuns claim can "restrain
the World without" (99), or their "holy Guard" described above,
it figuratively protects a false position. Its penetration by William
Fairfax signals Marvell's intention to repudiate the "supersti-
tions vainly fear'd" (260) which surround the current Lord Fairfax. That the cloister is immediately "dispossest" (272) is
figuratively true and literally false, for it was only in the next
generation that it came into the Fairfax family. Marvell's accomplishment in the lines—"The wasting Cloister with the rest /
Was in one instant dispossest" (271–72)—is to equate the order's
hypocrisy and evil with the cloister's physical decline. As a virgin building, Nunappleton is identified with Isabel: it has wasted
as she would have if she had remained with the nuns. So the

Fairfax line, Protestant warriors and English gentlemen, culminating in the Lord General of Parliamentary Army, would not exist. The next stanza ameliorates the impropriation and conveys the triumphant rightness of Isabel Thwaites's new possession of the cloister:

> At the demolishing, this Seat
> To *Fairfax* fell as by Escheat.
> And what both *Nuns* and *Founders* will'd
> 'Tis likely better thus fulfill'd.
> For if the *Virgin* prov'd not theirs,
> The *Cloyster* yet remained hers.
> Though many a *Nun* there made her Vow,
> 'Twas no *Religious House* till now.
>
> (273–80)

Marvell releases Nunappleton House to its destiny as the seat of a truly religious family, even as Isabel became that family's genetrix.

The garden is the Fairfax amendment to the estate, laid out in the shape of a fort, a pentagon, by the first Sir Thomas, son of William and Isabel. The present Fairfaxes' Edenic life there emphasizes the appropriateness of the family's possession. The house and grounds flourish; the only prodigality is nature's, who has "laid so sweetly wast" (78) the gardens and woods:

> From that blest Bed the *Heroe* came,
> Whom *France* and *Poland* yet does fame:
> Who, when retired here to Peace,
> His warlike Studies could not cease;
> But laid these Gardens out in sport
> In that just Figure of a Fort;
> And with five Bastions it did fence,
> As aiming one for ev'ry Sense.
>
> (281–88)

The bastions of the garden replace the cloister wall, and only the bees and flowers are the guardians of the Fairfax Eden:

> When in the *East* the Morning Ray
> Hangs out the Colours of the Day,
> The Bee through these known Allies hums,
> Beating the *Dian* with its *Drumms*.
> Then Flow'rs their drowsie Eylids raise,
> Their Silken Ensigns each displays,

And dries its Pan yet dank with Dew,
And fills its Flask with Odours new.

(289–96)

Marvell opposes this new Paradise to the "holy Guard" of the
nuns: he has the reality paradoxically parody the parody of the
nuns. The "vigilant *Patroul* / Of Stars" becomes the counterpart
to the fighting nuns, "the Tulip Pinke and Rose" to "their old
Holy-Water Brush," the "fragrant Vollyes" of the flowers to the
loud "Cannon" of the nuns' lungs, and the "Sentinel" bee who
"if once stir'd, . . . runs you through, or askes *the Word*" to the
sharp "Weapons" of "their Tongues" (298–320). Theirs is the
only protection now needed, for Fairfax's integrity is its own
holy guard, as was William Fairfax's. England, too, has had
such protection:

Oh Thou, that dear and happy Isle
The Garden of the World ere while,
Thou *Paradise* of four Seas,
Which *Heaven* planted us to please,
But, to exclude the World, did guard
With watry if not flaming Sword;
What luckless Apple did we tast,
To make us Mortal, and The Wast?

(321–28)

The protection of the sea, like the nuns' wall, is useless when
the degeneration lies within; with the associations that Marvell
has built up around *waste* in the poem, the false spirituality and
greed that caused the cloister to waste would seem transferable
to England's situation. The tour of the garden culminates in an
unpleasant image of England as a nation where "We Ord'nance
Plant and Powder sow" (344). It is Marvell's contention that Fairfax could have made England flourish like the garden at Nunappleton, but Marvell observes that it did not please Fairfax "and
God" (346) that he do so. The very qualities that are the basis of
his integrity, his conscience and his lack of personal ambition,
prevent this; implicitly, they prevented his participation in the
regicide and the invasion of Scotland, actions that he could not
reconcile with God's will. For, paradoxically, conscience provides only immortal protection with its "prickling leaf . . . [that]
Flowrs eternal, and divine": "Heaven" nurses this "Plant" (355–
59), not earth.
But Marvell presents earthly profit from Fairfax's conscience

continuing as a reality for England, for Fairfax's conscience would demand that he protect his country. The "sight" that watches may be interpreted as Fairfax's faithful guardianship from his Eden:

> The sight does from these *Bastions* ply,
> Th' invisible *Artilery;*
> And at proud *Cawood Castle* seems
> To point the *Battery* of its Beams.
> As if it quarrell'd in the Seat
> Th' Ambition of its *Prelate* great.

(361–66)

Marvell here presents the contemporary dichotomy between true and false religious houses, Nunappleton and Cawood Castle. The seat of the Archbishop of York was something of a bastion itself, one of the last of the bishops' lands, some of which had been used by Parliament as collateral to raise monies for the war.[13] At Laud's fall, King Charles had promoted Laud's long-standing enemy Bishop Williams to Archbishop of York; Marvell makes him the counterpart of the Abbess Lady Anna Langton, guardian of Isabel Thwaites. Analogous to William Fairfax's despoliation of the abbess, the present Lord Fairfax entered the war in 1642 to effect the deposing of the bishops.

In Marvell's allegorical landscape, he seems to present Fairfax as remaining ready to defend England, that war-wasted "Abbyss" ("Garden of the World ere while") represented by the meadow the reader enters. His protective gaze—"Th' invisible *Artilery*"— watches Cawood Castle with a bellicose eye, but benignly guards the countryside: "ore the Meads below it plays, / Or innocently seems to gaze" (367–68).

Marvell's naming of the meadow "the Abbyss" invites its comparison to the cloister of the Abbess, which wasted under her jurisdiction. The meadow wastes under the "massacre" (394) of the mower who "now commands the Field" (418). Unlike the undazzled sight of William Fairfax and the directed vision of the present Lord Fairfax, the perspective of no one in "the Abbyss" is reliable: "As, under Water, none does know / Whether he fall through it or go" (379–80). This untrustworthy perspective is characteristic of the land of grass and grasshoppers. Marvell has earlier created juxtapositions between the worthy and the unworthy; these frequently involve growth imagery which illuminates the poem's thesis that flowers and fruit prove the worth of what one does. The nuns' confine, where they artfully "dress the

Altars" (179) in flowers, but where their "Gardens yield" per-
verse "fruit" (219), has been juxtaposed to Fairfax's garden and
to Maria, who "Seems with the Flow'rs a Flow'r to be" (302).
The Fairfax garden guarded by the "Regiment . . . of the Tulip
Pinke and Rose" (311–12) has been juxtaposed to the remembrance of England when "Tulips . . . Were then the *Switzers* of
our *Guard*" (335–36). And, at the point of entry to the "Abbyss,"
Fairfax's good life, directed by an *"Ambition"*-free conscience of
the sort that is nurtured by heaven and "Flowrs eternal, and
divine" (354–58), is juxtaposed to the "Abbyss"-dwellers' existence, one so directed by ambition that they bring up "Flow'rs
so to be seen, / And prove they've at the Bottom been" (383–84).
This false position is equated with the unreliable vision; both
result from a separation from the providential guidance that Fairfax relies on. Yet Marvell does not specifically identify "The
sight" that plies "Th' invisible *Artilery*," and thus leaves it free
to be Fairfax's, ours, or his. If this indefinition constitutes a pre-
cursor of sorts of the shifting perspective that we are about to
experience, it also persuades the audience that a union of effort
can protect England.

When the reader enters the meadow, Marvell's allegorical fabric approaches the surreal:

And now to the Abbyss I pass
Of that unfathomable Grass,
Where Men like Grashoppers appear,
But Grashoppers are Gyants there:
They, in there squeking Laugh, contemn
Us as we walk more low then them:
And, from the Precipices tall
Of the green spir's, to us do call.

(369–76)

He presents a panorama that is confusing and purposefully so.
Rosalie Colie has likened it to a magic lantern show, dissolving
one thing into another so we lose the sense of discrete objects
and significances in the landscape.[14] The complex perspectives
permit Marvell to traverse time and interject bits of circumstance
that liken the meadow to England at civil war. Despite his first-
person reference to himself, Marvell remains true to his per-
sona—observer, not participant. Yet there is a sense of belea-
guerment: the grasshoppers laugh and "contemn" (373) him; the
"bloody *Thestylis*" seems to shout, "he call'd us *Israelites*; / But
now, to make his saying true, / Rails rain for Quails, for Manna

Dew" (401–8). This scorn sufficiently identifies him as prophet; having undergone this initial experience, he will during the course of his journey complete his metamorphosis to become the authority, the providential historian.

He takes "Sanctuary in the Wood" (482), hesitating in awe before this "double Wood of ancient Stocks" (489), that is, of Fairfaxes and Veres:

> When first the Eye this Forrest sees
> It seems indeed as *Wood* not *Trees:*
> As if their Neighbourhood so old
> To one great Trunk them all did mold.
> There the huge Bulk takes place, as ment
> To thrust up a *Fifth Element;*
> And stretches still so closely wedg'd
> As if the Night within were hedg'd.
> Dark all without it knits.
>
> (497–505)

The last three lines are reminiscent of the nuns' enclosure, where the walls repel "the World without, / But hedge our Liberty about" (99–100). Joseph Summers has observed that the cloister parodies retired life, whereas the wood provides a true retirement.[15] While it is true that sanctuary is present, due largely to the union of English families represented by the Fairfax–Vere connection, unions that protect ancient natural order and oppose the chaos of the meadow world, that "naked equal Flat, / Which *Levellers* take Pattern at" (449–50), sanctuary is not synonymous with retirement. There's a lot of activity in that wood, and Marvell has it become a temple, the birds a choir, which also indicates sanctuary rather than retirement.

Within the wood, Marvell creates an interior world as fantastic but not as threatening as the open meadow. The Thorn accommodates the nightingale by withdrawing its thorns. The Stock-doves "unto the Elms . . . moan" (526); the poet finds their music more pleasing than the nightingale's, yet wonders "why should such a Couple mourn, / That in so equal Flames do burn!" (527–28). The reader wonders, too, and wonders even more at "The hatching *Thrastles* shining Eye" (532). Rosalie Colie comments on Marvell's keen eye for detail: "the poet sees not the whole thrush upon her nest, but its 'shining Eye,' distinct from the surrounding leaves, a sharp eye which in its own right catches and holds the sharp eye of the poet. Montaigne and his cat; Marvell and the thrush—who plays with whom, who observes whom?"[16]

Marvell evokes the self-conscious nature of introspection in the image of the "shining Eye," conveying another world, another eye watching him as he watches, to insure that he doesn't disturb the good order. While the "hatching" thrush creates its family, the Hewel has the role of the trees' protector from parasites:

> But most the *Hewel's* wonders are,
> Who here has the *Holt-felsters* care.
> He walks still upright from the Root,
> Meas'ring the Timber with his Foot;
> And all the way, to keep it clean,
> Doth from the Bark the Wood-moths glean.
> He, with his Beak, examines well
> Which fit to stand and which to fell.
>
> (537–44)

He not only cleans the bark of parasites, but also claims "the hollow Oak . . . for his building . . . / And through the tainted Side he mines" (548–50). The tree itself "fed / A *Traitor-worm*, within it bred" (553–54). That the tree hosted the treacherous worm yet hated its treason—"the Oake seems to fall content, / Viewing the Treason's Punishment" (559–60)—may be seen as an interesting accolade for Charles I, for the passage may suggest his fall; Leah Marcus has observed that the oak was "a symbol closely tied to King Charles I and his family."[17] Since Marvell is justifying Fairfax's participation in the Civil War *and* his failure to save Charles I despite his advocacy of monarchy *and* his retirement as lord-general while also exalting the traditions of England, he does not condemn Charles. Instead, he bows gracefully to Fairfax's monarchist leaning in putting forth the proposition that there were traitor-counselors who corrupted the essentially good king and reduced him from a healthy state to a sick one. (And perhaps Marvell believed this. Many did.) As Marvell creates the allegory, the hewel cannot rescue the oak, so Fairfax was unable to rescue Charles. Equally, however, the passage suggests that the decision—made like the hewel's with the practical economy of nature—was both just and fruitful: "yet that Worm triumphs not long, / But serves to feed the *Hewels* young" (557–58).

Marvell's self-mockery in calling himself "*easie Philosopher*" (561) in the next stanza implies that the previous passage has too summarily accounted for the trauma England has experienced. The perspective that Marvell has prevail in this poem— necessary to oppose that of the nuns and produce a poem honoring Fairfax—prohibits all but occasional glimmers of the other view, the other eye watching. Here we find a slight parting of the surface as he subverts the perspective with "easie Philosopher," significantly inverts himself—"Or turn me but, and you shall see / I was but an inverted Tree" (567–68)—and enters that world of the "shining Eye."

> Already I begin to call
> In their most learned Original:
> And where I Language want, my Signs
> The Bird upon the Bough divines.
>
> (569–72)

In this union, he finds his place and his true names of poet, prophet, and priest. Unlike the legendary Sibyl, he knows where all the leaves belong: "No Leaf does tremble in the Wind / Which I returning cannot find" (575–76); therefore, his prophecy, though "strange," will be true:

> Out of these scatter'd *Sibyls* Leaves
> Strange *Prophecies* my Phancy weaves:
> And in one History consumes,
> Like *Mexique Paintings*, all the *Plumes.*
>
> (577–80)

He can read all of history, philosophy, and theology: "What *Rome, Greece, Palestine*, ere said" (581). With the understanding the light brings him through the leaves—the "light *Mosaick*" (582)—he assumes the "*antick Cope*" (591) and becomes the "great *Prelate of the Grove*" (592), the antithesis of the "*Prelate* great" (366), the archbishop of York.

He commands his communicants to hold him in the wood:

> Bind me ye *Woodbines* in your 'twines,
> Curle me about ye gadding *Vines*,
> And Oh so close your Circles lace,
> That I may never leave this Place.
>
> (609–12)

The temptation to remain ("Oh what a Pleasure 'tis to hedge / My Temples here with heavy sedge" (641–42)) echoes the pleasure the nuns felt in their wall that "hedged" (100) them about. But retirement of this sort is not possible; rules may not be bent as the nun proposed to Isabel Thwaites. Placidly waiting for an answer (fishing) gets no tolerance. Conscience must respond to the right—Maria, here, as a part of the Fairfax continuity that represents the conscience-guided role: "But now away my Hooks, my Quills, / And Angles, idle Utensils" (649–50). In a transferral of the guiding vision, Maria's "judicious Eyes" return him to the world of natural order she creates. She has been reared in a "*Domestick Heaven*" (722):

> Under the *Discipline* severe
> Of *Fairfax*, and the starry Vere;
> Where not one object can come nigh
> But pure, and spotless as the Eye.
>
> (723–26)

Moreover, her purity has God's generative power to direct nature:

> 'Tis *She* that to these Gardens gave
> That wondrous Beauty which they have;
> *She* streightness on the Woods bestows;
> To *Her* the Meadow sweetness owes;
> Nothing could make the River be
> So Chrystal-pure but only *She*;
> *She* yet more Pure, Sweet, Streight, and Fair,
> Then Gardens, Woods, Meads, Rivers are.
>
> (689–96)

This purity is demonstrably different from the nun's suggestion to Isabel Thwaites that she should with the other nuns lie hidden away in a self-indulgent inactivity, "Like Chrystal pure with Cotton warm" (192). *That* was a false retirement; Maria is active virtue, springing from active virtue; her future marriage will be "for some universal good" (741).

In the creation of this Protestant saint and this Edenic world, Fairfax has made a shrine worthy of pilgrimage; together they constitute "*Heaven's Center, Nature's Lap, / And Paradice's only Map*" (767–68). And this "more decent Order" (766) could possibly tame those "wild Creatures, called Men" (102).

In "Upon Appleton House," Marvell gives us cause to think his impulse to stay is equally strong as his desire to leave. Again, speculation would suggest that Marvell could have stayed on with Fairfax, not necessarily in the tutorial role to Maria, but more as an assistant to the amateur poet/translator Fairfax.

Marvell has illustrated that only a pure conscience able to create a fruitful life creates a truly religious house. An imposed purity or celibacy such as the nuns' culminates in self-indulgence. His panegyric evinces Fairfax's pure conscience and presents the Edenic existence of the Protestant holy family in the midst of a war-ravaged country. Nonetheless, the association of the nuns' celibacy and the overly sensitive conscience of General Fairfax is inescapable—or so it seems to me—and the parallel consequence of such emerges. Fairfax's record as a leader was not as pure as his conscience; he seems to have been chosen for lord-general by virtue of his usually innocuous disposition. Richard Baxter says of him that his appointment came about because he was thought "a man of no quickness of Parts, of no Elocution, of no suspicious plotting Wit, and therefore One that Cromwell could make use of at his pleasure."[18] He had great difficulty controlling the army during his command, particularly during 1647. Marvell would not have known this, nor needed to, for he could observe him at first hand. His lack of control was a notable characteristic; it had been a part of his battlefield performance. (Patterson has observed that it extended to his English syntax.[19]) Whitelocke draws a conservative portrait of Fairfax in the field: "I have seen him so highly transported, that scarce anyone durst speak a word to him, and he would seem more like a man distracted and furious, than of his ordinary mildness, and so far different temper."[20] At Nunappleton, Marvell presents Fairfax controlling his environment with his "*Discipline* severe . . . Where not one object can come nigh / But pure, and spotless as the Eye" (723–26).

England and its civil wars nonetheless intrude on "Paradice's only Map"; Marvell's imagery mirrors those conditions simultaneously with his presentation of this Eden, peopled with Protestant saints. The rest of England was once like this; Marvell asks how it has come to be *so* mortal:

Oh Thou, that dear and happy Isle
The Garden of the World ere while,
Thou *Paradise* of four Seas,
Which *Heaven* planted us to please,
But, to exclude the World, did guard
With watry if not flaming Sword;
What luckless Apple did we tast,
To make us Mortal, and The Wast?

(321–28)

The remarkably effective "Unhappy!" of the next stanza leads into another question of when England will return to its former garden state when "all the Garrisons were Flowrs" (332). Then "the *Gard'ner* had the *Souldiers* place" (337), but no longer. Yet the irony is that the lord-general of the parliamentary forces has chosen to become a gardener, to retire to make his own garden flourish, leaving England in its chaotic state. His portrait of Fairfax follows, and the tone challenges exact definition, but his encomium possesses some ambivalence at points:

> And yet their walks one on the Sod
> Who, had it pleased him and *God*,
> Might once have made our Gardens spring
> Fresh as his own and flourishing.
>
> (345–48)

Marvell's run-on line in which "spring" seems to mean renewed gardens and then evolves as reiteration when it attaches to "Fresh" is so brilliant that the completion of the line that tells us that Fairfax's only concern was that his own be "flourishing" is obscured. Moreover, Marvell has qualified Fairfax's choice by linking it to God's[21] and not only startled us with the rhyme of Sod and God, but reminded us that the decision *would* be made that way. The verse continues with Marvell's "But" that signals the demise here of the happy hope as it did in "The Garden." Any hope that England could exist as it had been is as imaginary as the former general's pretend forts:

> But he preferr'd to the *Cinque Ports*
> These five imaginary Forts:
> And, in those half-dry Trenches, spann'd
> Pow'r which the Ocean might command.
>
> (349–52)

Fairfax's extraordinarily sensitive "Conscience"—one "nursed" in Heaven—is responsible for this decision, a "Plant" with a leaf "such / As that which shrinks at ev'ry touch" (357–58), quite like the drop of dew in "On a Drop of Dew." A conscience such as Fairfax's is meant for Heaven alone, for it "Flowrs eternal, and divine, / That in the Crown of Saints do shine" (359–60).

Marvell emphasizes the deeply fallen, hellish world outside Nunappleton by referring to it as the "Abbyss" and placing it at the triumphal position. In his play on *Abbess* and *Abbyss* Marvell signals the association of the fallen world with the corrupt

spirituality that the Abbess represents in the poem in her urging
the young Isabel Thwaites to become a nun, thereby to remain a
virgin and to thwart her destiny. Marvell seems to disapprove
quite as much as Milton of a cloistered virtue. The separateness
that Fairfax has been able to achieve with his self-constructed
Eden would seem also, by extension, to be a corrupt spirituality,
relative since he cited his religious conscience as the reason for
his resignation. The central positioning of the Abbyss points up
the country's crucial need of someone who will behave in the
manner of the young warrior Fairfax who rescued Isabel because
he "would respect / Religion, but not Right neglect" (225–26).
Isabel herself might be said to represent England restrained from
its destiny by episcopacy. This line of thought makes apparent
Marvell's purpose in the repeated confusion of whether walls
and other boundaries close out or enclose. Fairfax has in a real
sense done both, shut himself away from the world and shut the
world away from him, as the nun tells Isabel they have done:

> 'Within this holy leisure we
> 'Live innocently as you see.
> 'These Walls restrain the World without,
> 'But hedge our Liberty about.
> 'These Bars inclose that wider Den
> 'Of those wild Creatures, called Men.
> 'The Cloyster outward shuts its Gates,
> 'And, from us, locks on them the Grates.
>
> (96–104)

Here perverted spirituality harbors virgins behind gates as they
keep themselves in readiness for "the great *Bridegroom*" (108),
analogous to Fairfax's retreat to preserve his conscience.

The "Abbyss" also suggests the uncreated world and a reen-
actment of creation—or a projection—of biblical history. A
miniature flood occurs as "Denton sets ope its *Cataracts*" (466).
The flood, too, can be evaded. This time, it is the poet who avoids:
"But, I, retiring from the Flood, / Take Sanctuary in the Wood"
(481–82). In some sixteen stanzas, he elucidates the pleasure of
his life in the woods—not in the garden. That is, he does not
base his own pleasure in the created pleasure of Fairfax's garden,
but rather in the wood that, sanctuary though it is, is not an
Eden, but a "yet green, yet growing Ark" (484). A part of the
fallen world, he is not Edenic Adam, but laboring man, "the
first Carpenter might best / Fit Timber for his Keel have Prest"
(485–86). He congratulates himself in a playfully ironic, appar-

ently self-deprecating manner; here he can continue his studies in a primeval solitude that seems eager to incorporate him:

And see how Chance's better Wit
Could with a Mask my studies hit!
The Oak-Leaves me embroyder all,
Between which Caterpillars crawl:
And Ivy, with familiar trails,
Me licks, and clasps, and curles, and hales.

(585–90)

Comfort is in the woods where he, "languishing with ease" (593), lies on the "Velvet Moss" (594), with the wind to fan him and "winnow from the Chaff my Head" (600). Here his mind is protected from the distractions and dangers of love and war. He continues to congratulate himself in exquisite verse: "How safe, methinks, and strong, behind / These Trees have I incamp'd my Mind" (601–2). I think the point of this witty revelation of selfishly guarded interests is to imply analogous motivation in his being at Nunappleton and Fairfax's retiring there.

We think he wrote "An Horatian Ode" before he went to Nunappleton.[22] If so, his decision was perhaps already made that his retreat into the paradise of the Fairfax estate to study and write poetry in that rarest commodity, leisure, could not, would not continue. "Languishing with ease" (593) he will, but enough had been "winnowed" from his head at Nunappleton that he realized that he had to move out of the shadows of the wood in which he had practiced his song with all those birds—not just the nightingale with the traditional song of the lover, but the doves, thrastle, heron, hewel—and into the sun of public life. No more the luxury of singing "His Numbers languishing." His "time to leave the Books in dust, / And oyl th'unused Armours rust" (4–6) would come.

Comparison between the two generals was inevitable. Rather than denigrating Fairfax with the poorer position that would emerge from a measuring of his attitude against Cromwell's, Marvell placed himself in this comparison to illustrate with his own confessional in "Upon Appleton House" the self-indulgence of the retired life.

Marvell chose Cromwell and the active life despite his awareness that his poetry would suffer for it. He knew the real temptation to return selfishly to an Edenic existence (limited of necessity) or to enter the fallen world led by Cromwell, a world that thought to improve itself to the point that a return to paradise—the millennium—would be its reward. Since he had experienced the confinement of Appleton and knew that such moral niceness imprisoned, he may have had little difficulty in making his decision to follow behind always the active man, the man who "Urged his active Star".[23]

4

"Mine own Precipice I go":
Marvell and the Active Life

ALTHOUGH the poems written during Marvell's time with the Fairfaxes express pleasure in his surroundings and company, they express also the impulse to rejoin the more active world. Fairfax may even have introduced him to Milton when he knew that Marvell sought to leave Appleton. However their acquaintance began, Milton seems to have immediately approved of Marvell's personality and talents sufficiently that he thought they could work together. His own secretaryship was still within his ability, he assured Bradshaw when he wrote the letter recommending Marvell, but if the Council were thinking of finding him an assistant in the event of Mr. Weckherlin's death, no one would be more fit. The Council of State was to exist only two months more, and perhaps had business more pressing than the appointment, which was not yet to be Marvell's. He had another acquaintance and perhaps friend in London, Marchamont Nedham, who may have introduced him to Milton initially; Milton had been Nedham's benefactor, visiting him during his three-month imprisonment in Newgate for "royalist scurrilities." (Because Nedham had been a royalist journalist who switched sides at a propitious moment, he has often been dismissed as a trimmer, really hardly fair in an age when changing sides was merely a matter of arriving at a different perspective.) Masson thinks Milton may have been responsible for Nedham's change from royalism and thus his quick release to write for the Commonwealth.[1] He had been editing the *Mercurius Politicus*, the state's official newspaper, since 13 June 1650 with Milton as his "censor, licenser, or supervising editor;" Pocock considers that "we are obliged to consider Nedham's *Mercurius Politicus* editorials a pioneer work in the application of republican theory to Commonwealth needs."[2] Masson comments that Milton's supervision of him "was in reality only such a friendly superintendence of the witty Needham, in his subsidized editorship of the *Mercurius,* as Milton might easily reconcile to his principles." He leaves it to conjecture whether Milton wrote in conjunction with Needham,[3] but some evidence exists that Marvell did, though it is tenuous. E. E. Duncan-Jones has illustrated that Needham's pamphlet *The Case of the Commonwealth of England Stated* (published mid-1650) from which Needham pulled his *Mercurius Politicus* writings for the first six months and "An Horatian Ode" present notable verbal similarities.[4] Reasonably, we may conclude that Marvell read it when it was first published. Needham also contributed, Blair Worden tells us, to the *Lachrymae Musarum,* the elegiac volume commemorating the young Lord Hastings' death, at the same time that Marvell did—late or at least after the book had gone to the printer. Worden sees evidence of the "possibility of collaboration" between the two writers. He compares "An Horatian Ode" to the early issues of Needham's *Mercurius Politicus* and discovers some startling parallels, going as far forward as 8 January 1652; he remarks during his argument that "The proximity of the ode to propaganda becomes striking in the nationalist conclusion to the poem."[5] His suggestion is that Marvell either collaborated with Needham or that Needham had read the poem.[6] It is Marvell, however, whom we characterize as a poet who "echos," which speaks against Needham's echoing Marvell's poem, but rather for the other way round. Perhaps the contact from 1650 with Needham continued during his time at Appleton, and "The First Anniversary" as propaganda—which we don't doubt—was an extension of what Marvell had already performed in a sense with "An Horatian Ode."

Marvell's penchant for echoing deserves consideration. In "Upon an Eunuch; a Poet," a Latin poem, he recommends echo as a poetic strategy. Apparently addressing another poet in need of encouragement, Marvell advances almost boundless poetic possibilities:

> Don't believe yourself sterile, although, an exile from
> women,
> You cannot thrust a sickle at the virgin harvest,
> And sin in our fashion. Fame will be continually
> pregnant by you,
> And you will snatch the Nine Sisters from the mountain;
> Echo too, often struck, will bring forth musical
> offspring.[7]

The predication of the last line implies that the directive was formulated from his own practice. As a tool for a poet-historian, echo or allusion serves a vital double function. Classical allusion provides precedent and parallel for contemporary issues, permitting the poet to place them on a recognized and accepted scale of value. Moreover, the echo of contemporary writers' lines and thoughts places those poets in a historic continuum of poetics. This last notion also allows the poet-historian to draw freely from the best poetry of others. Political history may be seen as the most vital of vehicles for the poet, for he is able to range through all of time for his echoes and to employ at will all poetic genre—in effect, to "snatch the Nine Sisters," all of them, "from the mountain." *Rapiesque*, translated as "snatch," connotes sexual assault. Thus any of the genre may be "forced" to accommodate the poet who seeks to gain "fame" through exertion of his poetic influence on public opinion or "fame."

Marvell strikes echo often and in various ways. His apparent fascination with reflection and resonance, perspective and inversion, suggests a desire to mirror simultaneously spiritual patterns and temporal particulars, to contract time on his own. He draws an incident as exactly as if he had seen it, uses a phrase or a line that contains an allusion involved with contemporary circumstance, creates a parallel with a biblical or classical allusion, and reverberates a theme through a poem to creat echoes that not only resound, but also elaborate. I have mentioned Rosalie Colie's comment on his keen eye for detail; so also C. V. Wedgwood has observed that Marvell's description of Charles in "An Horatian Ode" is so exact that he might have been observing him from the scaffold: "It is strange how small details noticed by an eye-witness on the scaffold are caught up into this poem—for it is recorded by one that he had never seen the king's eyes brighter than in his last moments, and by another that he more than once inquired about the sharpness of the axe."[8]

In the same context we can find an example of Marvell's contemporary allusiveness in the striking description of Charles's behavior at the point of decapitation: "But bow'd his comely Head, / Down as upon a Bed" (63–64). E. E. Duncan-Jones notes in *The Poems and Letters* that Browne uses this figure in *Religio Medici*, ii. 12; it was also, however, part of Lord-General Strafford's famous and often-repeated last words from his own scaffold: "I do as cheerfully put off my doublet at this time as ever I did when I went to bed." Since the responsibility for Strafford's death lay so heavily on Charles I's conscience that he thought his own downfall was God's punishment for it,[9] Marvell's echo may well have been intended to remind his audience of this. Whether Marvell knew Charles's anguish over Strafford's death does not matter (though Nedham was likely to have): Marvell almost certainly knew, as did many, that Strafford was innocent of treason and that Charles could have saved him and did not. (Since Strafford was a Yorkshireman, Marvell is likely to have had an even greater interest in his fate.) The notoriety of the event seemed to have made Strafford's phrase a common one. Richard Baxter uses it in his *Autobiography* to describe the death of Mr. Love, which took place some time after that of Charles: Love "was condemned and beheaded, dying neither timorously nor proudly in any desperate bravado, but with as great alacrity and fearless quietness and freedom of speech as if he had but gone to bed."[10]

In the "grateful Irish" segment of "An Horatian Ode," Marvell has been supposed ironic in his presentation of the Irish response to Cromwell; rather it probably presents a resonance, though whether Marvell's source was Nedham or Cromwell is hard to know. In "The First Anniversary," sufficient evidence exists to show that Marvell echoes Cromwell, and we know from "The Death of O.C." that he was charmed by Cromwell's "powerful language" (237). That he had spoken with him or heard him speak at this time is a possibility since Cromwell was elected to stand for Cambridge while Marvell was at Trinity. Marvell thus phrases the Irish situation:

And now the *Irish* are asham'd
To see themselves in one Year tam'd:
  So much one Man can do,
  That does both act and know.
They can affirm his Praises best,
And have, though overcome, confest
  How good he is, how just,
  And fit for highest Trust.

(73–80)

Cromwell himself was confident that he had brought about a much better situation for the Irish.[11]

"We find the people," he wrote, "very greedy after the word, and flocking to Christian meetings, much of that prejudice which lies upon people in England being a stranger to their minds. I mind you the rather of this because it is a sweet symptom if not an earnest of the good we expect."[12]

And he wrote to John Sadler in 1649:

"We have a great opportunity to set up . . . a way of doing justice among these poor people, which, for the uprightness and cheapness of it may exceedingly gain upon them, who have been accustomed to as much injustice, tyranny, and oppression from their landlords, the great men, and those that should have done them right as, I believe, any people in that which we call Christendom."[13]

Marvell's poetic statement reflects Cromwell's advocacy of his Irish accomplishment, however the information came to him.

Blair Worden writes that the seventeenth-century English conscience would have been little troubled by Drogheda and Wexford anyway; furthermore, that "In July 1650 the government published a prediction that the Irish leaders shall be made to think shame of themselves ('And now the Irish are asham'd')." Since Nedham was the official journalist, Marvell may echo Nedham, but the possibility exists that Nedham echoes Cromwell or even that Nedham echoes Marvell. The government itself had its fictions, and this may have been one. Worden cites a royalist publication that maintained that the government gave a falsified version of the battle at Clonmel in order to raise more money for Cromwell's coming Scots confrontation, and thus wrote that "the regicides 'confess thus much themselves, that they found in Clonmel the stoutest enemy that ever was found.'" Worden thinks that Marvell ironically inverts this statement in the line that speaks of the Irish as having "though overcome, confest" (78).[14] His argument is persuasive, but I am inclined to disagree; rather I read willingness in Marvell's statement, along the lines of what Michael Wilding presents in his essay "Marvell's 'An Horatian Ode upon Cromwell's Return from Ireland', the Levellers, and the Junta."

Wilding sees the ode as a propaganda piece of sorts as well; his premise is that "the poem's rhetoric" controls our response, that it "gives the impression of dispassionately considering all the political possibilities, but its full political nature lies not in its created 'impression of the mind detachedly at play over a number of possible choices' but in its skilful exclusion of certain possibilities and manipulation of others."[15] The army did not want to go to Ireland in 1647; even the officers balked. The civil war intervened, but when the issue came up again in 1649, they were equally recalcitrant. This time, however, the opposition was organized and seemed to consist for the most part of Levellers who argued that those who went would bring about the same rights for the English gentry in Ireland that they had achieved for them in England, and draw down even more oppression on the already burdened ordinary people. But, as Wilding points out, Marvell never mentions this: "The radical voices opposed to the Irish campaign are given no part in the ode . . . . a significant absence. But though their voices and their beliefs are excluded, their destruction by Cromwell is memorialized":[16]

> And, like the three-fork'd Lightning, first
> Breaking the Clouds where it was nurst,
> Did thorough his own side
> His fiery way divide.
> For 'tis all one to Courage high
> The Emulous or Enemy;
> And with such to inclose
> Is more then to oppose.

> (13–20)

Wilding contends that Cromwell's "destruction of the radical groups" in a number of mutinies, the main two of which were almost instantly quelled by Cromwell's immediate action, are the referent for the notion of his "breaking through his own side like lightning"[17] and that Marvell's use of "emulous" supports a reference to the lower-ranked army men.[18] Wilding quotes the response of the Levellers to Cromwell's Burford mutiny assault: "'the Sword convinceth not, it doth but enforce; it begetteth no love, but fomenteth and engendreth hatred and revenge; for bloud thirsteth after bloud, and vengeance rageth for vengeance, and this devoureth and destroyeth all where it cometh.'"[19] Cromwell was opposed to the philosophy: Maurice Ashley writes that he "expelled from the Army Council an officer who indiscreetly remarked that no visible authority was left in the kingdom but the power of the sword."[20] But generally it was a popular rationale; for example, Hugh Peters used it to justify the empowerment of the army over parliament when in 1648 Colonel Pride excluded those members who were "faint-hearted."[21] Peters, who rose from chaplain in the New Model Army to possess remarkable influence, espoused it without hesitation; Gooch and Laski cite an instance that Lilburne reports of a conversation with Peters in Newgate, in which Peters said "that Law was the sword and what it gave, and that there was no government in the world but what the sword maintained."[22] The phrase was used equally often by royalists. Worden comments that "Writers who favored the imposition of the engagement frequently cited Caesar and Nimrod as usurping tyrants to whom obedience was due by right of conquest, whatever the 'means or craft' by which they 'did obtain' their power."[23] Marvell's lines—"And for the last effect / Still keep thy Sword erect"—celebrate the sword, according to Wilding, who concludes his article with the assertion that the ode "makes better sense read as a wider appeal to support the military junta: as an appeal to the poet-intellectuals and other such members of the elite to identify with the Cromwellian army group."[24] Such an attitude on Marvell's part would seem to negate irony in the "grateful Irish" passage. Cromwell saw the Irish victory as having satisfied the Levellers' ideals, hence his expression of what had been accomplished in his letter to John Sadler, which I quote again:

> We have a great opportunity to set up . . . a way of doing justice among these poor people, which, for the uprightness and cheapness of it may exceedingly gain upon them, who have been accustomed to as much injustice, tyranny, and oppression from their landlords, the great men, and those that should have done them right as, I believe, any people in that which we call Christendom.

J. G. A. Pocock has written that the army men saw themselves as participants in a political process that was at the same time a spiritual process:

> they might see themselves as an elite of covenanted saints, or as the vanguard of some larger "people", but the essential fact in either case was that common men were presuming to act in politics on a basis not of magistracy, but of covenant and calling. . . . However, . . . the Agitators and Levellers . . . . On the one hand . . . affirmed that they had come to claim the birthright of free-born Englishmen; on the other, they reiterated the long-standing belief that England was elect, chosen by God . . . for some climactic struggle with a Roman Antichrist. But the chosen captain in that struggle was no longer to be the Godly Prince of the mainstream millenarian tradition, but a Godly People; the reclamation of that people's birthright merged in their minds with the taking up of the chiliastic calling. . . . To the saints . . . the moment was one of the liberation of the spirit, and whether this was conceived in terms of the fulfilment of prophecy or of natural human capacity . . . the action to be taken was one of the transformation of society by spiritual men acting in time.[25]

Representing the official stance, Nedham, however, in his editorials of 1650–52, many taken from his already published *The Case of the Commonwealth* as I have earlier mentioned, argues that "all governments are rooted in the sword. . . . the King resorted to the sword in asserting (unjustly) his disputed role in the mixed constitution, and having been defeated in a trial by battle, has forfeited all his rights to the victor."[26] In "An Horatian Ode," Marvell would seem in accord with Nedham that the "trial by battle" had gone by God's will to Cromwell, who as well as being chosen had personally "much" to do with his victory in that he knew how to handle fortune. If we consider "The Unfortunate Lover" as written at approximately the same time on essentially the same topic, we can see Marvell presenting the king as having both fortune and providence go against him; thus, in a sense, Marvell may be said to echo propaganda in these poems, perhaps consciously, perhaps not. We do know that he sought employment with the new government.

Milton's letter presents Marvell as a man who will be valuable to the state: "a man whom both by report and the converse I have had with him [is] of singular desert for the State to make use of." But Milton makes clear that Marvell also needs a job for which he would be paid: "who alsoe offers himselfe, if there be any imployment for him."[27] Employment as a state writer would have likely been a tacit agreement since Marvell was still untried. Cromwell hired him to tutor William Dutton whom he had earlier placed in the home of the Reverend John Oxenbridge at Eton. John Dixon Hunt thinks that Oliver St. John, to whom Oxenbridge's sister was married as his third wife and to whom Cromwell's beloved cousin Elizabeth Cromwell had been second wife and to whom another of Cromwell's cousins had been first wife, may have suggested to Cromwell "both his brother-in-law's house at Eton and Marvell as tutor for William Dutton." Hunt also comments that Marvell may have known Oxenbridge "during the latter's lectureship at Hull in the 1640s."[28] Oxenbridge and Marvell would have shared a dislike of Laud since Oxenbridge, rather than being threatened as Marvell's father had been, had actually lost his position as Oxford tutor in 1634 because of Laud.[29] St. John was also related to Lady Fairfax. Michael Craze includes the information that Lady Fairfax's sister Catherine was the wife of an older Oliver St. John who died comparatively young, an uncle of this Oliver."[30] Marvell's Latin poem "Upon the Embassy of Lord Oliver St John to the United Provinces" must have been written early in 1651, for St. John left England in March of that

year. It was in 1653 that Marvell went to tutor Dutton and live
with the Oxenbridges; he was to remain in this capacity for at
least three years. We can be assured that Marvell was considered
firmly Puritan or he should never have become Dutton's tutor.
Because of this association with the very Puritan Oxenbridges,
critics usually ascribe the religious poems to this period; Hunt,
for example, and I concur, assigns to it "On a Drop of Dew," "A
Dialogue Between The Resolved Soul, and Created Pleasure," "A
Dialogue between the Soul and Body," "The Coronet," and
"Bermudas."

Each of these poems continues the developing argument of the
poems previously discussed in the context of the retired versus
the active life, the overly fastidious conscience that shrinks from
earthly life to stay pure versus the active conscience that exerts
itself to create a purer earthly life. "On a Drop of Dew" presents
the Soul as imprisoning itself to avoid sin; contact with the world
makes it subject to contamination. As he has or will name his
"mistress" coy, so Marvell describes the Drop of Dew:

In how coy a Figure wound,
Every way it turns away:
So the World excluding round,
Yet receiving in the Day.
Dark beneath, but bright above:
Here disdaining, there in Love,
How loose and easie hence to go:
How girt and ready to ascend.

                                                    (27–34)

Dew dissolves in the warmth of the sun, for which the dew might
well be grateful since humans return to their essence by the less
elegant route of a "progress through a worm." The Drop of Dew
trembles "lest it grow impure: / Till the warm Sun pitty it's Pain, /
And to the Skies exhale it back again" (16–18). But, obviously,
life is sin. Marvell's Drop of Dew, metaphor for the sin-
apprehensive soul, "Shuns the sweet leaves and blossoms green"
(23); taking pleasure in them would be tantamount to physical
love. For that to exist, the Drop of Dew must release its fate to
the power of earthly time, which amounts, I suppose, literally to
a fall to earth to mingle with dust and undergo an alteration of
essence to become a part of earth's generative force. The Drop of
Dew values only its oneness that it so assiduously preserves that
it may be ever "ready to ascend" (34).

Under the Soul's strictures in "A Dialogue between the Soul

and Body," the Body is subject to the Soul's "coyness," but the Body's demand to live is as valid as that of the rose that holds the "Orient Dew" (1). In these terms, which Marvell exploits by way of illustrating the irreconcilable natures of the divine and the earthly, servitude to the both is inevitable in life, thus forcing the question of the freedom of any mind that resists the demands of the one or the other. For Marvell, the life at Appleton retained desirable qualities of its original identity as a cloister: time to study, think, and write, leisure and quiet. In "The Garden," he playfully tells us that man could have stayed there; in fact, "After a Place so pure, and sweet, / What other Help could yet be meet!" Why would Adam need a helpmate in such a satisfying place? "*But*" (61) signals the demise of Eden. The "helpmeet" was created and Adam fell, became mortal, thus "'twas beyond a Mortal's share / To wander solitary there." The equation of the female with death resounds the Renaissance commonplace that a little death occurred with every successful copulation, hence any woman brings death to any man. But Marvell makes clear that it is mortality that prevents a return to Eden. That is, "share" here has the meaning of "portion,"[31] and the four lines offer a rueful comment on man's fallen condition that makes a return to Eden impossible. Since the true state of existence is a fallen state, to seek to maintain an Edenic existence is to evade sin rather than to defeat it; in short, the cloistered virtue.

"Bermudas" also comments on Eden; it possesses more justification perhaps than the others to have been written while Marvell was with the Oxenbridges. John Oxenbridge had just received his appointment to the London Commission for the Bermudas' governing; he was quite familiar with the Bermudas, having been there as a minister from 1635 to 1641.[32] The opening and closing four lines present the English in a boat, singing of the new paradise that God has given them:

> He lands us on a grassy Stage;
> Safe from the Storms, and Prelat's rage.
> He gave us this eternal Spring,
> Which here enamells every thing;
> And sends the Fowl's to us in care,
> On daily Visits through the Air.

(11–16)

Their hymn includes features of "The Garden": "He makes the Figs our mouths to meet; And throws the Melons at our feet" (21–22), as well as looking forward to "The First Anniversary" in England's certainty that God intended the English to lead the world into the latter days (or so I interpret the line "He cast (of which we rather boast) / The Gospels Pearl upon our Coast"(29–30)). But the English are in a boat. And their song—"Chime" (39)—is measured by their "falling Oars" (40); they live in a fallen world in which time prevails despite their Eden. Moreover, since the English are in a boat, they would seem to need to escape their paradise. A part of their hymn is their prayer that their song will "arrive at Heavens Vault: / Which thence (perhaps) rebounding, may / Eccho beyond the *Mexique Bay*" (34–36). To stay in the sanctity of paradise is to retire; more important, it is to look on without concern, "spectators vain," thus to reject Christ's admonishment to teach others that they may be ready for the second coming.

Because critics have treated Marvell's poems, for the most part, as occasional and· not reflective of a cohesive philosophy, we have not perceived the consistency of his poetry in rejection of a return to Eden as a possibility and in his advocacy of the regeneration of man, or seasoning, as he terms it in "The First Anniversary." He equates a recreated Eden such as the Fairfax estate with false values and irresponsibility, the opposite of what "Upon Appleton House" seems to present. He does not reject artful gardens as temporary respites, however, despite his rejection of them as places of retirement.

The Drop of Dew confines itself, "Trembling lest it grow impure" (16) in the presence of the rose. The Resolved Soul, however, in "A Dialogue Between the Resolved Soul and Created Pleasure" resists temptation without experiencing bondage. Echoing Ephesians 6, the owner of the soul urges it to "learn to wield / The weight of thine immortal Shield" (1–2). If the soul is indeed "that thing Divine" (7), its hour has arrived in which it may "shew that Nature wants an Art / To conquer one resolved Heart" (9–10). "Nature" in the second stanza seems simply earth and its abundance; Created Pleasure's offerings include a temptation even to the Resolved Soul if he were not wholly resolute. Marvell's defining Pleasure as Created separates it from the pleasure the Resolved Soul experiences or aims to experience, which is primal pleasure or the reunion with God, that for which the Drop of Dew yearns. *Resolved* means *steadfast*, but Marvell seems to have intended the meaning of *to melt, dissolve*, as well, which meaning also points to a relation between the poem and "On a Drop of Dew." In a musical sense, *resolve* means "to cause (a discord) to pass into a concord" (*OED*); concord aptly describes the Resolved Soul's state.

Created Pleasure does not neglect flattery, calling the Resolved Soul the "Lord of Earth, and Heavens Heir" (12). Its offers are exquisitely framed; the Resolved Soul's replies are tersely restrictive. Velvety rose petals and "fragrant Clouds" of sweet scents are presented as gifts as well as reflections of the Resolved Soul's own beauty, which Created Pleasure sees as possessing the most "grace" (33), appropriately consistent with the Resolved Soul's appellation as "Heavens Heir" (12). Resolved Soul responds incisively: "When the Creator's skill is priz'd, / The rest is all but Earth disguis'd" (35–36). Created Pleasure has saved its most heavenly earthly delight until last—music that charms, able to turn the wind in its course with its "charming Aires" (38), to "suspend the Rivers Fall" (40). If there were time that the Resolved Soul wished to spend on earthly pleasures, that time would be granted only to music. Resolved Soul's earthly time must all be spent on his journey; he answers Created Pleasure with puns—"Had I but any time to lose, / On this I would it all dispose. / Cease Tempter. None can chain a mind / Whom this sweet Chordage cannot bind"(41–44). He has earlier emphasized his hurry in another punning response to the offer of "Nature's banquet" (14): "I sup above, and cannot stay / To bait so long upon the way"(17–18). Resolved Soul becomes appealing through the wit Marvell assigns him and his confession of weakness for music; that is, we become convinced that music has allured him, despite its being in a sense another pun in incorporating the commonplace notion that music speaks to the soul.

There are in the poem more offers intended to tempt before Resolved Soul will be "crown'd" (50). Pleasure would give Beauty and Gold; its final offers are Glory, Slaves, Friends, and the power to know the nature of things. (That Created Pleasure possesses this last seems beyond its realm.) Resolved Soul triumphs; the fiction of the poem was that temptation existed. The charm of "A Dialogue Between the Resolved Soul and Created Pleasure" lies in the witty responses of Resolved Soul, the hint of temptation that the reader has to consider to recall the temptation's validity, and the exquisite language of Created Pleasure.

I associate "The Fair Singer" with this period because it, too, concerns bondage and because its treatment contains the same exuberant wit that we experience in the two debate poems. The bondage is to beauty and music, which last would seem to lead the poet to write "Musicks Empire," or rework it, for he may have written it while he was with the Fairfaxes. In the perspective of this poem, the tempted speaks; he presents himself as assaulted with the double battery of the woman's eyes and voice:

> To make a final conquest of all me,
> Love did compose so sweet an Enemy,
> In whom both Beauties to my death agree,
> Joyning themselves in fatal Harmony;
> That while she with her Eyes my Heart does bind,
> She with her Voice might captivate my Mind.
>
> I could have fled from One but singly fair:
> My dis-intangled Soul it self might save,
> Breaking the curled trammels of her hair.
> But how should I avoid to be her Slave,
> Whose subtile Art invisibly can wreath
> My Fetters of the very Air I breathe?
>
> It had been easie fighting in some plain,
> Where Victory might hang in equal choice,
> But all resistance against her is vain,
> Who has th'advantage both of Eyes and Voice,
> And all my Forces needs must be undone,
> She having gained both the Wind and Sun.

In this apparent love poem, Marvell portrays himself as not only bound by the woman's eyes, but also captive to her voice. Since both sight and sound move invisibly through air, he is fettered by air. Marvell presents the charmed one as having lost the freedom of his mind because of the joined "fatal Harmony" of her "Eyes and Voice." He employs the Petrarchan strategy of the language of battle,[33] as if the Singer were the enemy, and he doomed to defeat, to being "trammel'd."

It's hard to resist the suspicion that the paradox of being fettered by air was fully as enchanting to him as the woman and to reason that this led him to write "A Dialogue between the Soul and the Body" in which he creates fascinating puns on the restraining properties of each:

> O who shall, from this Dungeon, raise
> A Soul inslav'd so many wayes?
> With bolts of Bones, that fetter'd stands
> In Feet; and manacled in Hands.
> Here blinded with an Eye; and there
> Deaf with the drumming of an Ear.

A Soul hung up, as 'twere, in Chains
Of Nerves, and Arteries, and Veins.
Tortur'd, besides each other part,
In a vain Head, and double Heart.

(1–10)

The bound Soul, enslaved "so many wayes" (2) is blinded by the
physical characteristics of Body with its "vain Head, and double
Heart" (10); Body, equally in bondage to Soul, has been "stretcht"
into the "upright" position to become its "own Precipice" from
which it "falls"—an impossibility had it remained in the on-four
state of other animals:

O who shall me deliver whole,
From bonds of this Tyrannic Soul?
Which, stretcht upright, impales me so,
That mine own Precipice I go;
And warms and moves this needless Frame:
(A Fever could but do the same.)
And, wanting where its spight to try,
Has made me live to let me dye.
A Body that could never rest,
Since this ill Spirit it possest.

(11–20)

As ever ready to depart as the Drop of Dew, Soul must instead
share Body's grief in its sickness and be used in Body's efforts
to regain health, the last thing that Soul wants:

What Magick could me thus confine
Within anothers Grief to pine?
Where, whatsoever it complain,
I feel, that cannot feel, the pain.
And all my Care its self employes,
That to preserve, which me destroys:
Constrain'd not only to indure
Diseases, but, whats worse, the Cure:
And ready oft the Port to gain,
Am Shipwrackt into Health again.

BODY.
But Physick yet could never reach
The Maladies Thou me dost teach;
Whom first the Cramp of Hope does Tear:
And then the Palsie Shakes of Fear.

The Pestilence of Love does heat:
Or Hatred's hidden Ulcer eat.
Joy's Chearful Madness does perplex:
Or Sorrow's other Madness vex.
Which Knowledge forces me to know;
And Memory will not forgoe.
What but a Soul could have the wit
To build me up for Sin so fit?
So Architects do square and hew,
Green Trees that in the Forest grew.

(31–44)

Their debate on who suffers most cannot be won, though some say that Body wins, by virtue of having the most lines and the last word, but this seems insufficient for such a declaration. In choosing the debate form and leaving it inconclusive, Marvell expresses the unceasing dynamic of the impossible combination. As Soul must "endure" (27) not just the sicknesses of the body, "but, whats worse, the Cure" (28), "Shipwrackt into Health again" (30), Body complains that the real "Maladies" arise in Soul, including the "Pestilence of Love" (32–35). The imbalance of the double forces of a divine soul housed in a body of clay is itself an imbalance never reconcilable apparently. Each has legitimate demands that deserve gratification; mutual happiness, extant before the fall, may be found now only in art, in the created garden. The often quoted lines from "The Garden" are relevant here since Marvell presents happiness of both body and soul occurring there: during the while—"Mean while"—of Body's pleasure in the garden, "the Mind" as well takes "its happiness"—equal but of a different nature:

Mean while the Mind, from pleasure less,
Withdraws into its happiness:
The Mind, that Ocean where each kind
Does streight its own resemblance find;
Yet it creates, transcending these,
Far other Worlds, and other Seas;
Annihilating all that's made
To a green Thought in a green Shade.

(40–49)

Since "Musicks Empire" possesses an equanimity reminiscent of "The Garden," it may have initially been written at Appleton. Its unequivocably peaceful tone, despite its exuberance, links it to the poems concerning the balance of body and mind/soul, earthly and divine. He may originally have directed it to Fairfax; he may later have meant it for Cromwell; he may purposely have left it ambiguous. Cromwell's love of music is frequently mentioned in accounts of his life; not so often noted is his fondness for poetry. James Heath, who had few good words for Cromwell, nonetheless, writes in *Flagellum* of Cromwell's cultivation of artists, including a poet:

> He was a great Lover of Musick, and entertained the skilfullest in that Science in his pay and Family; in that like wicked Saul, who when the evil spirit was upon him, thought to lay and still him with those Harmonious charms; but generally he respected or at least pretended a Love to all ingenious and eximious persons in any Arts, whom he procured to be sent or brought to him, but the niggardlinesse and incompetence of his reward shewed that this man was a personated Act of Greatness, and that private Cromwell yet governed Prince Oliver. Amongst the rest of those Virtuosi, He favoured a Poet too, who very elegantly saying his Marston-Moor *epininon* but with more misfortune then others, who made the Muses Slaves to his Triumphs, and Pegasus to draw his Chariot.[34]

Although the poet mentioned is probably Fitzpayne Fisher, not Marvell, Heath's accusation of "niggardlinesse" on Cromwell's part confirms as well that Cromwell, rather than providing the traditional patronage, placed Marvell in positions in which he earned his livelihood. Friendlier than Heath to Cromwell, Whitelocke verifies Cromwell's love of poetry, saying that Cromwell "'by way of diversion would make verses with us.'"[35]

In "Musick's Empire," Nature's music in the first stanza is single and "Jarring" (2); in the second stanza, Jubal, representing humankind, presides at music's birth, born from Jubal's imitations of nature—"He call'd the *Ecchoes* from their sullen Cell, / And built the Organs City where they dwell" (7–8)—the union of art and nature. The wedding of these two occupies the third and fourth stanzas; those that choose the "Cornet eloquent" sing "Mens Triumphs," those who practice "the Wire," the viol, practice for "Heavens quire" (13–16). "Musick, the Mosaique of the Air," the consequence of the harmonic union, reigns supreme over her dominion, all the air, "the Empire of the Ear"; the aural pun in "Air" and "Ear" (17–19) resonates to reiterate emphatically the realm of music, conqueror of all space—"all between the Earth and Sphear" (20). The sight puns in "Earth and Sphear" complete the delineation of music's realm in illustrating that it does indeed occupy all space. This greatest of conquerors is called on to "Homage do / Unto a gentler Conqueror" (21–22), who "flies" from what is usually thought of as music to human ears—praise—yet eagerly would praise Heaven. In an intriguing assessment, Jonathan Goldberg argues that the "gentler Conqueror" of "Musicks Empire" is Christ:[36] Cromwell *is* presented in "The First Anniversary" as Christlike, but "Musicks Empire" doesn't seem quite that complex—rather more a graceful compliment. In the union of earthly and spiritual music, the desired resolution of the poems discussed above occurs, as well as an element of the philosophy that we do hear in "The First Anniversary," that if a spiritually harmonious society were achieved and were led by Cromwell, the latter days and union with Christ could be achieved. Thus, "Musicks Empire" would appear to represent a link in Marvell's poetry between the private and the public poems. In "The First Anniversary," it is "indefatigable *Cromwell*" who "cuts his way still nearer to the Skyes, / Learning a Musique in the Region clear, / To tune this lower to that higher Sphere" (45–48), reiterating the thesis of "Musicks Empire" that Cromwell alone—the gentle-handed Amphion—can create an earthly realm harmonious with the divine.

5

"Cromwell alone":
Marvell as Cromwell's Poet

THE point at which Marvell chose to write "The First Anniversary" is interesting. The title indicates that it is a celebration of the end of Cromwell's first year as protector, yet other moments would seem more worthy of celebration: Cromwell's triumph in Scotland or at Worcester, for instance. Or if Marvell had been deeply involved in millenarianism, he might have chosen the moment of the first meeting of the Barebone's Parliament. He did not. "The First Anniversary," advertised in *Mercurius Politicus* of January 1654/55, defends Cromwell's actions as Lord Protector and unrelentingly accuses the English of being recalcitrant stoneheads. Cromwell's domestic decisions and his newly devised constitutional basis, the *Instrument of Government*, clearly stood in need of defense. The deposed royal family grew dearer in absence. The English mind seemed unwilling, even unable, to understand the requirements of the change from monarchical to republican government. They did, however, understand that the time was unique; Charles's decapitation had impressed that on them. Marvell takes advantage of this one glimmer and creates the logic by which he would turn them to cooperation with Cromwell, an inescapable conclusion: "If these the Times, then this must be the Man" (144).

Cromwell was more than ordinarily beleaguered by what seemed the eternal resistance of parliaments to action, as well as by royalist plots against his life and harangues from the religious sects. One plot uncovered in February of 1654 had taken most of the year to unravel and was finally estimated to involve five or six hundred people. The object of the plot was to destroy the Cromwellian government and to bring in Charles Stuart; it was said to have originated in France.[1] The *Weekly Intelligencer* of 8–15 August expresses some of the frustration that Cromwell himself must have felt:

The Plots and Repinements against this present Government are like the Heads of Hydra, no sooner one is cut off, but another ariseth. This day a Pavier in Grubstreet was by a Warrants from the Council apprehended, for having an intent to stab the Lord Protector, and that the way whereby he would accomplish his wicked Design, was by taking an opportunity to come unto him with a petition, pretended to be of great, and remarkable importance.[2]

Early in the year, Cromwell had issued a declaration delineating the boundaries of treason. In part, it said,

if any person shall compasse, or imagine the death of the Lord Protector, . . . or if any person or persons shall maliciously, or advisedly, either by writing, printing, openly declaring, preaching, teaching, or otherwise publish, that the Lord Protector, and the people in Parliament assembled, are not the Supream authority of the Common wealth, or if any person or persons whatsoever, shall proclaim, declare, publish, or any way promote Charles Stuart eldest Son the late King, or James Stuart one other of his Sons, or any other person or persons, claiming by, from, or under him or them.[3]

After the conspiracy, the restrictions were even tighter.

In addition to the conspiracies, the religious sects rumbled constantly, though their proclamations became much more discreet after the arrests of the Fifth Monarchists Feake and Simpson in late January on charges of treason. They were both sent to Windsor, and the newspapers' regular reports on them must have galled Cromwell. The following from *The Faithful Scout*, 3–10 February, is typical of the newspapers' attitudes:

thus much I desire, that the Series [sic] of Providence may guide and protect those two faithful Saints, and Ministers of the Gospel, pious Mr. Feak, and zealous Mr. Simpson . . . I hope it is no Treason to pray for them, although some hold it not reason to act with them; yet I could wish, that if it might stand with the honour of God, and the glory of his Church, that all men would submit in peace and love.[4]

A reading of Feake's and Simpson's mental and emotional health seems to have been taken about every two weeks and published as the news from Windsor. For example, *The Every dayes Intelligence*, 28 April–5 May, announced that "Mr: Sympson and Mr: Feake are very cheerful at Winsor, and as confident as ever." As close and sympathetic a watch was kept on the Leveller John Lilburne. News involving the royal family, only slightly less overtly sympathetic, was even more frequent. Henrietta Maria was referred to in most accounts as "the little Queen," which has an affectionate ring to it.

An incident of importance occurred that may have given added stimulus to Marvell's desire to defend Cromwell. In the spring of 1654, three army colonels met to discuss their grievances with the Cromwellian government, which they considered as "contrary to parliamentary government," and the imposing of the *Instrument of Government*, which had been drawn up by only a few officers.[5] Cromwell heard of it and had Colonel Matthew Alured removed from his command in Ireland by Lieutenant-General Fleetwood to whom Alured confessed that some of the army were meeting in London against Cromwell.[6] Colonel Matthew Alured was the nephew of Marvell's stepmother Lucy Alured and the father of Mary, wife of Marvell's nephew William Popple, and though the association may have been no embarrassment to Marvell, still it may have reinforced his loyalty to Cromwell. John Alured, brother to Matthew, was a member of the Long Parliament and the Rump, but he died in 1654. Perhaps Matthew Alured's ire was aroused as much by grief over his brother's death as irritation with Cromwell's delay in dissolving the House and then abruptly dismissing it. Alured himself would be elected to the House from Hedon in 1658/59, but in 1660, he failed to win the election that Marvell, one of his opponents, won.[7] In her article on the petition, Barbara Taft recounts the complicated story of the dissident colonels, which began apparently with a meeting in London of the Colonels Alured, John Okey, and Thomas Saunders who signed a petition that denounced "Cromwell's unfettered control over a standing army and demanded successive Parliaments, freely chosen by the people and holding the supreme power in the state." John Wildman had written the petition; he and Okey and Saunders had won election to the first Parliament under Cromwell to convene on 3 September 1654. Cromwell, however, seems to have prevented their sitting, along with several others, through his order that any who refused to sign a "recognition of the government" would be excluded.[8] Before the petition could be circulated for other signatures, Alured was arrested, "imprisoned in the Mews and the petition was taken from his chamber."[9] Taft surmises that the petition was published by John Wildman, the writer of the document, whose dislike for "powerful executives, military might, and Oliver Cromwell" had been confirmed by "the exclusion of properly elected members—himself among them—from the Parliament of 1654."[10] The three colonels were trusted officers of notable accomplishment. Only the year before Alured had been given "command of all the forces in western Scotland,"[11] but Taft judges that he alone was imprisoned (for a year) because he was "clearly the most meddlesome."[12] They had all been loyal to Cromwell prior to the Protectorate. Their petition was circulated throughout the army across England and into Scotland and Ireland. Taft comments that the army officers represented "the only critics who could destroy [Cromwell's] regime,"[13] that the "printed copies probably ran into the thousands, and [that] the zeal with which Protectorate authorities seized and destroyed the manifesto is suggested by the character of contemporary comment on the contents."[14] Major-General Robert Overton, friend of Milton and Marvell (and another possibility as introducer of the two poets), governor of Hull until 1650, and Fifth Monarchist, became involved through the discussion generated by the petition and "reportedly" met with Wildman. Overton had gone to Scotland from London late in 1654 to meet with similarly "disaffected officers" who signed a letter advertising a meeting in Edinburgh "'to assert the freedomes of the people in the priviledges of parliament.'"[15] Copies of the petition signed by the colonels were found in Overton's quarters. He was imprisoned for four years or longer in the Tower for his part in the proposed insurrection. John Wildman continued to spread the petition; he was imprisoned early in 1655, but his *Declaration of the Free-born People of England, Now in Armes against the Tyrannie . . . of Oliver Cromwell* nonetheless was published and at about the same time that he was arrested. Taft comments that "Wildman's arrest had marked the end of the wave of hostile plots which had been the principal concern of Cromwell and his councilors since the discovery of the meetings which produced the *Petition of Several Colonels*."[16]

The army had been patient in a sense with the House and the House with the army, primarily because their membership "overlapped": there were officers who also sat in the House, there were House members who had served during the civil war and kept their military titles. Blair Worden observes that "There were broad areas of cooperation between army and parliament, . . . [yet] parliament and army still seemed to themselves and each other to be distinct and often opposing institutions."[17] Worden explains their divergent perspectives of the political power due each group:

The civil war had been a split within the governing classes represented in parliament. Both sides had been obliged to employ men
from outside the governing classes to fight their battles for them, but
neither had questioned the divine right of those classes to govern or
had imagined that the war had anything to do with the remedy of
social inequalities. The demand for social reform advanced by the
parliamentary army, and especially by Cromwell's increasingly
prominent New Model forces, transformed the nature of the revolution. The troops, grievously underpaid, exhorted by their officers and
their chaplains to regard themselves as God's chosen instruments of
victory, provided fertile ground for the dissemination of social
radicalism.[18]

The House resisted the army's requests for social reform and the
doing of "the Lord's work" by slowing down even more than the
burden of administrative detail they dealt with made necessary.
One can hardly argue with Worden's observation that "politi-
cians who give much of their time to mundane administrative
tasks cannot be expected to sustain an unrelieved sense of apocalyptic urgency for more than four years."[19] Worden has no doubt
but that "the inertia which afflicted the Rump in its later stages
is to be explained more by the conflict between parliament and
army than by an endemic resistance to hard work on the part of
the rumpers."[20] Yet, as Worden goes on to consider, the army
never lost faith in the parliament as an institution, rather they
advocated "frequent parliamentary elections as the cure to all
evils, but rarely seem to have asked themselves what kind of
men parliamentary elections would return."[21] And the elections
continued to return the same sorts. The bill that caused Cromwell to dissolve the Rump in 1653 had concerned setting the
date for their adjournment and "'for the calling and settling of
future and successive parliaments.'"[22] Agreeing that the qualifi-
cations for the representative (which was what the new parliament was to be called) should be only those "'such as are persons
of known integrity, fearing God, and not scandalous in their conversation,'" they decided to meet in November before the newly
elected group met, thus they could screen the new members'
political bents. Recognizing this as a ploy to insure that the same
kind continued to sit, the army knew they would make moot the
reforms they had urged for so long. The night before the bill was
to be passed, Cromwell held a meeting with the army leaders
and some twenty of the most powerful of the House members.
He suggested bringing to a close the present House and installing
a smaller governing group comprised equally of army men and

parliament members who should function until a new parliament convened. The movement toward the education of the electorate to choose men who were worthy to govern the Commonwealth could grow, or so Cromwell envisioned, through the careful selection and empowering of God-fearing men of integrity who would reform the inequities of law and wield justice fairly. With that kind of ruling body, the hope could exist that monarchy would be seen as inferior and thus forgotten. Enlightened by these governors of integrity, the necessity of keeping a standing army would cease. The Barebone's was to be the disillusioning consequence of Cromwell's hope, but the hope itself was admirable. The House members there that evening agreed that the present ruling group should not be "permitted to prolong their own power," and agreed as well "to suspend farther proceedings about the bill." [23] Instead, the next morning they went straight to proceedings to pass the bill. Cromwell gathered a group of soldiers, went to the House, listened to the session for a while, and dissolved them.

The expulsion of the Rump had not shaken the army's loyalty to Cromwell, but the acceptance of the Protectorate after the unfortunate Barebone's Parliament and "in accordance with an *Instrument of Government* drawn up by a small group of officers" prompted what Taft calls "emerging disaffection"[24] for Cromwell. In the poem, Marvell's contempt for the general English populace's inability to determine anything evinces itself immediately. He softens his contumely by substituting "Man" for the English and by assuming a philosophical attitude:

Like the vain Curlings of the Watry maze,
Which in smooth streams a sinking Weight does raise;
So Man, declining alwayes, disappears
In the weak Circles of increasing Years;
And his short Tumults of themselves Compose,
While flowing Time above his Head does close.

                                                             (1–6)

Man, like a rock, a "Weight," drops into the "smooth"—that is, continuous—stream of time; the circles formed by his entry into the stream dissolve themselves; he, "declining always," merely sinks. And time, with its never-ceasing flow, closes above his head. Man does not move with time, but instead falls through it, perpendicular in his relation rather than parallel. Marvell reduces the uprisings that may be said to have precipitated the poem by presenting them as man's "short Tumults [that] of them-

selves Compose" (5). "Man" has neither the power to disturb the
stream nor the power to calm it, and "flowing Time" will continue its undisturbed course. Only Cromwell can effect change.

Because he "alone" moves parallel to time (and of course with
the times), "*Cromwell* alone" increases. Man "disappears / In the
weak Circles of increasing Years":

> *Cromwell* alone with greater Vigour runs,
> (Sun-like) the Stages of succeeding Suns:
> And still the Day which he doth next restore,
> Is the just Wonder of the Day before.
> *Cromwell* alone doth with new Lustre spring,
> And shines the Jewel of the yearly Ring.
>
> (7–12)

The phrase "*Cromwell* alone" suggests not only that Cromwell
could achieve single-handedly all that he would do since God
favors his efforts, but also that he alone of all English people
and monarchs would build and restore England. The ability and
desire lie nowhere else than with Cromwell. In his creative role,
Cromwell not only restores but regenerates, so that beneath his
hand, all grow more perfect. In the attributing to Cromwell the
ability to "restore" days, Marvell expands *restore* sufficiently that
it assumes the meaning of returning mankind from its fallen and
ever-falling condition to a state of grace; thus, the implication is
that Cromwell is capable of fulfilling Daniel 9.25 to restore and
to build Jerusalem.

Marvell continues to enrich the aggregate of meanings of *restore* with the denial that any king ever restored and that to
restore a king would be to destroy rather than restore:

> 'Tis he the force of scatter'd Time contracts,
> And in one Year the work of Ages acts:
> While heavy Monarchs make a wide Return,
> Longer, and more Malignant then *Saturn*:
> And though they all *Platonique* years should raign,
> In the same Posture would be found again.
> Their earthy Projects under ground they lay,
> More slow and brittle then the *China* clay:
> Well may they strive to leave them to their Son,
> For one Thing never was by one King don.
>
> (13–22)

With no mention of Charles II, Marvell has linked all monarchs
with malice, incompetence, stupidity, and godlessness. The slant

of the lines "While heavy Monarchs make a wide Return, / Longer, and more Malignant then Saturn" (15–16) ominously reminds his audience of the nature of a Stuart reign, as well as of the retribution that a restored Stuart would likely exact. As Marvell would have it, a Stuart restoration means backward movement, and throughout Marvell reiterates relentlessly the value of forward movement. Saturn speaks to this as well; the astrologically oriented age, fully familiar with its meandering, often retrogressive, path, considered Saturn a malignant influence only when it moved backward.[25] Thus, Marvell creates the equation of a Stuart restoration as the exemplar of backward movement with its implications and Cromwell of forward movement. Only Cromwell has the ability to use Time as his instrument because only he can compress its force to unite time and work to achieve in his first year what monarchs cannot in a lifetime: "'Tis he the force of scatter'd Time contracts, / And in one Year the work of Ages acts" (13–14). "Man" cannot influence time; nor can kings. Marvell overtly and frequently repeats the point in this poem to make ever present the awareness that kings have no more power over time than ordinary men: "And though they all *Platonique* years should raign, / In the same Posture would be found again" (17–18). Those "earthy Projects" of the monarchs that take so long that they must "leave them to their Son" remind the audience of the great sums that monarchs require to maintain their "state" and the vast amounts they pass on to their heirs, all state monies. "Earthy" also stands in opposition to "spiritual."

Even in what kings seem to accomplish—victory in war—they in fact do not even do that without a severe toll on their subjects. They consider themselves to have won if they lose only their kingdom's resources:

> Yet some more active for a Frontier Town
> Took in by Proxie, beggs a false Renown;
> Another triumphs at the publick Cost,
> And will have Wonn, if he no more have Lost.
>
> (23–26)

Thus only against their own subjects do they actually war. The irony is that the foreign wars are touted as protective measures; in reality, monarchs with their wars exhaust money and citizenry to the point of devastation; their "Common Enemy" is their own people:

They fight by Others, but in person wrong,
And only against their Subjects strong;
Their other Wars seem but a feign'd contest,
This Common Enemy is still opprest;
If Conquerors, on them they turn their might;
If Conquered, on them they wreak their Spight.

                                                        (27–32)

Secular recriminations comprise Marvell's explicit list thus far, and any might have been directed against Charles I. A particular exploitation that encompasses both the earthly and divine will lead to the spiritual objection:

They neither built the Temple in their dayes,
Nor Matter for succeeding Founders raise;
Nor sacred Prophecies consult within,
Much less themselves to perfect them begin;
No other care they bear of things above,
But with Astrologers divine, and *Jove*,
To know how long their Planet yet Reprives
From the deserved Fate their guilty lives:
Thus (Image-like) an useless time they tell,
And with vain Scepter, strike the hourly Bell;
Nor more contribute to the state of Things,
Then wooden Heads unto the Viols strings.

                                                        (33–44)

Refuting Ruth Nevo's contention that Marvell emulates Waller's "Upon his Majesty's repairing St. Paul's" (1635), Annabel Patterson points out that "Marvell is *replying* to Waller's poem, rather than merely echoing it."[26] Among the numerous 1654 happenings interpreted as ominous for Cromwell's government, one was the partial fall of St. Paul's south wall. Marvell may have intended that the allusion and reply to Waller bring his audience to connect Charles's repairs with James's work and the ineffectiveness of both (for the south wall continued to crumble). This is to interpret rather literally, but their failed efforts in "building the temple" and the disrepair of St. Paul's at the time would seem to manifest a monarchical as against a Cromwellian failure. The repair of St. Paul's had been an issue for Charles I since at least 1631. St. Paul's was very nearly completely desecrated. Charles Carlton writes that "the nave had become a short cut for meat porters carrying freshly slaughtered, dripping carcases from Smithfield Market, it was a playground for children, . . . a place where writers of news letters could garner the latest intelligence, and a rendezvous where [whores] ... found bountiful business." In 1631, the king instituted a commission and commissioners to "solicit contributions," and raised forty thousand pounds. Laud enthusiastically joined him in fund raising, sending "letters urging contributions" to bishops, cities, mayors, justices of the peace, whomever he might squeeze. He went further; he persuaded the king "to donate all fines levied by High Commission ... [and thus corrupted] it 'from an ecclesiastical court for the reformation of manners to a court of revenue.'" He was ruthless in his fining. Their use of the funds was as subject to criticism as Laud's garnering of them had been. They had Inigo Jones design the west front, which he did "in the Palladian style, using as his model the facade of Il Gesu, the mother church of the Jesuits in Rome." The contributions flowed in, nonetheless, amounting to between sixty and a hundred thousand pounds more through 1639, in addition to the forty thousand pounds from the king's initial effort.[27] Physically, Anglican churches all over England "needed reform."[28] The cosmetic work on St. Paul's that might have been done with those kinds of monies was poorly done or done insensitively for the time. The point would seem to be that the king's concern had been with a crumbling structure, comparable to his concern with the Church of England, also a crumbling structure, and that he had merely cobbled it up. Cromwell's work, as Patterson points out, "is not only construction of the constitutional framework of the Commonwealth but also the building of the Temple ... a common Puritan metaphor for the achievement of a new church polity."[29]

The "sacred Prophecies" (35) seem to be those of Daniel, including the admonishment of Daniel 9.25 to restore and to build Jerusalem, matters of no concern to monarchs. Their only involvement with the spiritual lies in seeking to "divine" with astrologers "and *Jove*" (38) their own fate, not that of their kingdom. The ruler's higher obligation is concern with eternal life rather than temporal, as well as with the spiritual life of the state. Moreover, it implies that Charles as a monarch "deserved" as his "Fate" the loss of his "guilty" life. Oppositely, the consulting of "sacred Prophecies" suggests Cromwell's procedure of attuning himself to God's direction. Charles Firth explains:

> For his own part, Cromwell believed in "dispensations" rather than "revelations." Since all things which happened in the world were determined by God's will, the statesman's problem was to discover the hidden purpose which underlay events. ... "Seek to know what

the mind of God is in all that chain of Providence," was his counsel. . . . With Cromwell, in every political crisis this attempt to interpret the meaning of events was part of the mental process which
preceded action. As it was difficult to be sure what that meaning
was, he was often slow to make up his mind, preferring to watch
events a little longer and to allow them to develop in order to get
more light. This slowness was not the result of indecision, but a
deliberate suspension of judgment. When his mind was made up
there was no hesitation, no looking back; he struck with the same
energy in politics as in war . . . [a] "sudden engaging for and sudden
turning from things."[30]

With each negative statement about monarchs or men, Marvell
posits Cromwell as the positive.

In reality, Cromwell was well aware that this 'sudden engaging
for and sudden turning from things,' the speed with which he
moved once his way was clear to him, appeared unusual to
others: "'I am very often judged for one that goes too fast. . . . It
is the property of men that are as I am, to be full of apprehensions
that dangers are not so real as imaginary.'"[31] Cromwell's speed
is a topic in the poem as a whole: "in one Year the work of Ages
acts" (14), "Indefatigable Cromwell hies" (45), "Angelic Cromwell who outwings the wind" (126), "The ill delaying what the
elected hastes" (156). Conversely, the monarchs' dominant attri-
bute is their stillness, their inactivity: "In the same Posture
would be found again" (18), "one Thing never was by one King
don" (22), "(Image-like) an useless time they tell" (41), "wooden
Heads" (44). Marvell makes this comparison explicit, even to the
point of employing parallel parentheses in lines 8 and 41:

> Cromwell alone with greater Vigour runs,
> (Sun-like) the Stages of succeeding Suns:
> And still the Day which he doth next restore,
> Is the just Wonder of the Day before.
>
> (7–10)

> Thus (Image-like) an useless time they tell,
> And with vain Scepter, strike the hourly Bell;
> Nor more contribute to the state of Things,
> Then wooden Heads unto the Viols strings.
>
> (41–4)

"(Image-like)" also suggests Catholicism and the adoration of
saints, figures to the Puritan mind as incapable of efficacious
response as the effigies of saints, christs, and death marking the

time of the great clocks in England's public squares. Monarchs are useless except to denote the passage of time; they are incapable of restoration. Cromwell, however, exerts himself with unremitting perseverance to reach higher and higher goals, to understand what God wishes, to hear the heavenly voice, the music of the spheres, so that he can bring earth in tune with heaven, to create a political and spiritual concord:

> While indefatigable *Cromwell* hyes,
> And cuts his way still nearer to the Skyes,
> Learning a Musique in the Region clear,
> To tune this lower to that higher Sphere.
> So when *Amphion* did the Lute command,
> Which the God gave him, with his gentle hand,
> The rougher Stones, unto his Measures hew'd,
> Dans'd up in order from the Quarreys rude;
> This took a Lower, that an Higher place,
> As he the Treble alter'd, or the Base:
> No Note he struck, but a new Story lay'd,
> And the great Work ascended while he play'd.
> The listning Structures he with Wonder ey'd,
> And still new Stopps to various Time apply'd:
> Now through the Strings a Martial rage he throws,
> And joyning streight the *Theban* Tow'r arose;
> Then as he strokes them with a Touch more sweet,
> The flocking Marbles in a Palace meet;
> But, for he most the graver Notes did try,
> Therefore the Temples rear'd their Columns high:
> Thus, ere he ceas'd, his sacred Lute creates
> Th'harmonious City of the seven Gates.
>
> (45–66)

The identification of Cromwell with Amphion[32] arises naturally from the lines in their emphasis on speed and skill. "The rougher Stones" reflect Cromwell's penchant for choosing men only on the basis of their devotion to God and their ability, that is, their usefulness to God's purpose. He shaped such "rougher Stones" into fine soldiers and extended their usefulness as statesmen when the war was over, in a sense retrieving them from their fallen state and restoring them to a right and useful life. Even his enemies had to admire his ability to place the right men in the right places: "Hyde wrote from Paris, with grudging admiration, that 'Cromwell proceeds with strange dexterity towards the reconciling all sorts of persons, and chooses those out of all parties whose abilities are most eminent.'"[33] The whole of Marvell's passage reflects the trait that Hyde comments on—Cromwell's ability to bring men of disparate views into service in his government. Generally, each believed Cromwell's opinions to be in tune with his own, or at least sympathetic. Rather than duplicity on Cromwell's part, his wide tolerance and his custom of listening attentively created this perception in others. In contrast to the "wooden Heads unto the Viols strings" (44) of monarchs, who are functionless other than as props or holders of office, Cromwell harmonizes even as he builds the new state.

Moreover, Cromwell has recreated time in recreating circumstance: "The listning Structures he with Wonder ey'd, / And still new Stopps to various Time apply'd" (57–58); that is, in remolding the government into a commonwealth from a monarchy, he creates a new context for English life. The historic Cromwell's sudden turnings to or from action seem to match well with the nervous energy of these lines. As I mentioned earlier, he had the habit of waiting and watching "with Wonder" to see how God intended events to develop. Marvell's description of time as "various" reflects Cromwell's flexibility in applying himself to a variety of circumstance. Charles Firth considers this trait an argument against the accusation that he was calculating:

> He was too much taken up with the necessities of the present to devise a deep-laid scheme for making himself great. . . . more practical and less visionary than other statesmen of his party; more open-minded and better able to adapt his policy to the changing circumstances and changing needs of the times. . . . The persistent adhesion . . . to . . . old formulas, in spite of defeats and altered conditions, Cromwell regarded as blind to the teaching of events.[34]

Marvell presents Cromwell as having turned his transforming attention to every facet of government in creating the *Instrument of Government*, which name Marvell himself plays on:

> Such was that wondrous Order and Consent,
> When *Cromwell* tun'd the ruling Instrument;
> While tedious Statesmen many years did hack,
> Framing a Liberty that still went back.
>
> (67–70)

The "tedious Statesmen" may be identified as the Long Parliament and the Rump, particularly the Rump, whose pace should have been quickened since rarely were more than fifty members present to fulfill their obligations. But they knew nothing except monarchy and the parliament as governmental structures, and thus clung unimaginatively to what they knew, searching for precedents for an event unprecedented. Even the Barebone's could not lift itself from the monarchical morass. Their slowness is akin to the Saturnian-paced monarchs of the past and represents dangerous backward movement. They "hack" over the years looking for precedent to guide them, in contrast to the pioneering Cromwell who "cuts his way still nearer to the Skyes" (46). As I have earlier mentioned, the army's demands for reforming legislation caused the House to move even slower. Blair Worden gives an explicit picture of the parliamentary circumstance:

> After the summer of 1649 there is a steady decline in the amount of legislation passed, in the number of committees appointed and, to a lesser extent, in the frequency with which the House sat. . . . Once the royalist threat had faded, the bond which had held the regime together simply snapped. As army pressure for reform increased, business and legislation became ever more bogged down in parliamentary dissension, until long delays became the norm rather than the exception. Division and delay promoted each other, and the decline in the number of committees appointed was closely paralleled by an increase in the number of occasions on which motions were put to the vote. . . . The government had run out of steam. Yet the inertia which afflicted the Rump in its later stages is to be explained more by the conflict between parliament and army than by any endemic resistance to hard work on the part of the rumpers.[35]

In addition to diminished attendance, the enormous membership of the House was a problem long wrestled with; by 1640 there were five hundred and seven members of the House,[36] thus the "num'rous Gorge [which] could swallow in an hour / That Island, which the Sea cannot devour: / Then our *Amphion* issues out and sings, / And once he struck, and twice, the pow'rful Strings (71–74). Much of the House time had been occupied with electoral reform; Marvell does not focus on that though, nor is his implication concerning the vast membership's insatiable greed primary. His main motive here is to point up the state's danger in the numerous and divisive House members' inability to govern the Commonwealth. In contrast, Cromwell has the ability not only to rule alone, but also to create concord out of their self-serving cacophony:

> The Commonwealth then first together came,
> And each one enter'd in the willing Frame;

All other Matter yields, and may be rul'd;
But who the Minds of stubborn Men can build?
No Quarry bears a Stone so hardly wrought,
Nor with such labour from its Center brought;
None to be sunk in the Foundation bends,
Each in the House the highest Place contends,
And each the Hand that lays him will direct,
And some fall back upon the Architect;
Yet all compos'd by his attractive Song,
Into the Animated City throng.
   The Common-wealth does through their Centers all
Draw the Circumf'rence of the publique Wall;
The crossest Spirits here do take their part,
Fast'ning the Contignation which they thwart;
And they, whose Nature leads them to divide,
Uphold, this one, and that the other Side;
But the most Equal still sustein the Height,
And they as Pillars keep the Work upright;
While the resistance of opposed Minds,
The Fabrick as with Arches stronger binds,
Which on the Basis of a Senate free,
Knit by the Roofs Protecting weight agree.

                                        (67–98)

Obviously, he echoes Milton's *Areopagitica*, but his own genius
evinces itself in the figure of Amphion and the play on "instrument." The passage should have convinced anyone who understood harmony; Cromwell however, might have found irony in
Marvell's assertion of "Consent" (67). Though Marvell presents
Cromwell himself as God's "ruling Instrument" (68) and the creator of the instrument as well, Cromwell waited and looked for
consent in vain. He had been recently accused by Major-General
Ludlow (perhaps out of personal animus at having been relegated
to General of the Horse in Ireland) of not possessing the people's
consent. "Where shall we find the consent?" Cromwell asked in
seriousness.[37] Finding no consensus, Cromwell could look only
to events, and as long as they could be read as favoring his rule,
he found consent in God.

   To prevent what he foresaw as catastrophe, Cromwell by this
time had dissolved parliament twice; Marvell gives the most
positive coloration possible to this action: "Then our Amphion
issues out and sings, / And once he struck, and twice, the
pow'rful Strings" (73–74). In "The First Anniversary," Marvell
would have it that that strong action has enabled Cromwell to
create a "willing Frame," that is, the *Instrument of Government*,

by which the English can achieve freedom from monarchy and a new, better order. *Willing* carries both the meaning of *consent*, thus referring to "that wondrous Order and Consent, / When *Cromwell* tun'd the ruling Instrument," and the meaning of *to will*, in the sense of to grant or concede. In other words, Cromwell's desire in the *Instrument* is to reflect the desires of all the English insofar as possible. Their own attitude stands in his way, or their obtuseness: "But who the Minds of stubborn Men can build? / No Quarry bears a Stone so hardly wrought" (78–79). This last resounds Cromwell's preliminary construction of "The rougher Stones," who "Dans'd up in order from the Quarreys rude" (51–52), with the undertone of reminder that it was he who created a path for them. In further reiteration of theme, the lines remember Man, the first figure in the poem, described as "a sinking Weight" or rock thrown into the stream of circumstance, "flowing Time." These stoneheads are determined only in one thing, to be what they cannot be, to place themselves out of their element, the ground, the quarry, the foundation, which to be of value must remain the bottom. Their intractability and rigidity are virtues in the foundation. If they cannot bend by their nature, they should look to their architect to place them. If they can bend, as Cromwell with his flexibility and "gentle hand," the implication is that they may then be deserving of higher place than the foundation. Marvell indicts them with the accusation that "All other Matter yields, and may be rul'd," and then, reminding them more strongly of their ingratitude for what Cromwell has done, sounds again the theme of Cromwell's shaping hand : "each the Hand that lays him will direct, / And some fall back upon the Architect" (83–84). The image of the stones falling creates an ominous context in the awareness of not only direction based solely on stupid opportunism, but also the fall of the government. Yet having the frame, the *Instrument*, Cromwell can actually draw the government into a whole, using the "crossest Spirits" as beams to join all together, creating the tension capable of "Fast'ning the Contignation which they thwart" (90). Cromwell as the "Roofs Protecting weight" (98) provides both ballast and protection.

6

"Angelique *Cromwell.* . . . *Angel* of our Commonweal": the Raised Leader and the Fallen Populace

Given his place as head of state, Cromwell can reconstruct the world in Cromwellian order:

> When for his Foot he thus a place had found,
> He hurles e'r since the World about him round;
> And in his sev'ral Aspects, like a Star,
> Here shines in Peace, and thither shoots a War.
> While by his Beams observing Princes steer,
> And wisely court the Influence they fear;
> O would they rather by his Pattern won
> Kiss the approaching, nor yet angry Son;
> And in their numbred Footsteps humbly tread
> The path where holy Oracles do lead;
> How might they under such a Captain raise
> The great Designes kept for the latter Dayes!
> But mad with Reason, so miscall'd, of State
> They know them not, and what they know not, hate.
> Hence still they sing Hosanna to the Whore,
> And her whom they should Massacre adore:
> But Indians whom they should convert, subdue;
> Nor teach, but traffique with, or burn the Jew.
>
> (99–116)

Cromwell's position is unique: steadying the country and settling the government to some partial extent gave Cromwell a base from which to continue his divinely appointed work. Marvell resumes here, in a slightly altered form, the star image of "An Horatian Ode." Rather than urging "his active Star," Cromwell has become "like a Star" and the traditional lore of stars describes the range of Cromwell's "sev'ral Aspects," which may portend peace or signal war. As sailors observe the stars to chart their course, so rulers of other countries watch closely his actions and fashion their courses by "his Beams." Marvell's reference to the directing beams of light from Cromwell's starlike influence continues the "contignation" theme of joining together with beams. Because of their opposition to Cromwell, the actions of the "observing Princes" represent responses to his governance of the Commonwealth, similar to those of the governing body of England taking its shape under Cromwell's hand through the holding tension created by opposites who are "Fast'ning" with their cross "Spirits ... the Contignation which they thwart" (89–90).

That those foreign princes "fear" the "Influence" they "wisely court" is, however, an inappropriate response. Rather than fear Cromwell, they should truly follow with him his guide, the "holy Oracles" (108). Cromwell "by his Pattern" or example is "such a Captain" that they might redeem "The great Designs kept for the latter dayes!" Marvell accomplishes here the separation of Cromwell from his merely national role and translates him into the international and prophesied spiritual leader, that one who would destroy the Beast and bring about the millennium. Lacking faith, the foreign princes have lost their true sense of purpose as God's rational representatives and leaders of men and become intent instead on "Reason, so miscall'd, of State" (111), which is at the farthest remove from "right reason." Cromwell's deep-seated desire to promote the "Protestant Interest" throughout Europe and to have England lead all other nations into the latter days was unrelenting.[1] Marvell's imagery here alludes to contemporary events. *Massacre* (114), for example, suggests the massacre of the Indians by the Spaniards, an issue on which Marvell may have had privy knowledge. It also serves as an example, as do the Jews, of the atrocities that "Reason, so miscall'd, of State" (111) can create. The latter days required greater preparation than just England's rejection of the Beast. A contignation of all countries and the conversion of the Jews were necessary, all to follow the Pope's overturning.

In the fall of 1654, when the conditions to which Marvell speaks were developing, Cromwell's influence was increasing rapidly abroad: fear of Cromwell had grown to such a degree in France that the French were reported to be showing greater favor to the Huguenots. Yet in Parliament, his position continued to be debated, the "hacking" to which the poem refers. Abbott says that "There, over and over again, the old questions of his authority, its basis and its limitations, were threshed out in the House with endless and seemingly purposeless reiteration."[2] During this time, Cromwell had given the Council a paper advocating the readmission of Jews to England, but the Council was not yet ready to act on this issue.[3] In December, he quietly commissioned and instructed commanders for a West Indian fleet, and the expedition was put to sea. "There is no better tribute," Abbott observes, "to the skill and discretion of Cromwell and his associates than the fact that, though the preparations for an expedition were known to the foreign representatives in England, the destination of this force was kept such a profound secret."[4] Cromwell's instructions to Penn and Venables included orders "to lead and conduct the said army and forces . . . against the king of Spain, his people, and subjects, in any part of America . . . . to pursue, invade, kill, and destroy by all means whatsoever.[5] Instructions of this nature were also given for "ships and vessels of the . . . . French king, or any of his subjects."[6] But in the *Commission of the Commissioners for the West Indian Expedition*, addressed not only to Venables and Penn, but also to Edward Winslowe, Daniel Searle (governor of Barbadoes), and Gregory Butler, the description of the expedition had quite another color:

> Wee . . . hold our self Obliged in Justice to the People of these Nations for the Cruelties, Wrongs, and Injuries done and exercised uppon them by the Spaniards in those parts, Haveing a respect likewise in this our undertaking to the Miserable Thraldome and Bondage, both Spirituall and Civill, which the natives and others in the Dominions of the said King [of Spain] in America are subjected to and lye under by meanes of the Popish and cruell Inquisition and otherwise, from which if it shall please God to make us instrumentall in any measure to deliver them and uppon this occasion to make way for the bringing in the light of the Gospell and power of true Religion and Godliness into these parts, wee shall esteeme it the best and most Glorious part of any Successe or Acquisition it shall please God to blesse us with."[7]

"The First Anniversary" echoes this eloquent statement of noble principles. Though there is no hint in the poem of the content of the directive addressed only to Penn and Venables, Marvell's suggestive positioning of "Massacre" in relation to Indians—"her whom they should Massacre adore: / But Indians whom they should convert, subdue" (114–15)—indicates that he may have had information about the preparation of the West Indian fleet, which was "known to very few," as Abbott says. Marvell's possession of this information could argue for a greater acquaintance with Cromwell than he had previously had.

The next section of the poem, addressed to those "Unhappy Princes" (117), may relate as much to Cromwell's ambitions as to Marvell's:

> Unhappy Princes, ignorantly bred,
> By Malice some, by Errour more misled;
> If gracious Heaven to my Life give length,
> Leisure to Time, and to my Weakness Strength,
> Then shall I once with graver Accents shake
> Your Regal sloth, and your long Slumbers wake:
> Like the shrill Huntsman that prevents the East,
> Winding his Horn to Kings that chase the Beast.
> Till then my Muse shall hollow far behind
> Angelique *Cromwell* who outwings the wind;
> And in dark Nights, and in cold Dayes alone
> Pursues the Monster thorough every Throne:
> Which shrinking to her *Roman* Den impure,
> Gnashes her Goary teeth; nor there secure.
>
> (117–30)

Cromwell reportedly said to General Lambert, "'Were I as young as you, I should not doubt, ere I died, to knock at the gates of Rome,'"[8] and that "as he had better motives than the late King of Sweden he believed himself capable of doing more for the good of nations than the other did for his own ambition."[9] Marvell, as Cromwell's poet, would then speak with strength to wake those "ignorantly bred" princes, urging them to battle against popery.

Until that point, his Muse shall fulfill that role for Cromwell, but "far behind" (125): Cromwell needs no urging. Cromwell alone is not subject to weariness or fatigue in his pursuit of the "Monster" (128). Marvell places the burden and the hope of the millennium on the English (the highest spiritual achievement), for they alone have a ruler in possession of "High Grace," or so the previous lines suggest in saying that he "alone / Pursues the Monster thorough every Throne":

> Hence oft I think, if in some happy Hour
> High Grace should meet in one with highest Pow'r,
> And then a seasonable People still
> Should bend to his, as he to Heavens will,
> What we might hope, what wonderful Effect
> From such a wish'd Conjuncture might reflect.

Sure, the mysterious Work, where none withstand,
Would forthwith finish under such a Hand:
Fore-shortned Time its useless Course would stay,
And soon precipitate the latest Day.
But a thick Cloud about that Morning lyes,
And intercepts the Beams of Mortal eyes,
That 'tis the most which we determine can,
If these the Times, then this must be the Man.

                                                    (131–44)

God has conferred "High Grace" on Cromwell and directed his
actions, but the House then sitting could not bring itself to do
the same; the numerous religious sects were certain their claims
were more worthy than his and at the least withheld their support and often reviled him. The general populace did nothing
except complain. "Seasonable People" or properly seasoned
people—that is, the people as a whole united in support of
Cromwell—are necessary, Marvell maintains. His use of "Con-
juncture" sustains for the reader the image of the star that Cromwell has become in this poem, and emphasizes that the
fulfillment of that high destiny depends on the people's correct
response to that force. Marvell reminds his audience that "Mortal eyes" (142) are clouded. The implicit question in Marvell's
supposition, "If these the Times, then this must be the Man"
(144), is what other man exists on whom this "High Grace" has
been bestowed? God chose him for this destiny. Cromwell waits
now only for mortals to allot "highest Pow'r, / And then a seasonable People" (132–33).

Marvell's sounding of the fallen man theme in the mention of
the clouded mortal vision is reminiscent of Cromwell's eloquent
greeting to the Barebone's Parliament, a speech full of faith and
grand hope for the millennium:

If any man should ask you one by one, and tender a book to you,
you would dare to swear that neither directly nor indirectly did you
seek to come hither. You have been passive in coming hither; being
called,—and that's an active work. . . . Therefore, own your call! . . .
And therefore I may say also, never a people so formed, for such a
purpose, so called,—if it were a time to compare your standing with
those that have been called by the suffrages of the people. Who can
tell how soon God may fit the people for such a thing, and none can
desire it more than I! Would all the Lord's people were prophets. I
would all were fit to be called, and fit to call. . . . I say, own your
call; for indeed it is marvellous and it is of God, and it hath been
unprojected, unthought of by you and us. And indeed it hath been

the way God hath dealt with us all along, to keep things from our
eyes, that in which we have acted we have seen nothing before us;
which is also a witness in some measure to our integrity. I say, you
are called with a high call. And why should we be afraid to say or
think, that this may be the door to usher in the things that God has
promised; which have been prophesied of; which He has set the
hearts of His people to wait for and expect? We know who they are
that shall war with the lamb, against his enemies; they shall be a
people called, and chosen and faithful. And God hath, in a military
way—we may speak it without flattering ourselves, and I believe you
know it—He hath appeared with them and for them; and now in
these civil powers and authorities does not He appear? These are
not ill prognostications of that good we wait for. Indeed I do think
something is at the door: we are at the threshold; and therefore it
becomes us to lift up our heads, and encourage ourselves in the Lord.
And we have some of us thought, That it is our duty to endeavour
this way; not vainly to look at that prophecy in Daniel, "and the
kingdom shall not be delivered to another people." Truly God hath
brought this to your hands; by the owning of your call; blessing the
military power. The Lord hath directed their hearts to be instrumental to call you; and to set it upon our hearts to deliver over the power
to another people.[10]

Cromwell's identification of not just the Darebone's but the English nation as the "called" to fulfill the prophesy of the latter
days was not unique to him, but possessed by many who strove
to interpret the meaning of the time. The necessary condition,
however, was that the people be "seasonable," fit for the
millennium.

Cromwell has lived in readiness:

And well he therefore does, and well has guest,
Who in his Age has always forward prest:
And knowing not where Heavens choice may light,
Girds yet his Sword, and ready stands to fight.

                                                            (145–48)

The reference here extends beyond Cromwell's forward movement and fitness to the stance prescribed in Ephesians 6.13, that
verse so seminal to Marvell and Milton: "Wherefore take unto
you the whole armour of God, that ye may be able to withstand
in the evil day, and having done all, to stand." As no mortal can,
Cromwell did not know that "Heavens choice" would light on
him, but he was ready when it came to him, accepted it, and was
firm enough in his faith to "own" it. His own experience stood

behind his words to the Barebone's to "own your call; for indeed it is marvellous and it is of God, and it hath been unprojected, unthought of by you and us."

Yet if not alone the fit man, Cromwell, it seems, is virtually so:

> But Men alas, as if they nothing car'd,
> Look on, all unconcern'd, or unprepar'd;
> And Stars still fall, and still the Dragons Tail
> Swinges the Volumes of its horrid Flail.
>
> (149–53)

Failing to stand in readiness, men may lose the time of grace; Cromwell is not invincible. "Stars still fall," and Satan stands ever in readiness to achieve revenge on man. Others have noted the influence of Milton's "Ode on the Morning of Christ's Nativity" in the last two lines. I quote the whole of Milton's stanza because Marvell's echo seems to indicate that he intends the allusion to include not just Satan but Satan's state as Milton portrays it:

> And then at last our bliss
> Full and perfect is,
>   But now begins; for from this happy day
> Th'old Dragon under ground,
> In straiter limits bound,
>   Not half so far casts his usurped sway,
> And wroth to see his Kingdom fail,
> Swinges the scaly Horror of his folded tail.
>
> (165–72)[11]

In the world where men fail to involve themselves in their own salvation but "Look on, all unconcern'd, or unprepar'd," Satan has retained his position from Christ's birth to the present of this poem. Little advance, Marvell implies, has been made against Satan since Christ except by Cromwell (the poem's focus is limited to him), the only true warfaring Christian of the time.

The "Day" waits for men, a vital point since most Fifth Monarchists,[12] and perhaps millenarians in general, waited for the day:

> Hence that blest Day still counterpoysed wastes,
> The Ill delaying, what th'Elected hastes;
> Hence landing Nature to new Seas is tost,
> And good Designes still with their Authors lost.
>
> (155–58)

The "blest Day" has been possible any time since Christ, but like Satan and like the monarchs, man has remained in the same position, himself wasting the blessing that waits only for his readiness. Marvell's double use of *hence* suggests cause and effect—one thing leading to another to another, each dependent on the other—but the effect has been a perpetual stalemate. Only Cromwell could break it. But not just the "Day" wastes; Cromwell is also "wasting" in that he has not been given the "highest Pow'r" to effect his "good Designes." "Hence landing Nature to new Seas is tost" indicates that the "blest Day" is like a ship thwarted at the point of landing, pushed back to sea, and more important, tossed to new seas: hence the blest Day may be lost to England and bestowed on another country. Cromwell had touched on this possible loss in his Barebone's speech (see note on speech). If the opportunity for England is lost, the "good Designes" of Cromwell and those united with him will also be lost before their purpose is fulfilled. Despite Marvell's generalizing this, Cromwell is unquestionably the repository of "good Designes" in this poem, and I think Marvell creates the circular reasoning to make it apparent that if the author of those is lost, all is lost. He thus illustrates his own good design in this transitional passage leading to the midpoint accent, the overturn of Cromwell's carriage.

The near-fatal carriage accident that Cromwell has just experienced could have left England bereft. Marvell approaches that crucial occurrence with an account of Cromwell's heritage. The narrative involving Cromwell's mother and her longevity seems intended to illustrate that Cromwell as well has the potential for a very long life:

> And thou, great *Cromwell*, for whose happy birth
> A Mold was chosen out of better Earth;
> Whose Saint-like Mother we did lately see
> Live out an Age, long as a Pedigree;
> That she might seem, could we the Fall dispute,
> T'have smelt the Blossome, and not eat the Fruit;
> Though none does of more lasting Parents grow,
> But never any did them Honor so.

(159–66)

The implication is of a natural aristocracy that God rewards with a long life. In addition to this evidence of a strong hereditary pattern, Marvell presents what amounts to proof that Cromwell's "whole armour of God" has protected him through all dangers:

Though thou thine Heart from Evil still unstain'd,
And always hast thy Tongue from fraud refrain'd;
Thou, who so oft through Storms of thundring Lead
Hast born securely thine undaunted Head,
Thy Brest through ponyarding Conspiracies,
Drawn from the Sheath of lying Prophecies;
Thee proof beyond all other Force or Skill,
Our Sins endanger, and shall one day kill.

(167–74)

God has bestowed "High Grace" and long life; Cromwell has lived spiritually pure. Only the "Sins" of the English, their obdurate allegiance to sin and thus to death and Satan rather than God and Cromwell, "endanger [him], and shall one day kill."

"Sins" are generalized in the definition of "Our brutish fury strugling to be Free" (177). Earlier passages have identified the commissioners of these sins: the tedious statesmen, the thankless men, all headstrong people, as headstrong as Cromwell's carriage horses. They have "Hurry'd" Cromwell's "Horses while they hurry'd" him (178): The association of runaway horses and "Hurry'd" creates the denotation of directionless and frenzied movement, which may be likened to the "short Tumults" of the first lines and contrasted to the fast, directed movement that belongs to Cromwell. "Hurry'd" has as well the sense of *to agitate, disturb, excite; to molest, harass, worry (OED)*. As representative of acts against order, against forward movement under Cromwell's guidance, they can be seen as "Sins." Marvell's analogy works beautifully: the horses moved orderly under Cromwell's reins until spooked; England could do the same. But as the carriage overturned when the horses took the control from Cromwell, so England is in danger of overturn if the "headstrong people" take the reins from Cromwell.

Nature itself seems overturned at Cromwell's fall when he is considered dead (as he was at first rumored to be):

And all about was heard a Panique groan,
As if that Natures self were overthrown.
It seem'd the Earth did from the Center tear;
It seem'd the Sun was faln out of the Sphere:
Justice obstructed lay, and Reason fool'd;
Courage disheartned, and Religion cool'd.

(203–8)

Thus not simply one man is destroyed but God's plan. The repetition of Nature at this point brings back "landing Nature" as a figure for the millennium. That prospect too will be destroyed with Cromwell.

Continuing the impression of a calamity amounting to a universal quake, the rest of the passage—"And to deaf Seas, and ruthless Tempests mourns, / When now they sink, and now the plundring Streams / Break up each Deck, and rip the Oaken seams" (212–14)—echoes the sea imagery of the "landing Nature" line, and gives added dimension to the introductory theme of man's sinking always in the "Streams" of time, forever falling and fallen.

Cromwell alone does not fall. As his upward movement has always opposed that of other men, he ascends:

> But thee triumphant hence the firy Carr,
> And firy Steeds had born out of the Warr,
> From the low World, and thankless Men above.
>
>   (215–17)

The brightness of his transport, harmonious with the approaching "Peoples Charioteer" image, also echoes the "Sunlike" Cromwell of the opening passage. After this seeming apotheosis, Marvell asserts that Cromwell's only descent ever has been his assumption of England's governance: he dimmed himself to rule, for "to be Cromwell was a greater thing, / Then ought below, or yet above a King" (225–26). For him it has been a self-immolating act—"For all delight of Life thou then didst lose" (221) and "Therefore thou rather didst thy Self depress, / Yielding to Rule, because it made thee Less" (227–28).

The poem continues with something of a recapitulation of Cromwell's life, but one becomes unsure as the passage progresses whether Marvell speaks of Cromwell or God. In addition, in the middle of the section, Marvell shifts from the second to the third person in his address to Cromwell:

> For, neither didst thou from the first apply
> Thy sober Spirit unto things too High,
> But in thine own Fields exercisedst long,
> And healthful Mind with a Body strong;
> Till at the Seventh time thou in the Skyes,
> As a small Cloud, like a Mans hand didst rise;
> Then did thick Mists and Winds the air deform,
> And down at last thou pow'rdst the fertile Storm;
> Which to the thirsty Land did plenty bring,

But though forewarn'd, o'r-took and wet the King.
  What since he did, an higher Force him push'd
Still from behind, and it before him rush'd,
Though undiscern'd among the tumult blind,
Who think those high Decrees by Man design'd.
'Twas Heav'n would not that his Pow'r should cease.

(229–43)

Marvell's purpose seems to be to blur the distinction between God's acts and Cromwell's and thus to illustrate God's power working through Cromwell. His use of *pow'rdst* (236) and *Pow'r* (243) is deliberate, and the purpose of using the spelling *pow'rdst* rather than *pour'dst*, as he might have done, suggests the power that has been exhibited in Cromwell's deeds, power out of the ordinary. By this point in the poem, the "tumult blind" is a familiar theme that resounds the opening and Man's "short Tumults [that] of themselves Compose, / While flowing Time above his Head does close." "Man" in his undiscerning nature supposes "those high Decrees by Man design'd" rather than understanding that they are God's "good Designes" supporting and impelling Cromwell. Marvell's use of "higher Force" in this passage also echoes "An Horatian Ode" in which the "forced Power" (66) seems to acquire a similar meaning to account for the death of Charles. An alteration has occurred, as it did with the star image. In this poem, Marvell unquestionably attributes the regicide to a higher design than that of the parliamentarians. But he does not stop with that; the answer to why Cromwell *must* rule is that it is his fate to build the Commonwealth:

'Twas Heav'n would not that his Pow'r should cease,
But walk still middle betwixt War and Peace;
Choosing each Stone, and poysing every weight,
Trying the Measures of the Bredth and Height;
Here pulling down, and there erecting New,
Founding a firm State by Proportions true.

(243–48)

In this consideration of just what God has decreed as Cromwell's fate, Marvell seems to follow Cromwell's determination in his decision not to accept the crown. Since all previous laws had been created for a nation with a king, Cromwell chose to place himself beyond or outside those laws by taking a title other than king. He searched for a title that had never before been used by a ruler because "A name that the law knows not," he said, "is

boundless, is that under which a man exerciseth more arbitrari-
ness."[13] Cromwell's statement sounds tyrannical, but as Carlyle
has observed, he was "very careless about . . . [his] words."[14] The
measure was more a matter of expedience, something difficult to
achieve at any time, and it is well to keep in mind that Cromwell
made no decision without much deliberation and prayer. His
refusal to accept the title may be seen as a brilliant strategy,
allowing him to bypass those laws that might have proved an
impediment to his designs for the Commonwealth. Thus a rationale exists for Marvell's argument that Cromwell became a law
to himself:

> Thou with the same strength, and an Heart as plain,
> Didst (like thine Olive) still refuse to Reign;
> Though why should others all thy Labor spoil,
> And Brambles be anointed with thine Oyl,
> Whose climbing Flame, without a timely stop,
> Had quickly Levell'd every Cedar's top.
> Therefore first growing to thy self a Law,
> Th'ambitious Shrubs thou in just time didst aw.
>
> (257–64)

Marvell's questioning of why lesser men—"Brambles"—should
receive the anointment that rightfully belongs to Cromwell
seems to indicate that he is urging Cromwell to accept the crown.
In the context of this section, however, Marvell is accounting for
or justifying the necessity of Cromwell's actions in refusing the
crown while positioning himself as ruler and architect of the
Commonwealth. I have mentioned earlier the accusation that
Cromwell had replaced one arbitrary power with another. Marvell counters this opinion by presenting evidence of the necessity
of Cromwell's being a law to himself, and enhances his argument
by representing the rule Cromwell has created as a "just time."
This term—"just time"—has more than one application in the
passage, but its primary purpose seems to be to name what
Cromwell has designed. It is the last of a series of parallel phrases
describing time in the poem: the others are "flowing time" (6),
"scatter'd time" (13), "useless time" (41), "various time" (58), and
"fore-shortned Time" (139). Outside of Cromwell's control, time
was described as flowing, scattered, or useless; in his creation as
Amphion of the Commonwealth's structure, he "still new Stopps
to various Time apply'd." And "under such a Hand" as his, "Fore-
shortned Time its useless Course would stay, / And soon precipitate the latest Day." Thus, as architect in the first example, as the

captain under whom the millennium may occur in the second example, as a ruler under whom a "just time" is created in the third,[15] Cromwell achieves what Marvell has asserted: "'Tis he the force of scatter'd Time contracts, / And in one Year the work of Ages acts."

Marvell's use of "Levell'd" suggests reference to the Levellers, and evidence exists for this assumption. John Lilburne had been given his "timely stop" (261) by Cromwell and sent off to the Isle of Jersey where, as the *Weekly Post* (2–8 May) said, he deported "himself with abundance of patience and humility." The next passage is the "lusty mate" section and it analogously vivifies the mistaken vision of the Levellers who supposed that the revolution was to achieve economic and social reform. Cromwell had much better judged the way that reform must advance in time than Lilburne had. A "just time" perhaps of necessity had to come before an equal time. Interestingly, it is from an "artless Steersman" that the "lusty Mate" takes the "Helm"; Lilburne was ardent but artless, as the truly ardent often are. (Despite Cromwell's appearing as the exception to this, he also had his artless moments.) Marvell's references to the Levellers have a rather gentle quality; he describes their objections without acerbity—"What though a while they grumble discontent, / Saving himself he does their loss prevent" (277–78).

Ending this parabolic analogy, Marvell concludes:

> 'Tis not a Freedome, that where All command;
> Nor Tyranny, where One does them withstand:
> But who of both the Bounders knows to lay
> Him as their Father must the State obey.
>
> (279–82)

This passage, as has the one that refers to the Levellers, reiterates the matter of an earlier section of the poem: "Each in the House the highest Place contends, / And each the hand that lays him will direct." The Fifth Monarchists were the greatest single cause of the failure of the Barebone's: however much the poem is a general castigation of all the sects, the primary accusation is against the Fifth Monarchists (that against the "tedious Statesmen" (69) includes the army in that army men and former army men also were Fifth Monarchists and House members). Evidence for this contention may be found in Marvell's description of "ambitious Shrubs." Anna Trapnel, the Fifth Monarchy prophetess,

referred to her people as "Shrubs" in an early section of her long
spate of prophesying at Whitehall in January of 1653/54:

> Another Vision I had at the same time, of many Oaks, with spreading
> branches full of leaves, very great limmed; I looking to the root,
> which lay but very little in the ground, & look't dry, as if it were
> crumbling to dust, and above the ground was only a little dry bark,
> on which limmed and spreading Oaks were set; a few shrubs which
> being by, were very lovely and green, these great Oaks fell suddenly
> down, and cover'd the other; presently I saw a very lovely tree for
> stature & compleatness every way not to be paralleld by any thing
> that ever I saw, and before which the great Oaks crumbled to dust,
> and the little shrubs were raised up, growing and thriving exceed-
> ingly; then I desired Scripture to this Vision; Reply was, in the first
> of Isaiah it is said, *They shall be confounded in the Oaks that they
> have desired:* And as to that lovely Tree, it was declared to me to be
> the Lord Jesus, which I had sometimes seen in the new Jerusalem,
> which is spoken of in the Rev. ult. [sic] That that Tree was the very
> same that is there mentioned whose fruit should be very many and
> beautiful, held forth to the Shrubs, which they feeding upon, should
> immediately grow up to a lovely Stature; which said the Lord to me,
> thou here seest, that no sooner doth this Tree appear, which repre-
> sents my Son, but immediately those despised Shrubs that the great
> Oaks endeavored to scatter and hide in their holes, they shall come
> forth, and all the Oaks shall crumble into dust; this is not by Might,
> nor by Power, or Arms, but brought in through the pourings out of
> my Spirit.[16]

To Trapnel and the Fifth Monarchists, Cromwell was the prime
oppressive "Oak." As I have mentioned earlier, "Oak" was the
traditional symbol for the king, and they perceived Cromwell as
greedy for monarchical power. Following this vision, she describes a vision of Cromwell's persecuting "many precious
Saints that stood in the way of him." Marvell's chastisement of
the Fifth Monarchists will be resounded in later lines.

His reference to Cromwell as "Father" in the lines defining the
knowledge that a ruler must possess—"who of both the Bounders [of freedom and tyranny] knows to lay / Him as their Father
must the State obey"—leads naturally into the Noah section. The
image of Cromwell and his family being "Left by the Wars Flood
on the Mountains crest" (284) presents another figural expression of "Cromwell alone," as well as the concept of God's having
chosen Cromwell, something most of those associated with him
believed as did Cromwell himself. His exasperated speech to the
first elected parliament on 12 September 1654, was occasioned

by their seeming certain so to reduce his power[17] that his position as Protector would be impossible. In this speech, he stated
repeatedly that he had not chosen himself, but that he had
been chosen:

> I called not myself to this place. I say again, I called not myself to
> this place; of that, God is witness. And I have many witnesses who,
> I do believe, could readily lay down their lives to bear witness to the
> truth of that, that is to say, that I called not myself to this place. . . .
> If my calling be from God, and my testimony from the people, God
> and the people shall take it from me, else I will not part with it. I
> should be false to the trust that God hath placed upon me, and to
> the interest of the people of these nations, if I should. . . . I can say
> in the simplicity of my soul, I love not, I love not, (I declined it in
> my former speech) I say I love not to rake into sores or to discover
> nakednesses. . . . I say to you, I hoped to have had leave to have
> retired to a private life. I begged to be dismissed of my charge; I
> begged it again and again.[18]

Cromwell would receive little in return for the advantages he
offered England as its leader; Marvell has earlier pointed out that
Cromwell gave up "all delight of Life" in taking "Command" and
turning "the headstrong Peoples Charioteer." Marvell's image of
him in the "Noah" passage is Cromwell as the good "Husband-
man" of England, conserving, judicious, devoted to bringing the
land to prosperity for its own sake:

> And the large Vale lay subject to thy Will,
> Which thou but as an Husbandman wouldst Till:
> And only didst for others plant the Vine
> Of Liberty, not drunken with its Wine.

(285—88)

Cromwell is contrasted to Noah, who *did* get drunk on the wine.
The fruit of Cromwell's husbandry is liberty, but not unbounded
liberty. Marvell's vine image and the association of pruning and
fruitfulness reflect the need for restraints on liberty to assure
that it does not grow wantonly into license. The passage thus
elaborates the previous lines ("who of both [Freedom and Tyr-
anny] the Bounders knows to lay / Him as their Father must
the State obey.") Cromwell is extraordinary in his self-denying
dedication; most men have no comprehension of restraint:

> That sober Liberty which men may have,
> That they enjoy, but more they vainly crave:

And such as to their Parents Tents do press,
May shew their own, not see his Nakedness.

(289–92)

Drunk on the "Wine" of liberty that Cromwell has given them,
they demand more with the self-indulgent attitude of children.
Marvell's terms—*drunken, crave, press*—all have to do with the
irresponsible urgency of those with unbridled desire. Their arguments and accusations to the supposed hinderer of those desires
have basis only in their own impulse. Marvell maintains that
those who look for flaws in Cromwell expose themselves in doing
so, and like Ham, they bring the curse of darkness on themselves.

Among many offenders, the Fifth Monarchists seem the greatest of the Ham-like:

Yet such a *Chammish* issue still does rage,
The Shame and Plague both of the Land and Age,
Who watch'd thy halting, and thy Fall deride,
Rejoycing when thy Foot had slipt aside;
That their new King might the fifth Scepter shake,
And make the World, by his Example, Quake:
Whose frantique Army should they want for Men
Might muster Heresies, so one were ten.
What thy Misfortune, they the Spirit call,
And their Religion only is to Fall.
Oh, Mahomet! now couldst thou rise again,
Thy Falling-sickness should have made thee Reign,
While Feake and Simpson would in many a Tome,
Have writ the Comments of thy sacred Foame:
For soon thou mightst have past among their Rant
Wer't but for thine unmoved Tulipant;
As thou must needs have own'd them of thy band
For prophecies fit to be *Alcorand.*

(293–310)

This castigation might be considered general (as it is to some
extent) were it not for the numerous Fifth Monarchy references.
Issue here has the meaning of *offspring* and points to the Fifth
Monarchists since many were army men and many of those were
Cromwell's officers and proteges. The derision that followed
Cromwell's carriage accident was widespread, but the Fifth Monarchists had loudly pronounced derisive prophecies and con-
demnations of Cromwell for some time before the accident. Thus
their predictions seemed fulfilled by it: God agreed with their
contention that Cromwell had betrayed them and the millen-

nium. With some good reason, they had thought Cromwell with them in the dissolution of the Rump, and in that action they had supported him in no small capacity. James Heath comments on the apparent concerted thrust of Cromwell and the Fifth Monarchists:

> Every other day almost more Fasts, or some such religious Exercise was managed by Cromwell and Harrison, who mainly promoted the same Proposals for a new Representative, in order for the personal Raign of Christ, and that therefore it was high time the Government was placed in the Hands of his Saints, for all the glorious Prophesies thereof were now ready to be fulfilled, and this was cryed up as the Doctrine of the Times. Cromwell seemed to be of the same judgement and of that Millenary Principle, designing (as he said) nothing in the Mutations of Government which were agitation, but in tendency to that great Revolution, so that he had absolutely fooled Harrison into a confidence of his good Intentions, and that he aimed not at his own greatnesse: and thereupon all the party Harrison could make, which was Feaks, Rogers, and Sympsons Congregations, were impatient to have the Parliament outed, and their fine module to take place, wherein Righteousnesse and Holynesse should be exalted in the Kingdomes of the World. And now the Turke and the Pope were horribly threatned, and Oliver look'd upon as the great Instrument that should confound Antichrist.[19]

The Fifth Monarchists' demands during the Barebone's Parliament and Cromwell's refusal to support them rid both parties of their illusions about each other. Militancy was not really characteristic of the Fifth Monarchists, not even of Major-General Harrison and Major-General Overton. Their tendency had been to wait, but they began to understand that they would have to seek actively what they wanted. Major-General Overton, often referred to as Colonel Overton and the sometime governor of Hull, established in Hull one of the few outposts of the Fifth Monarchists, a primarily urban movement. Marvell's "affectionate Curiosity" about "Overtons businesse" expressed in his letter to Milton of 2 June 1654,[20] referred to Overton's presence in London, recalled from Scotland to discuss his "favouring a Republican or Anabaptist revolt among the northern soldiery"[21] with Cromwell. He promised Cromwell that he would inform him "if conscience forbade faithful service."[22] He didn't. (See above discussion on his interaction with Wildman). Marvell's interest would not preclude his disapproval of the movement's actions against Cromwell. The Fifth Monarchists' clamor was erosive to Cromwell's power in England and their desires were counter to his larger goals for the Commonwealth: they were strongly against the peace with Holland and the war with Spain, and for very self-serving reasons in some segments of the group.[23]

The primary preacher-leaders of the Fifth Monarchists, Feake and Simpson, mentioned in line 305, were strong and strident in the pulpit. Simpson was a prophet as well, although that role was generally dominated by the women of the group,[24] of whom Anna Trapnel was the most renowned. Major-General Harrison was probably the strongest of the army men. They were all four involved in the meetings held at Blackfriars from whence, Bernard Capp says, "the most determined opposition to Cromwell came predictably from Feake." Dubious even before the Barebone's Parliament convened, Feake "preached at Christ Church on 8 May that 'although the General [Cromwell] had fought their Battles with successe, yet he was not the Man, that the Lord had chosen, to sitt at the Helme.'"[25] I hardly need point out that Marvell echoes Feake's words in the now famous line "If these the Times, then this must be the Man" (144).

After the opening of the Barebone's in July, the House issued a declaration "with a strongly millenarian tone, comparing the age to that immediately before the birth of Christ. It expected Christ's 'glorious coming, who is King of kings, and Lord of lords, ... who is still to ride on prosperously, conquering, and to conquer, till he hath subdued all his enemies.'"[26] The twelve identified Fifth Monarchists in the Barebone's worked closely together as members of that parliament. Their aims were not only the abolition of tithes, but also the abolition of the right to presentation of benefices, the court of Chancery, and allegedly a standing army, plus the granting of complete liberty for preachers to preach in public and the continuation of the Dutch War.[27] Bernard Capp observes that "They discussed tactics among themselves and with the Blackfriars preachers. Cromwell said later that 'the persons that led in the meeting were Mr. Feake and his meeting in Blackfriars, Major-General Harrison, and those that associated with him at one Mr. Squibb's house; and there were all the resolutions taken that were acted in that House day by day.'"[28] None of their aims was achieved, and the moderates in the Barebone's were so threatened by the propositions of the radicals—which included many who were not Fifth Monarchists, but who shared some of their goals—that they determined to turn over their power to Cromwell. After this, perpetual war existed between the Fifth Monarchists and Cromwell, though

Cromwell continued to treat them with more tolerance than he was given.

In the fall of 1654, while the first elected parliament under the Protectorate was convened, Feake and Simpson were in prison at Windsor. Simpson had been arrested for prophesying that Cromwell's rule would only last six months, and perhaps Feake's treason somehow involved prophet Anna Trapnel. Both Feake and Simpson were vociferous on Cromwell's "treason," and Feake seems to have been particularly fond of calling Cromwell "'the man of sin, the old dragon, and many other scripture ill names.'"[29] Trapnel, after her much publicized prophesying at Whitehall, left London for Cornwall and remained free until spring. As the government's inquiry into the conspiracy against Cromwell (uncovered early in the year) grew more and more complex, the Council arrested and committed her to Bridewell. Around the middle of December, while Marvell was almost certainly writing this poem, Simpson escaped and spoke at Allhallows. Within a day or so of this event, Feake's condemnation of Cromwell appeared, entitled *The Oppressed Close Prisoner in Windsor Castle, his Defiance to the Father of Lies*. John Rogers, formerly a strong supporter of Cromwell became an even stronger opponent in 1654. He preached constantly from Lambeth Palace where he was imprisoned; Feake railed from inside Windsor. They both ranted sermons, halting only, it would seem, to write letters to their congregations.[30] Many, either devoted or curious, went to Lambeth and later to Windsor specifically to hear Rogers. After Simpson's appearance at Allhallows, Cromwell ordered him brought before him; rather than pleading for anything, the audacious Simpson harangued Cromwell for not keeping his promise to take tithes away before 3 September. Their three-hour conversation was like most of those "between the Protector and the more extreme sectaries, . . . a heated exchange of opinions and admonitions."[31] Cromwell was reported to have said after this interview, "Where shall wee have men of a Universall Spirit? Every one desires to have liberty, but none will give it."[32] Cromwell later met with Feake and ten of the saints for an even longer session.

Concurrently, Parliament was approaching the finish of its consideration of the *Instrument*. Abbott says, "It seems . . . from some of the steps which it took that it contemplated the removal of Cromwell."[33] Fearing more escapes such as Simpson's, Cromwell now ordered additional fortification supplies for Windsor

Castle and the Tower.[34] Conspiracies abounded. Abbott assesses the situation:

> It is apparent from every piece of information that we have that as the end of 1654 approached, Protector and Council were taking the information in regard to a new effort to overthrow their government with the utmost seriousness. Pains were taken to see that the soldiers guarding Whitehall and its approaches were paid promptly to secure their fidelity. The "great and bloody plot" which was reported to come to a head on Christmas Day was given full publicity in the newsbooks. Harrison and Rich were relieved of their commands and Harrison was summoned before Cromwell but released on his assurance that he did not contemplate any action against the government.[35]

In all, the first year of the Protectorate had been very shaky; at the end of it, Cromwell had still to cope with Parliament's determination to reduce his power or depose him completely, and he also had conspirators and the Fifth Monarchists' constant harassment to deal with. Marvell condemns them for their "Rejoycing" at Cromwell's carriage accident because to them the incident meant their "new King might the fifth Scepter shake, / And make the World, by his Example, Quake" (297–98). Derision seems to have been a kind of hallmark of the movement (the Quakers were not alone in refusing to remove their hats). A pamphlet directed mainly against Feake complained:

> Now for the singing of Psalms, I mean that which Mr. Feake derides; I am confident, that for all their scoffes; as when I have come to Christ Church, onely in contempt of the Ordinance, I have beheld a great part of the people to sit with their hats on in a deriding posture: This it seems is one of Mr. Christopher Feake's Exhortations, and indeed it is not a comly one, when I compare it with that of the Apostle, 2 Cor.8.24. Paul was of that heavenly condiscending [sic] temper, that if by eating meat his brother was offended, he would never eat meat more. And does Mr. Feake think that this hat-waring and laughing (at our howling as they call it) doth not offend us that sing?[36]

Marvell himself is derisive in his wordplay on "Quake," which also echoes the earlier quake of the earth when Cromwell was thought dead. There is, however, a vast difference in an image of the earth quaking and an image of a man quaking; one is quite serious, the other but amusing. Marvell hardly confused the Fifth Monarchists with the Quakers, but he probably wished to include the Quakers in his satiric description of Cromwell's enemies. Marvell's evident fear that the structure of society would be severely shaken, perhaps destroyed, if the Fifth Monarchists achieved power was well founded. They were not an altruistic group; their concern was only for themselves. They imagined a world not too different from the one that existed, with their pet changes instituted, and with the Fifth Monarchists in control. Pertinent also to Marvell's reference to the Quakers, and to the general condemnation in lines 311–20, was the rumor prominent in the second half of 1654—that all the sects were uniting in a conspiracy against Cromwell.[37]

Marvell's description of their "frantique Army" is witty, but their chances of raising an army were not so slight as his ridicule indicates: "Whose frantique Army should they want for Men / Might muster Heresies, so one were ten" (299–300). Part of the rumor concerning the union of the sects placed Major-General Harrison at the head of a Fifth Monarchy uprising, and had he been a more bellicose sort, he might have garnered a respectable force with the help of the army men who were Fifth Monarchists. But despite their vocal leaders, the Fifth Monarchists were not particularly united, not even in their beliefs. Marvell's statement that "their Religion only is to Fall" has ironic truth beyond the humor. Their interpretations of the Scriptures rarely agreed one with the other, but instead were a matter of individual conception (not rare actually, but rare in a sect). Marvell's judgment— that "their Religion only is to Fall"—is ironic in that their desire for vision (which some might call forbidden knowledge), their certainty that they possessed the true vision, and that they had the single right to possess it, all smack of the first fall.

Though Anna Trapnel is not mentioned, the sayings from her twelve-day trance at Whitehall in January 1653/4 had been published as a book, to which it is likely that Marvell refers:

> Oh Mahomet! now couldst thou rise again,
> Thy Falling-sickness should have made thee Reign,
> While Feake and Simpson would in many a Tome,
> Have writ the Comments of thy sacred Foame.
>
> (303–6)

She was a member of Simpson's congregation and had been prophesying since 1647. During her long trances, she sometimes uttered songs and prayers for five hours at a stretch, most of which were directed against Cromwell. A "relator" who claimed he was slow of hand captured what he could of her words, and that—plus her account of herself and her visions—amounts to more than seventy pages, published in 1654 as *The Cry of a Stone*. Whether Simpson was instrumental in the publication of her prophecies is not known, but the incident of her prophesying attracted much attention and many went to hear her and believed that her words came from God.

Marvell's tone becomes more vituperative than derisive as he ends the section with a general condemnation:

> Accursed Locusts, whom your King does spit
> Out of the Center of th' unbottom'd Pit;
> Wand'rers, Adult'rers, Lyers, *Munser's* rest,
> Sorcerers, Atheists, Jesuites, Possest;
> You who the Scriptures and the Laws deface
> With the same liberty as Points and Lace;
> Of Race most hypocritically strict!
> Bent to reduce us to the ancient Pict;
> Well may you act the *Adam* and the *Eve*;
> Ay, and the Serpent too that did deceive.
>
> (311–20)

Many of the pamphlets of the sects gave the bottomless pit of Revelation as part of their title;[38] "Accursed Locusts" was a common epithet. Marvell here uses terms that frequently appeared in the pamphlets and newspapers. His appellations of lines 313–14 constitute a derogatory roll call of the sects—that is, he attacks one or another of them in each of the names. "*Munser's* rest" possibly has some relation to the Fifth Monarchists: those who defended the Barebone's Parliament moderates for their decision to dissolve "claimed there had been in Barebone's a radical party, comparable to the Munster Anabaptists, 'laying all waste that they might enter and devour at pleasure.'"[39] Marvell's point seems to be that whatever the sect, they were hypocrites one and all—"Oh Race most hypocritically strict!"—as well as deceivers. Their common goal would seem to be to enclose others in a rigid purism, "Bent to reduce us to the ancient Pict," that would resurrect the simplicity of Adam and Eve. What they all want, Marvell suggests, is power over the habits, manners, language, behavior of others, yet they least deserve any kind of power: they are "Wand'rers, Adult'rers, Lyers." The passage resounds, as well, the charge of backwardness levied against kings and the parliaments. The sects' view is narrow and in a fair way to demolish all achievements of the civil war, even to return time to its begin-

ning and man, one would think, to his state *after* the fall rather
than before. Marvell returns in line 321 to Cromwell as the great
Captain, the title given him in the "lusty Mate" section; Cromwell with his "careful Eye" (273) has guided the ship of state to
safe harbor and saved them all. The line also promises punishment of another quake to the sects: "But the great Captain, now
the danger's ore, / Makes you for his sake Tremble one fit
more" (321–22).

The story of the first man and his sorrow at the disappearance
of the sun and subsequent joy at its reappearance is a brilliant
transition from the homely scope of the previous forty-five lines.
For at least two reasons, Marvell needed to illustrate that Cromwell's image abroad has grown to a magnitude that has obliter-
ated the impression of him as simply the usurper of the English
throne. One reason is that the "man" who will guide England to
the millennium (with the rest of the world to follow) must of
necessity have a global reputation. Cromwell's foreign achievements, of course, were more than respectable; he *had* gained for
the Commonwealth recognition as a government, a position that
seemed nearly impossible at the time of Salmasius's first attack
on it as a "bunch of tyrants." The English have been given a
second chance, despite their stubborn stone minds, grasping and
ambitious determinations, backward-moving, self-seeking, fac-
tious ways, any one of which qualities might have eclipsed their
destiny as the leaders of the millennium. For Cromwell "Does
with himself all that is good revive" (324). Here we have a reiteration of the "Cromwell as restorer" theme, which effects the transition into the story of "first Man" (325):

> So when first Man did through the Morning new
> See the bright Sun his shining Race pursue,
> All day he follow'd with unwearied sight,
> Pleas'd with that other World of moving Light;
> But thought him when he miss'd his setting beams,
> Sunk in the Hills, or plung'd below the Streams.
> While dismal blacks hung round the Universe,
> And Stars (like Tapers) burn'd upon his Herse:
> And Owls and Ravens with their screeching noyse
> Did make the fun'rals sadder by their Joyes.
> His weeping Eyes the doleful Vigils keep,
> Not knowing yet the Night was made for sleep:
> Still to the West, where he him lost, he turn'd,
> And with such accents, as Despairing, mourn'd:
> Why did mine Eyes once see so bright a Ray;

Or why Day last no longer then a Day?
When streight the Sun behind him he descry'd,
Smiling serenely from the further side.

(325–42)

But "first Man" plays a role in this analogy only insofar as he
responds to the sun: he is innocent and therefore sad at its loss;
when he discovers it has risen the next day behind him to shine
once more, he is happy as well as wiser. Consistent with the
comparison throughout the poem, the analogy is of Cromwell
and the sun, the sun that seems briefly to have left the earth, as
he has at first seemed dead because of the carriage accident. Yet
both return "Smiling serenely from the further side." Like the
jubilation of Cromwell's enemies, the "Owls and Ravens . . .
[and] their Joyes" (333–34) are no more than "screeching noyse"
in the night, which the sun silences with its reappearance.

The first man segment startlingly repeats an image from the
Eikon Basilike:

> For mine honor, I am well assured that, as mine innocency is clear
> before God in point of any calumnies they object, so my reputation
> shall, like the sun (after owls and bats have had their freedom in the
> night and darker times), rise and recover itself to such a degree of
> splendor as those feral birds shall be grieved to behold and unable
> to bear. For never were any princes more glorious than those whom
> God hath suffered to be tried in the furnace of afflictions by their
> injurious subjects.[40]

This portion from the Eikon Basilike occurs at the very center;
the writer of the Eikon Basilike was as conscious of the midpoint accent that looks forward to triumph as Marvell was. The
triumph that would restore Charles I in Charles II could have
happened had Cromwell died in the carriage accident. Or if he
were removed by the House. But Cromwell has not died nor
been removed; God allows this man to stand. Cromwell rises in
triumph and proves his divinity as Charles I could not. Marvell
would not leave the voice of the king unheard since the Eikon
Basilike was and had been from its publication so widely read
and sympathized with. Equally pertinent, the echo sounds to
refute the current indictment that Cromwell's excluding parliaments so often and retaining unfettered control over a standing
army amounted to one tyrant's having been exchanged for another. Marvell's counters to the Eikon Basilike pervade the poem.
Charles I's presented complaint that his subjects are his ene-

mies—"If they had been my open and foreign enemies, I could have borne it; but they must be my own subjects, who are, next to my children, dear to me"[41]—Marvell inverts in an early passage that strikingly convicts kings of being strong only against their subjects:

> They fight by Others, but in Person wrong,
> And only are against their Subjects strong;
> Their other Wars seem but a feigned contest,
> This Common Enemy is still opprest;
> If Conquerors, on them they turn their might;
> If Conquered, on them they wreak their Spight.
>
> (27–32)

The king writes of his subjects' desires for liberty, reductively terming it licentiousness. Marvell counters this in a somewhat different manner, since his accusation against the people is essentially the same. He appropriates the meaning of the king's statement that "Time will best inform my subjects that those are the best preservers of their true liberties who allow themselves the least licentiousness against or beyond the laws"[42] in that he presents Cromwell exemplifying it:

> Thou, and thine House, like *Noah's* Eight did rest,
> Left by the Wars Flood on the Mountains crest:
> And the large Vale lay subject to thy Will,
> Which thou but as an Husbandman wouldst Till:
> And only didst for others plant the Vine
> Of Liberty, not drunken with its Wine.
> That sober Liberty which men may have,
> That they enjoy, but more they vainly crave:
> And such as to their Parents Tents do press,
> May shew their own, not see his Nakedness.
>
> (283–92)

If Marvell's refutations of the king's voice jogged the memory of those who had read sympathetically the *Eikon Basilike*, perhaps they read again the prayer, which might be seen to reflect Cromwell's present tribulations as much as they had the king's and thus illustrate that "the people" have not moved forward with "the time"; they are, in fact, referred to as "stone" in the prayer:

> Thou, O Lord, knowest my reproach and my dishonor; my adversaries are all before Thee.

My soul is among lions, among them that are set on fire, even the sons of men, whose teeth are spears and arrows, their tongue a sharp sword.

Mine enemies reproach me all the day long, and those that are mad against me are sworn together.

O my God, how long shall the sons of men turn my glory into shame? How long shall they love vanity and seek after lies?

Thou hast heard the reproaches of wicked men on every side. Hold not Thy peace, lest my enemies prevail against me and lay mine honor in the dust.

. . . .

Make my righteousness to appear as the light and mine innocency to shine forth as the sun at noonday.

Though they curse, do Thou bless, and I shall be blessed and made a blessing to my people.

That the stone which some builders refuse may become the head-stone of the corner.

Look down from heaven and save me from the reproach of them that would swallow me up.[43]

Cromwell as England's "Star" brings back to England "Light and Heat"; the king prayed his "righteousness" would "appear as the light and [his] innocency . . . shine forth as the sun." But Cromwell's star—the sun—firmly fixed as the most favored of the time shines despite his detractors. In fact, "his Flame" startles the world—"foreign princes." Marvell presents the contemporary astronomical notion of the sun as a star rather than the Ptolemaic reckoning of it as a planet. By extension, Cromwell is "Sun-like," for he is the paragon of men, as the sun is the paragon of stars. Thus he not only generates life for England as the sun, but regenerates life in returning himself to them—for their sake, not his own. (A Christ analogy is all but inescapable.) To foreign princes, his restorative powers have become abundantly evident:

> 'Is this, saith one, the Nation that we read
> 'Spent with both Wars, under a Captain dead?
> 'Yet rig a Navy while we dress us late;
> 'And ere we Dine, rase and rebuild their State.

> (349–52)

The comments of the foreign prince are like proofs offered for the poem's asseverations, a superb strategy for proving that which cannot be proved.

Cromwell's regenerative powers can replenish forests, coffers, and troops: "'What Oaken Forrests, and what golden Mines! /

'What Mints of Men, what Union of Designes!'" (353–54).
"Union of Designes," however, has resonance of another theme—
that of Cromwell as the architect of the Commonwealth and the
leader under whom the millennium may occur. Foreign princes
have been the subject of an earlier passage relating to Cromwell
in this role:

> 'While by his Beams observing Princes steer,
> 'And wisely court the Influence they fear;
> 'O would they rather by his Pattern won
> 'Kiss the approaching, nor yet angry Son;
> 'And in their numbred Footsteps humbly tread
> 'The path where holy Oracles do lead;
> 'How might they under such a Captain raise
> 'The great Designes kept for the latter Dayes!
>
> (102–10)

The foreign prince of lines 349–94 refers to Cromwell as "Captain" (350). His wonder at the "Union of Designes" rests, it would
seem, on the expectation that Cromwell's "good Designes" (158)
would at least have been diminished, or "Spent" by his brush
with death, as the nation has been "'Spent with both Wars" (347).
His amazement focuses then on the British Navy,[44] the symbol
of the regeneration:

> 'Theirs are not Ships, but rather Arks of War,
> 'And beaked Promontories sail'd from far;
> 'Of floting Islands a new Hatched Nest;
> 'A Fleet of Worlds, of other Worlds in quest.
>
> (357–60)

The comparison of the British fleet to "Arks" reinforces the earlier identification of Cromwell with Noah and, by extension,
Noah's rescue of the worthy few from destruction. So complete
are the battleships of the English that they might each be entities,
"floting Islands," or each a "World"; this elaboration seems intended to make the allusion very clear. Marvell, however, seems
also to enjoy the reversal of water and earth he creates (reminiscent of the meadow and river in "Upon Appleton House") in
envisioning a new world controlled from the sea:

> 'An hideous shole of wood-Leviathans,
> 'Arm'd with three Tire of brazen Hurricans;
> 'That through the Center shoot their thundring side

'And sink the Earth that does at Anchor ride.
'What refuse to escape them can be found,
'Whose watry Leaguers all the world surround?
'Needs must we all their Tributaries be,
'Whose Navies hold the Sluces of the Sea.
'The Ocean is the Fountain of Command,
'But that once took, we Captives are on Land.
'And those that have the Waters for their share,
'Can quickly leave us neither Earth nor Air.

(361–71)

Despite the prince's fear of the British Navy, his greatest concern lies with Cromwell:

'Yet if through these our Fears could find a pass;
'Through double Oak, & lin'd with treble Brass;
'That one Man still, although but nam'd, alarms
'More then all Men, all Navies, and all Arms.
'Him, all the Day, Him, in late Nights I dread,
'And still his Sword seems hanging o're my head.

(373–78)

As I have indicated earlier, Cromwell as "Star" has reference both to day and night, since Marvell seems to consider the sun as a star and Cromwell as "Sun-like" in his capacity as a "Star." The foreign prince is one who harbors the Beast, and his fear conclusively illustrates Cromwell's effectiveness as he "in dark Nights, and in cold Dayes alone / Pursues the Monster thorough every Throne" (127–28).

But Cromwell's effectiveness extends to creative rule as well, for a kingless England would have been conquered but for Cromwell: "'The Nation had been ours, but his one Soul / 'Moves the great Bulk, and animates the whole" (379–80). This last line resounds the Cromwell/Amphion theme and positively underscores it in a conclusive way. In addition, the loss of England to an outside force (had it not been for Cromwell) is implicit in the poem, and perhaps explicit in that the king might well have been recalled and monarchy reestablished in the absence of Cromwell. While Charles II was far from being a foreign force, he was supported by Catholic countries or would have been had they thought he had a chance of regaining the throne. The foreign prince's statement is an ominous reminder that under less adroit military leadership, the return of monarchy could not have been prevented. This leads to a summation of Cromwell's martial prowess:

'He Secrecy with Number hath inchas'd,
'Courage with Age, Maturity with Hast:
'The Valiants Terror, Riddle of the Wise;
'And still his Fauchion all our Knots unties.
'Where did he learn those Arts that cost us dear?
'Where below Earth, or where above the Sphere?

(381–86)

The first line of this passage may involve the West Indian fleet mentioned earlier, known to the foreign-power representatives in England. The prince has little doubt that Cromwell's military strategies are more than earthly, and Marvell has supplied his own suggestion of this more than once—that Cromwell has learned "a Musique in the Region clear, / To tune this lower to that higher Sphere" (47–48) or "'Twas Heav'n would not that his Pow'r should cease, / But walk still middle betwixt War and Peace" (243–44).

The prince's observation that Cromwell "seems a King by long Succession born" (387) recalls the pedigree that Marvell accords Cromwell in placing him in the line of Elijah, Gideon, and Noah. His astonishment that Cromwell "to be a King does scorn" (388) recalls the lines, "For to be Cromwell was a greater thing, / Then ought below, or yet above a King" (225–26). The "greater thing" that Cromwell is is evident to him, too: "Abroad a King ... seems, and something more" (389); the prince's vague "something more" speaks to his awareness of the guidance and support that God has bestowed on Cromwell.

The crescendo of amazement presented in the foreign prince's remarks reaches its climax in "'O could I once him with our Title see, / 'So should I hope yet he might Dye as wee" (391–92). These lines exemplify the "Fear and Spight" of line 395; more important, they confer greater significance on the apotheosis that Marvell has created: to the prince Cromwell's recovery is a miracle. Most obviously, they imply that if Cromwell would take the title of king, "we" could have the hope that he could die like other kings, like Charles I. The perception of the prince, even springing from his "Fear and Spight," presents a more just view of Cromwell than that of the English who, despite their "Love and Duty" (396) cannot see the extraordinary gift they have been given in Cromwell. Stated differently, the astounding Cromwell shines clearly to the rest of the world however much the English vision is blinded and "all unconcern'd" (150) in its "Malice." Marvell concludes his symphonic resonances with the aural repetition in "*Angel* of our Commonweal" of the earlier "Angelique Cromwell" (126)—plus a thematic echo in the last line. Cromwell, "Troubling the Waters, yearly mak'st them Heal";[45] as the poem stated initially and has iterated throughout, he alone has the power both to disturb and to heal.

7

"Spectators vain": the Death of Cromwell

I<small>F</small> Marvell had not considered providential historiographer his
primary role, and I think from the evidence of "Upon Appleton
House" that he did, his role as Cromwell's poet would soon have
convinced him of the necessity. The Interregnum saw many in-
terpreters of Providence; however, God's intentions were difficult
to assess correctly, and prophecy by its nature was not understood until it was fulfilled. Moreover, no one could be sure when
the fulfillment had actually occurred: a man such as Cromwell
who appeared designated by God as the captain to lead England
into the millennium might be a prefigurement rather than the
actual figure. Many were convinced that he was not "the man."
Joseph H. Summers has written that "Whether panegyrist or sati-
rist, the poet must appropriate, undermine, or destroy those visions and attitudes in the external world which oppose or differ
from the central visions and judgments of his poem."[1] In "Upon
Appleton House," Marvell destroys any sense of Nunappleton's
having been a holy place under the Cistercians and proves Fairfax's true right to the property; in "The First Anniversary," Marvell condemns monarchy as ineffectual and tyrannical and
presents England as doomed to fall unless Cromwell, whose
natural movement is to ascend, continues to rule and to create
the harmony that only he can in the troubled state. Cromwell's
right to rule England is thus justified, and if the English would
but grow "seasonable" (133)—that is, in harmony with the time
that Cromwell has created—he is the man to lead them into the
latter days. In the poem, Cromwell manages most capably all
points of domestic and foreign government, yet must struggle
simultaneously against the inordinate demands of the sects and
ominous prophecies of the punishments that God would soon
visit on him. The poem castigates the sects, refutes indirectly
the prophesying, and dispels the idea that the carriage accident
showed Providence acting against Cromwell. The centrality of

the carriage accident in the poem indicates the importance that Marvell formally assigns the incident. His strategy is to establish firmly the carriage accident and the loss of Cromwell as God's threat to the English, as well as to emphasize the providential nature of Cromwell's deliverance. Another poetic difficulty lay in Cromwell's not dying. Despite its conventionality, the poem of praise for one who almost died but did not is anticlimactic.[2] Marvell's strategy is to weave a "shining wave" (184) of praise through the poem on the thread of suppositions. From "what if Cromwell died" to "what if foreign princes spoke of Cromwell," and "what 'if in some happy Hour / High Grace should meet in one with highest Pow'r'" (131–32), the whole of the argument is couched in hypothetical terms. Thus Marvell shapes the year as glorious with only "one Sorrow" (181)—the fall from the carriage, caused by the sins of the people, who are characterized in the poem by their tendency to fall, ever sinking in their torpor. Of course, the Protectorate's first year had not been glorious but disappointing even to those who tempered their expectations (or failed even to possess them) of a re-creation of government worthy of the suffering that had gone before. Praise of Cromwell and condemnation of almost everyone else was the logical, indeed the only, option. But the poem could condemn only obliquely the "prophetic" interpretation of the accident as a foreboding of worse for Cromwell. To condemn prophecy openly would foil his effort, since everyone believed in it to some degree.

Like most devout persons, Cromwell was particularly sensitive to workings of Providence, and he seems bound to have interpreted the event, as others did, as a possible sign of God's displeasure. He was also extraordinarily punctilious in scrutinizing his own sins, with a much heightened sense of what Keith Thomas describes as an "essential feature of Puritanism"—"the sense of being God's especial preoccupation."[3]

Undoubtedly, Cromwell's schoolmaster Thomas Beard influenced his attitude. Beard had written the definitive compilation of the actions of Providence—*The Theatre of Gods Judgments* (1597). In this virtual encyclopedia of the various sins and the likely punishments that God would exact for each sin, the probability of the particular punishment was based on biblical, classical, and contemporary precedents.[4] Beard asserts unequivocally in his Preface that "nothing in the world commeth to passe by chance or adventure, but onely and alwaies by the prescription of his will; according to the which he ordereth and disposeth by a strait and direct motion." God's judgment was not hidden but open, and anyone might "perceive [it] if he would but marke and consider the whole bodie, but especially the end and issue of things." By these signs, and in them, "the great and mervailous vertues of God, as his bounty, justice, and power, does most cleerly shine; when he exalteth and favoreth some, and debaseth and frowneth upon others, blesseth and prospereith whom he please, and on the contrarie, curseth and destroieth whom he please, and that deserve it." A believer did not question God's evident frowns or curses—if they were received, they were deserved.

Cromwell's carriage accident was violent; he had not previously driven the six Friesland horses, gifts of the Count of Oldenburg. Others of the Hyde Park picnic party tried to dissuade him, but he insisted. Perhaps he wanted to show that he could still drive spirited horses; perhaps he urged them too strongly—whatever the circumstance, he lost control, was pulled off the carriage and dragged with his foot caught in the reins. His shoe came off, which saved him, although his pistol discharged. Secretary of State Thurloe suffered an injured ankle, and Cromwell was in bed for three weeks with severe stomach bruises and a leg wound.[5]

In those three weeks, with the deluge of derisive comment, Cromwell's schoolmaster's final warning in The Theatre of Gods Judgments to the "mightie, puissant, and fearefull," that God was always ready "to hurle you downe and overturne you"[6] may have occurred to him and added to his discomfort. Whether he remembered Beard or not, Cromwell would examine himself for the cause, a practice common not only to him. Because of his position, however, he saw himself and any sins he might commit as more serious than those of others. Late in 1655, he assumed the entire blame for the Hispaniola loss: "It is not to be denied but the Lord hath greatly humbled us in that sad loss sustained . . . ; no doubt but we have provoked the Lord, and it is good for us to know so, and to be abased for the same."[7] Thus, in "The First Anniversary," we have the fascinating situation of Marvell's blaming the carriage accident on the sins of the people, while Cromwell was likely to have been assiduously searching his conscience to discover the sin for which God had punished him. If the disaster were singular and personal, it arose as a result of particular sin; if it were collective, such as plague, it represented divine retribution for public sins. Wiser heads viewed it as Marvell did, a potential national disaster that could only be caused by the sins of the people.

In fact, the prophetic poet George Wither treated the situation similarly, though Marvell's poem is incomparably superior to his. On the day of the accident, intent on maintaining his self-appointed role as a public corrector and advisor to Cromwell, Wither was waiting to see Cromwell. Wither's poem counters the same public attitude that Marvell condemns, maintaining also with Marvell that rightly understood the accident exhibits providential favor:

> why is it conceiv'd, as if, to Us,
> Or, unto him, his fall were Ominous?
> . . . .
> When he did Fall, was it not wondrous well,
> That, from his seat, into GOD's Armes he fell?
> And, that, He falling, fell not in such wise,
> As they, who Rise, to fall; but, Fell, to Rise?
> And to Arise with an improvement too,
> By Thankfulnesse, for having scaped so?
> As also, with that Mark, upon him set,
> Of being God's especial Favourite?[8]
>
> (29–42)

"A Jolt on Michaelmas Day 1654" more nearly characterizes popular comment on the accident. James Heath ascribes it to "Birkenhead";[9] the twelve-stanza satire jibes at Cromwell's ineptitude as the people's charioteer: for one who had the "power of the Sword, / He had no command of the Whip" (59–60). Nor is the pistol forgotten:

> But O how they snuff
> When his Pistol flew off,
> For which all the Saints suspect him,
> Doth Providence attend him,
> Thirty thousand defend him,
> Yet a poor Pocket-pistol protect him.[10]
>
> (19–24)

Though to the Fifth Monarchists the pistol may have made Cromwell appear wavering, they were more involved in their own accusations that the incident fulfilled their prophecies, particularly those of Anna Trapnel. In January of 1654, whether by intention or by Providence, she fell into a trance at Whitehall while waiting for Vavasour Powell, whom Cromwell had summoned for what amounted to treason: he had prophesied from his pulpit that Cromwell's regime would be short-lived and would topple through a "small matter."[11] Having come to Whitehall with Powell, Trapnel waited until he came out from his meeting with Cromwell to fall into her twelve-day trance. Her eyes were closed for the entire period; she prayed, sang, and prophesied for up to five hours each day. She was a member of Fifth Monarchist Simpson's congregation, and he had brought her to her moment of recognition that she had been chosen by God to deliver His messages.[12] Her six years of prophesying before her debut at Whitehall had gained her something of a following, but Whitehall was her prime performance. Louise Fargo Brown says Trapnel's impact was so great because those who heard her believed that her utterances "were directly inspired of God"; to her believers, her inspired words were congruent with other signs taken to denote God's displeasure with Cromwell's government: "the miraculous ebb and flow of the Thames, the fall of one of the walls of St. Paul's, the comet, and the reputed appearance of Charles I's ghost at Whitehall."[13] She had long had visions about the army, and the name she gave Cromwell— Gideon—exemplified nothing unusual; that is, numerous others had made the comparison. But she was unique for two reasons other than those named: she had Whitehall as a theatre and she gave a stunning performance for which she received good press. In fact, on a weekly basis for some long time afterward, the newspapers continued to report on her. Employing imagery drawn largely from Daniel, she gained the advantage of her utterances seeming more meaningful because they were familiar to her audience, who also had no difficulty in understanding her entranced speaking of a text so well known to them.[14]

In the published version of her prayers and songs at Whitehall, *The Cry of a Stone*, Trapnel related her history in a preface. She tells of prophesying from a vision Cromwell's victory at Dunbar six weeks before the event, as well as the Lord's telling her "that he had raised up a Gideon, bringing that of Judges 7. to me, to prove Oliver Cromwell, then Lord General, was as that Gideon . . . that God had appointed him for the work of that present day to serve this Nation."[15] She saw in a vision the dissolution of the Rump, then that of the Barebone's—"the Lord gave me Visions of their breaking up"—but she now had visions "of the deadness of Gideons spirit towards the work of the Lord, shewing me that he was laid aside, as to any great matters, the Lord having finished the great business that he would employ him in."[16] Two nights before Cromwell was established as Protector, she had another vision (actually several in that one night); this came to be her most important vision, or at least the one for which she said she was later arrested. In it, she saw "a great company of Cattel, some like Buls, and others like Oxen, and so lesser, their faces and heads like men, having each of them a horn on either side their heads; For the foremost, his Countenance was perfectly like unto *Oliver Cromwell*." All the others humbled themselves before him, and at the urging of the others, the Cromwell bull ran at her, but God reached down and caught her in his arms. The Cromwell bull "run at many precious Saints that stood in the way of him, . . . gave them many pushes, scratching them with his horn, and driving them"; but from the clouds came a "great fury" to scatter the cattle, break their horns, and tumble them "into Graves."[17]

Christopher Feake also enjoyed success as a prophet. He was the first to doubt Cromwell publicly when he declared him in the spring of 1654 "'not the Man, that the Lord had chosen, to sitt at the Helme.'"[18] By December of that year, Feake implied in a sermon that Cromwell was the little horn. By the middle of 1654, most Fifth Monarchist preachers had announced the same, that Cromwell was the Antichrist. Even John Rogers, who had seen in Cromwell another Moses, accused him of violating all the ten commandments: "'O thou black Whitehall,' he stormed, 'Fah, fah, it stinks of the brimstone of Sodome, and the smoke of the bottomless pit.'"[19] This sudden shift in the identity of the Antichrist must have startled Cromwell, but it didn't faze the Fifth Monarchists. Their confidence in their prophetic ability remained unshaken, and they retained sufficient credibility for many to accept that Cromwell's "fall" had been foreseen and in part accomplished.

Marvell ascribes Cromwell's fall to the collective sins of the people, emphasizing in various ways that Cromwell alone cannot fall. He is heaven's favorite, and all his movement inclines upward. Marvell moves from the carriage accident to the subsequent rise through comparisons with "impossible" events, such as the sun's falling "out of the Sphere" (206). Cromwell can only rise, and Marvell presents the apotheosis "Unto the Kingdom blest of Peace and Love" (218) that would have occurred had Cromwell died. Cromwell has been the sun that redeemed the English from the darkness following Charles's execution; his providentially guided rise has been for that purpose. He "runs" (7), "shines" (12), "acts" (14), "hyes" (45), "hurles" (100), "shoots" (102), "does" (145), "girds yet his Sword, and ready stands" (148), and "Moves the great Bulk, and animates the whole" (380). His only descent has been "To turn the headstrong Peoples Charioteer" (224), to guide the fallen English. Thus the carriage accident indeed portends disaster but not for Cromwell. The warning from God is for the "Chammish issue" who have rejoiced at Cromwell's accident, failing to understand that it is a prefigurement of their overturning their chariot of state from which there can be no rise. God is unlikely to send another savior to such ingrates. As John Wallace has commented, the "'Panique groan' (203) which greets Cromwell's/Nature's fall is the more pointed an allusion in that no Christ-like successor was born at the instant of Cromwell's death; justice, reason, courage, religion—the virtues Christ came at the original panic moment to restore—lie obstructed and disheartened."[20]

Marvell's inveighing against the "sins of the people" and wishing for "a seasonable People" that Cromwell's plans might go forth and the millennium be achieved reflects the frustration the revolution's leaders felt with a populace conditioned to the servitude of monarchy that called for no individual responsibility. Marvell's use of "seasonable" is particularly fitting, for the people—not merely the ignorant and the poor—had not been seasoned to freedom or religious toleration. Most had no comprehension of the ideals of their leaders. As Christopher Hill points out, "the English Revolution had no predecessors. . . . So whereas the trinities of the later revolutions—liberty, equality, fraternity; peace, bread and land—demanded something new, something to be fought for and achieved *in the future*, the trinity of the English revolutionaries—religion, liberty and property—was intended to defend what already existed, or was believed to exist." The paradoxical situation, according to Hill, had been created by the achievements of the revolution itself. The destruction of episcopacy with its controls and doctrinal rigidity meant the demise of "institutional restraints" without a "disciplinary system" to replace them. Cromwell's rule had of necessity to grow more and more restrictive, but paradoxically, and perhaps unfortunately, it was marked just as much by his tolerance of religious and political differences. Hill observes that "religious toleration and the lack of an effective ecclesiastical censorship allowed wholly unorthodox groups claiming to be visible saints to propagate their subversive ideas."[21] Thus dissension remained the greatest of Cromwell's domestic problems (other than the ubiquitous financial difficulties). Despite his assurance to the Second Protectoral Parliament in his opening speech on 17 September 1656, that England's "great enemy is the Spaniard,"[22] he directed much of his discourse to the reformation of manners "and those abuses that are in this nation through disorder." He was "confident that the liberty and prosperity"[23] of England depended on that reform. He maintained that the Major-Generals "hath been more effectual towards the discountenancing of vice and seething religion, than anything done these fifty years. . . . you had not had peace two months together [without it]."[24] He drew in his conclusion on the 85th Psalm, a constant favorite of his:

'I will hear what the Lord will speak: for he will speak [peace] unto his people and to his saints: but let them not turn again to folly. . . . If you be the people of God, and be for the people of God, he will speak peace, and we will not again return to folly, [as to] which [there] is a great deal of grudging in the nation, that we cannot have our horse-races, cock-fightings, and the like. I do not think these are unlawful, but to make them recreations, that they will not endure to be abridged of them, [is folly]. . . . If God give you a spirit of reformation, you will preserve this nation from turning again to these fooleries. And what will the end be? Comfort and blessing. Then "mercy and truth shall meet together." Here is a great deal of truth among professors, but very little mercy. They are ready to cut the throats of one another; but when we are brought unto the right way, we shall be merciful as well as orthodox.[25]

In "A Poem Upon the Death of O.C.," Marvell indicts "The People" as Cromwell's enemy. As in "Upon Appleton House" and "The First Anniversary," the anti–ideal, the foe of the poem's hero, as well as the hero, the ideal, are created in the first ten to twenty lines. The anti–ideal is, in a sense, every man except the hero (and the poet); as every man he represents the ordinary, the accepted; only the hero is extraordinary and, by extension, unaccepted.

In "Upon Appleton House," man undoes his hope of eternity in building mansions to house himself; in that expanse his vanity grows equally large, so that his tomorrow is lost in his ambitious today. What other animal than "Man unrul'd / Such unproportion'd dwellings build?" (9–10), spreading himself "superfluously" (17), expressing himself as a much greater being than he is and one too large to enter the kingdom of heaven, the opposite of the truly great man who practices expressing himself in small places to acquire the humility to enter "Heavens Gate" (32)? In contrast, Fairfax exemplifies the "greater . . . in less contain'd" (44) as he forces his modest hall to hold him, distressing the dwelling more by "his Magnitude" than he is troubled by its smallness (this is the "natural" reason to move to a larger dwelling, as Fairfax was to do). The "low Things . . . [that] clownishly ascend" (60) are the anti–ideal. Fairfax is the specific of the ideal that "Height with a certain Grace does bend" (59), but the anti–ideal remains general until the center of the poem. At that point, the Archbishop of York and Cawood Castle may be said to represent "the Wanton Mote of Dust" (22) imparked by the "Marble Crust" (21) mentioned in this early section of the poem.

In "The First Anniversary," the first seven lines define man as characterized by his tendency to fall, destined to sink through his torpor. As in "Upon Appleton House," social rank has no bearing on this malady, which extends from man in general to kings. "Cromwell alone" is not subject to the characteristic sinking. Falling men, fallen men, falling stars, every variation possible Marvell assays to create the foe—fallen man—who causes Cromwell's fall from the carriage. Cromwell's only descent has been to command the English people, the fallen who have pulled him down, or would do so. They are the anti–ideal. Their only hope is Cromwell; he alone prevents their sinking.

In "A Poem Upon the Death of O.C.," the counter to the foe (other than Heaven and the poet), since Cromwell is dead, must be the "succeeding Ages" who will "mourn, / As long as Grief shall weep, or Love shall burn" (27–28). In this poem, Marvell handles a more delicate situation, perhaps for himself as well as Cromwell's family; almost certainly this explains his more subtle castigation of the foe than in the previous two poems. Yet he continues to shape circumstance to present an heroic portrait of Cromwell.

John Wallace has commented in relation to "Upon Appleton House" that "the temptation simply to annotate Marvell's poem is irresistible,"[26] and this holds true for his Cromwell poems as well. The temptation springs from Marvell's surrounding his ideal figures with a wealth of certifiable detail, such as Cromwell's speed and his love of horses and wild deer. As a result, his portraits emerge as realistic, lending credence to his alteration of circumstance.

A review of the historical situation has value in that the detail that emerges speaks to Marvell's shaping of "A Poem Upon the Death of O.C." The Venetian envoy Giavarina's letters to his government are sensitive and "well-informed."[27] In February of 1658, he said of Cromwell that "'not knowing whom he can trust, he is thinking out the steps which he ought to take by himself

... Cromwell is so deeply plunged in embarrassment and distress that he is now even taking his meals alone. ... in eight days he has only once sat at table with his wife and family, whereas he used to do so every morning and evening.'"[28] Cromwell's immediate circle was disintegrating as well. In that month, Frances's husband, Robert Rich, died; on the same day, Cromwell's niece Lavinia Whetstone Beke died. Secretary of State Thurloe seemed on the point of death, and Cromwell himself was so ill that he was unable even to sleep. Young Rich's father and grandfather, Cromwell's friend of thirty years, were to die within the next few months, as well Elizabeth Claypole, Cromwell's best-loved daughter, and her son Oliver. The Anglican priest Dr. Hewitt was beheaded; he had privately performed Mary Cromwell and Lord Fauconberg's wedding and probably that of Frances Cromwell and Robert Rich as well. To worsen this circumstance, Fauconberg's uncle was executed with Hewitt for their conspiracy against Cromwell. Fauconberg pleaded with his father-in-law for his uncle, and Mary, perhaps Frances, and surely Elizabeth, in her own right Hewitt's friend, interceded on Hewitt's behalf with Cromwell. Elizabeth's emotions concerning her father are evident in a letter that she wrote to her brother Henry's wife after the execution of Hewitt.[29] Abbott accepts the report that Elizabeth did intercede and was able to get the men's sentences transmuted from disembowelling to beheading, a far more humane death. Her intercession and the death of Hewitt caused her sufficient anguish that it was said to contribute to her own death.[30] Abbott also includes the report that on her deathbed, Elizabeth "reproached" Cromwell for Hewitt's *and* Charles I's deaths.[31] A sad irony presents itself in the visions of Cromwell's beloved daughter not only pleading for those who conspired to effect his deposition and death, but also blaming him for such deaths.

Cromwell's mental state disturbed his family. Henry Cromwell wrote to Broghill in April that he wished his father "were equally distant from both his childhoods,"[32] which suggests that his father is in his second childhood or has regressed to his first. Abbott cites an account of Cromwell's striking a servant and calling him "'a presbyterian rascal.'" (This does not necessarily reflect madness.) The frightened man ran for help; returning with some of his fellows, they discovered Cromwell "crying and howling."[33] This was unusual behavior indeed for Cromwell, of whom John Maidstone, his steward and treasurer of his household, onetime army officer, and member of parliament said—in an often quoted passage:

He was naturally compassionate to objects in distress even to an effeminate measure; though God had given him a heart, wherein was left little room for any fear but what was due to himself, of which there was a large proportion, yet did he exceed in tenderness towards sufferers. A larger soul, I think, Hath seldom dwelt in a house of clay than his was.[34]

And the eloquent Giavarina wrote to his government that "'The people . . . are so nauseated with the present government, largely owing to the dissolution of the last parliament . . . that they only desire to throw off the yoke and cast themselves on the clemency of their natural prince, feeling that they have suffered enough for the faults committed, which they now realise and wish to amend. . . . At present all men speak of him [Cromwell] with contempt and scorn, without the slightest respect.'"[35] Most were certain that without Cromwell, the Protectorate would crumble quickly.[36] Ludlow reports that Cromwell's great concern when he was near death was for the "'reproaches he said men would cast upon his name, in trampling on his ashes when dead.'"[37] And Cromwell's relentless troubles did plague him even after death, for the embalming failed, and since the stench could not be contained, the body had to be buried quickly. Cromwell's state coffin was almost certainly empty. In *Oliver Cromwell's Latter End*, F. J. Varley states that "all accounts agree that the body was disposed of privately and secretly, and . . . there is no specific statement in any of the accounts that it was so disposed of in Westminster Abbey. The Abbey muniments have no record of any such burial. . . . The place and date of the burial of his actual body was known only to a small inner circle, and the secret has been well preserved."[38] It is quite unlikely, according to Varley, that Cromwell's body, or Ireton's either, was that body hanged, decapitated, and buried under the gallows at Tyburn. Ireton died in Ireland of the plague, and plague victims were not embalmed and were also buried immediately, so that his coffin was shipped empty to England.[39] If Marvell knew about Cromwell's body, and Ireton's, too, for that matter, it would explain his apparent lack of concern in his letter to Hull of 4 December 1660 over the impending exhuming and hanging up of Cromwell and Ireton's bodies. He presents the event merely as news:

To day our house was upon the Bill of Attaindor of those that haue bin executed, those that are fled, & of Cromwell Bradshaw Ireton & Pride And tis orderd that the Carkasses & coffins of the foure last named shall be drawn, with wt expedition possible, upon an hurdle to Tyburn, there be hangd up for a while & then buryed under the gallows. The Act for the Militia hath not been calld for of late men not being forward to confirme such perpetuall & exorbitant powrs by a law as it would be in danger if that Bill should be carryed on. Tis better to trust.[40]

What Marvell may not have known then or he should not have been so casual was that Cromwell's mother and daughter Elizabeth were among those that "were dug out of their tombs in the Abbey and cast into a pit."[41] Cromwell's funeral did not occur until 23 November, and cost "tens of thousands of pounds."[42] Parliament seems to have ordered the regal burial, but their reason is not clear. Evelyn recorded it as "the joyfullest funerall that ever I saw, for there was none that Cried, but dogs, which the souldiers hooted away with a barbarous noise; drinking, & taking Tabacco in the streetes as they went."[43]

In summary, disaster was for Cromwell the keynote of 1658, the year of his death. His government was bankrupt, or nearly so, and hated. He was accused of being a madman and a tyrant.[44] Bowed down by the regime's troubles and likely to lose control through the apparently impending insurrection of the entire army (heralded by the actual insurrection of his own troop of horse), the ailing Cromwell no longer had at his command either the energy or the strength that had carried him through crises before. Indeed the last months of Cromwell's life seemed to fulfill Montaigne's words that "it seemeth Fortune doth sometimes narrowly watch the last day of our life, thereby to shew her power, and in one moment to overthrow what for many yeares together she had been erecting, and makes us crie after Laberius. . . . *I have lived longer by this one day than I should*." Montaigne concludes that no man should be considered fortunate "untill he have been seene play the last act."[45] Cromwell's circumstances would seem to reflect that God's judgment had gone against him. Marvell derails this connection by linking Cromwell's death to Charles's death and employing the "last Act"[46] as a controlling image, as well as drawing the people's character as unchanged by circumstances:

The People, which what most they fear esteem,
Death when more horrid so more noble deem;
And blame the last Act, like Spectators vain,
Unless the *Prince* whom they applaud be slain.

(7–10)

Marvell would have it that Cromwell's death has not been violent enough for the people, who behave as if they were merely an audience, "like *Spectators* vain," taking no responsibility for the scene before them except to applaud or hiss. Marvell is consistent in his creation of the people's character with "An Horatian Ode" in which they "clap their bloody hands" (56) at Charles's death and with "The First Anniversary" in which they, "as if they nothing car'd, / Look on, all unconcern'd" (149–50) while Cromwell effects virtual miracles to bring about the new state. Their judgment is doomed to err. Here they are so craven they can esteem only what they fear. Because the *Prince*, the "*Royal Actor*" Charles, was slain, they revered him and considered his life noble. No relation existed. Charles was an actor/king, assuming the trappings of majesty without fulfilling its responsibilities as Cromwell has done. Their fallen vision cannot see Cromwell's death or any other as noble unless it is violent. Marvell will tell the history of Cromwell's true last act and illustrate the truth of the maxim in relation to Cromwell as he shows also how little the people understand of Cromwell's actions.

His opening lines propose that Providence continues to preside over Cromwell's life by closing it with a death that reflects his character:

> That Providence which had so long the care
> Of *Cromwell's* head, and numbered ev'ry hair,
> Now in its self (the Glass where all appears)
> Had seen the period of his golden Years:
> And thenceforth onely did attend to trace,
> What death might least so fair a Life deface.
>
> (1–6)

With this congeries of meanings on Providence, Marvell ensures that every interpretation of Providence applies. Divine nurturing had protected him—"numbered ev'ry hair"; foresight "Had seen the period of his golden Years"; timely care "did attend to trace, / What death might least so fair a Life deface." Beyond firmly grounding the proposal, Marvell also fashions an implicit allusion to the Puritan conviction that once a man possessed grace, that grace did not depart from him.[47]

Marvell maintains Cromwell could not die in fight, for his personal bravery was so great that there were none "left that could / Indanger him, or Clemency that would" (13–14). His own mercy, like his valor, was boundless. Typical of the hero guided by God, his was not a warlike nature. Only heaven's force, sway,

could have made him enter war. He set aside his personal prefer-
ence for God's way. Heaven honors his sacrifice by creating his
last act a fitting one to the man Cromwell: "an End whose ev'ry
part / Should speak the wondrous softness of his Heart" (16–17).
Marvell sculpts a complete communion between Eliza and
Cromwell to illustrate the Cromwell whose motivation has always been love, for his daughter, his family, his country. Love is
not the motivation of a tyrant nor a madman. Impervious to all
else, Cromwell can be overcome only by love and grief: "in himself so oft immortal try'd, / Yet in compassion of another dy'd"
(87–88).

Marvell thus leads into the account of the symbiotic relationship between Cromwell and Elizabeth, or "Eliza," as she is called
in the poem, illustrating how Cromwell has been the subject and
object of love. The providential decree reveals itself in Eliza's
illness, but it is not a last act matter. Enchanted even with her
infant "charms" (31), Cromwell knows intuitively when she
grows up, as does she, that their fates are inextricably bound:
"they by sence, not knowing, comprehend / How on each other
both their Fates depend" (45–46). Loving him, she virtually
knows his soul. Loving her more each day, he doubles "that knot
which Destiny had ty'd" (44). As his mirror fate, her pain is as
his own: "A silent fire now wasts those Limbs of Wax, / And him
within his tortur'd Image racks" (53–54). Providentially joined
as they are, when her life goes, his cannot stay:

> And now his Life, suspended by her breath,
> Ran out impetuously to hasting Death.
> Like polish'd Mirrours, so his steely Brest
> Had ev'ry figure of her woes exprest;
> And with the damp of her last Gasps obscur'd,
> Had drawn such staines as were not to be cur'd.
> Fate could not either reach with single stroke,
> But the dear Image fled the Mirrour broke.
>
> (71–78)

Eliza is traditionally the name associated with England. *Historia*
may be translated into *allegoria*[48] here for an analogous connection between Elizabeth and England. That is, Marvell makes the
symbiosis that exists between Eliza and Cromwell represent that
between the Commonwealth and Cromwell. Thus, his life also
is "suspended by" the "breath" of the Commonwealth, and will
run out just as "impetuously to hasting Death" with its demise.
He has always considered the people as his children,[49] and the

disintegration of his government has caused him great anguish. Marvell has again leveled the loss against the people—not Providence—and made the death of their loyalty the cause of Cromwell's death.

The roles can be assigned with one of the sets reversed, since Marvell makes clear that the relationship is symbiotic; in other words, as Eliza has been to Cromwell, so Cromwell has been to the Commonwealth. His life has been the Commonwealth, and the life of the Commonwealth has been Cromwell. The hopes of a monarchy-free state die with him. Devising the allegory as Marvell does allows him to have it both ways.

With the figure of the protecting vine, Marvell extends the motif of paternalism:

> So I have seen a Vine, whose lasting Age
> Of many a Winter hath surviv'd the rage.
> Under whose shady tent Men ev'ry year
> At its rich bloods expence their Sorrow chear.
>
> (89–92)

In "The First Anniversary," Cromwell "only didst for others plant the Vine / Of Liberty" (287–88). Marvell expands the meaning to include sustenance and comfort as well as protection—lifeblood. The vine, despite its great resistance, will often succumb, as Cromwell has, to death through grief for a "dear branch . . . prun'd by an untimely knife" (93–94).

Nature's anguish at Cromwell's death seems to extend to the point of death as Cromwell's has at that of his "children." To portend and to commemorate Cromwell's death, Marvell employs an historically horrendous storm that occurred four days before.[50] Not only the topography of England suffers, but men and horses die[51] mysteriously. The sense of an England scourged is inescapable.[52] Nature, gone berserk with the death of Cromwell, has torn the "Elements" from their normal relations, so that they are "unfix'd / Troubled to part where so exactly mix'd" (129–30). Such a state in nature is akin to suicide: as grief has caused Cromwell's death, nature grieves so that it seems ready for death—"Nature it seem'd with him would Nature vye; / He with *Eliza*, It with him would dye" (133–34).

Said to have been the worst in over a century, the storm destroyed totally harvests, forests, and ships; thus as Cromwell's death, the death of the "spreading Vine, / Frustrates the Autumn and the hopes of Wine" (99–100), so Nature's near-death because of his loss destroys the fruit that the autumn should have brought:

> He unconcern'd the dreadful passage crost;
> But oh what pangs that Death did Nature cost!
> First the great *Thunder* was shot off, and sent
> The Signal from the starry Battlement.
> The *Winds* receive it, and its force out-do,
> As practising how they could thunder too:
> Out of the Binders Hand the Sheaves they tore,
> And thrash'd the Harvest in the airy floore;
> Or of huge Trees, whose growth with his did rise,
> The deep foundations open'd to the Skyes.
>
> (113–20)

Cromwell and the Commonwealth are gone, too, Marvell indicates, without their fruitful autumn. The earlier weeping of the vine, "Trickling in watry drops, whose flowing shape / Weeps that it falls ere fix'd into a Grape" (97–98) has been a prefigurement of the storm and its devastation as well as reflective of the sorrow of England's protective vine of liberty and strength, Cromwell. The storm also providentially punishes, for the onus of its ravishment of the landscape and the consequent deprivation falls on the people.

In contrast to Nature's thunderous upheavals, Cromwell goes silently: "He without noise still travell'd to his End, / As silent Suns to meet the Night descend" (135–36).[53] This stunning passage continues the sun/star association by which Marvell has characterized Cromwell throughout. The stars now "determine" the hour of death for one of their own (137–38). Since they cannot prevent his death, their gift is a death date that memorializes his past glories, 3 September, the day of his great victories at Dunbar and Worcester. Marvell adds "the *Belgick Coast*" (154) to the 3 September victories, for as Marvell fashions it, on the day of Cromwell's death, "his victorious *Ghost*" (153) pushed an English contingent to help defeat the Prince de Ligne.

The midpoint fall is Cromwell's death, after his spirit—still active for England—has effected his final victory: "Here ended all his mortal toyles: He lay'd / And slept in Peace under the Lawrel shade" (155–56). On earth, peace and all the glory the laurel entails are high rewards, but they are paltry in comparison to those to which he goes. He ascends with no essential change. He has been "Heavens Favorite" on earth; the honors heaven shows at his death are proof that he ascends to be the favored there:

> To none
> Have such high honours from above been shown:
> For whom the Elements we Mourners see,
> And *Heav'n* it self would the great *Herald* be;
> Which with more Care set forth his Obsequies
> Then those of *Moses* hid from humane Eyes;
> As jealous only here lest all be less,
> That we could to his Memory express.
>
> (157–64)

Heaven honors Cromwell more than it did even Moses,[54] simultaneously heralding and celebrating his "Obsequies."[55] The distinction that Marvell makes between Cromwell's public and Moses's private obsequies gives additional purpose to his having employed the storm as heavenly herald and celebrant of Cromwell's death. After Moses was shown the Promised Land, but told that he could not pass over, he died and was buried "in a valley in the land of Moab, over against Bethpeor; but no man knoweth of his sepulchre unto this day" (Deut. 34.6). The comparison between Cromwell and Moses is rich, and fully extended by the knowledge that Cromwell's grave, too, is hidden and, according to Varley, still unknown.

Marvell's exhortation—"let us to our course of Mourning Keep: / Where *Heaven* leads, 'tis *Piety* to weep" (165–66)—is strong, almost strident. Historical evidence suggests that tears for Cromwell were not copious.[56] Heaven has compensated for any lack of mourning on earth (163–64). Though Marvell maintains that "our Tears suffice" (170) and that none will be needed from the "Seas" (167), the clause is buried in the stanza. The seas are commanded to mourn for their monarch, and Marvell begins his account of Cromwell's glory. Cromwell is England's greatest hero, more valiant than Arthur, more holy than Edward the Confessor: his "greater *Truths* obscure the Fables old / Whether of *British Saints* or *Worthy's* told" (175–76). Like Moses, Cromwell has been their leader and their teacher:

> He first put Armes into *Religions* hand,
> And tim'rous *Conscience* unto *Courage* man'd:
> The Souldier taught that inward Mail to wear,
> And *fearing God* how they should *nothing fear.*
>
> (179–82)

He created true Christian soldiers, "men of a spirit" and "well
armed within by the satisfaction of their consciences,"[57] "godly,
precious men."[58] Cromwell thought that "he that prays and
preaches best will fight best," and he had evidence that prayer
won battles. Firth has commented on Marvell's noting the
"proved efficacy"[59] of the day of public prayer coinciding with
the victory day of the Dunes:

> Astonish'd armyes did their flight prepare,
> And cityes strong were stormed by his prayer;
> Of that for ever Preston's field shall tell
> The story, and impregnable Clonmell.
> And where the sandy mountain Fenwick scal'd,
> The sea between, yet hence his pray'r prevail'd.
>
> (185–90)

Cromwell's invincibility sprang from his having "conquer'd
God, still ere he fought with men" (194). He saw himself as having struggled for his salvation: he wrote in 1645 of "'the people
of God . . . all England over, who have wrestled with God for a
blessing.'"[60] After such a battle as that, or "Hence," as Marvell
has it, "though in battle none so brave or fierce, / Yet him the
adverse steel could never pierce" (195–96).

Marvell then gives further examples of Cromwell's compassionate nature even in the midst of violent circumstance: though
he was impervious in battle to the physical attacks of others,

> Pity it seem'd to hurt him more that felt
> Each wound himself which he to others delt;
> Danger itself refusing to offend
> So loose an enemy, so fast a friend.
>
> (197–200)

From Cromwell's magnanimity issued "tendernesse extended
unto all" (204), and after instances of this, Marvell turns again
to the opposite, also the opposition of the great man, who have
failed so notably in compassion and gratitude. Although he died
for his daughter, yet he did that only once; whereas he risked
his life—"adventur'd every day" (214)—for the people. His grief
for them was "deepest," despite his sorrow for Eliza being "last"
(216); his love for them had called for "prudence more than
humane" (217) "To keep so deare, so diff'ring minds agreed"
(218). In "The First Anniversary," Marvell portrays Cromwell as
advantageously employing the tension created by the "resistance

of opposed Minds" (95). Whereas Marvell does not say that Cromwell has been unable to continue to do so, here his admonishment of those who do not respect his obsequies grows harsher:

Oh! ill advis'd, if not for love, for shame,
Spare yet your own, if you neglect his fame;
Least others dare to think your zeale a maske,
And you to govern only Heaven's taske.

(223–26)

He urged grief as a matter of piety earlier; he now shames them for neglecting one who loved them as Cromwell has, and warns them they are in danger of hypocrisy or worse. Perhaps Marvell argues, too, that only Heaven can govern the English since "Valour, religion, friendship, prudence" (22)—requisite and embodied only in Cromwell—have not succeeded and are now lost to them. An indictment of *all* the people would have thrown into disarray Marvell's premise that the relationship between Cromwell and the Commonwealth has been more vital and beneficial to the people than to Cromwell. Some have loved him, and they are desolate without the animation of his presence:

we (so once we us'd) shall now no more,
To fetch day, presse about his chamber-door;
From which he issu'd with that awfull state,
It seem'd Mars broke through Janus' double gate;
Yet always temper'd with an aire so mild,
No April sunns that e'er so gently smil'd.

(231–36)

Cromwell rises again as the sun in this reminiscent passage, a preamble to the death portrait in the following passage. Marvell's friendship with Cromwell is clear in the next lines: he remembers the power of his language; Cromwell's devotion to England's business and to his own spiritual business of "pray'r and praise" (240); his insistence on doing anything to advance God's cause— "Whose meanest acts he would himself advance, / An ungirt David to the arke did dance" (241–42); and finally his personal pleasure in the world of horses, hunting (of which Marvell's stag seal may have been a memento), armor, and music.

The next portrait evinces a rather special knowledge of Cromwell:

I saw him dead, a leaden slumber lyes,
And mortal sleep over those wakefull eyes:
Those gentle rays under the lids were fled,
Which through his looks that piercing sweetnesse shed;
That port which so majestique was and strong,
Loose and depriv'd of vigour, stretch'd along:
All wither'd, all discolour'd, pale and wan,
How much another thing, no more that man?

                                                        (247–54)

This expression clearly has to do with the actual body of Cromwell, not the effigy lying on a bed of state. Though the figure is greatly changed from the man that was Cromwell, it has a power greater than death—"in his alter'd face you something faigne / That threatens death, he yet will live again" (259–60). Cromwell shows greater in death than in life (as the final heavenly portrait will show), like "the sacred oak, which shoots / To Heav'n its branches, and through earth its roots: / Whose spacious boughs are hung with trophies round, / And honour'd wreaths have oft the victour crown'd" (261–64). In using the oak, symbol of kings, as well as his sanctifying of it, Marvell confers on Cromwell a greater kingship than that he refused in life. Magnificent though the tree was, its true height could not be perceived while it stood; indeed, Cromwell's great stature may not be measured for many years: "So shall his praise to after times encrease, / When truth shall be allow'd, and faction cease, / And his own shadows with him fall; the eye / Detracts from objects than itself more high:" (271–74). His detractors misunderstand him because he is so much the greater man; "his own shadows" are perhaps his illness, his grief, his paranoia. Marvell's perspective is superb: he understood well that Cromwell had not yet been correctly viewed, that time would refine his image. He prophesies that the English soldier shall always remember and invoke Cromwell's name to "inflame" his fighting spirit and that "As long as future time succeeds the past, / Always thy honour, praise and name, shall last" (285–86). Marvell presents then his final portrait of Cromwell who now "tow'rst" (287) beyond all his earthly honor, in a "world" that is "Spacious enough, and pure enough" for the "great soule" (291–92) for whom death held no fears. There he finds his own kindred, Moses, Joshua, and David.

But for England, Marvell sees little promise, with "neither sight nor mind / To guide us upward through this region blinde" (301–2). He puts forth the hope that Richard will "in an hour a prince . . . grow" (312). But he is quite aware that the time that

Richard has to prove himself is short.[61] Marvell's covert premise in this poem that the Commonwealth and Cromwell were doomed to die together, as he presents Eliza and Cromwell fated to do, undermines that hope. Other than the inspiration his memory may bring the English in the future, this fall has been fortunate only for Cromwell.

8

"That Majesty which through thy Work doth Reign": Marvell and Milton

MARVELL remained as Latin Secretary for a year after the death of Cromwell, but he must have taken sanctuary in Hull, in a sense, some time in that period to work out the details of his standing for parliament. He emerges from this dim period as an M.P., and around 1667–68 as a satiric poet whose manuscript of "The Last Instructions to a Painter" was circulated. That he became more interested in circulation and publication speaks to his intentions. For Marvell assumed an individual responsibility that included turning to satiric poetry in an attempt to "season" the people through the derision of public figures' foibles, as well as becoming a participant in the governing of England. In what has seemed to some a radical departure, he actually placed himself in a far more influential position than he had held as Cromwell's poet. For he spoke to the people, in a language accessible to them, in a mode that amused them while it unburdened them of illusions about English monarchy and courtiers. His work continues as both history and prophecy, now in the satiric rather than the epideictic mode. The change is the audience to whom it is directed.

Yet there was still one great man left, although for a time it was unsafe to praise Milton. Marvell had been effective in saving Milton's life, though we don't quite understand why his efforts were as efficacious as they were. Christopher Hill surmises that Marvell's earlier association with Fairfax gave him "Fairfax's ear, and Fairfax was an important man in 1660."[1] In the House of Commons, Marvell also objected to the jailer's having exacted an unseemly amount of Milton and succeeded in restoring the money. Hill adds that others helped in the enterprise of saving Milton's life—"Sir William Davenant and the Boyles," for example—and that Marvell's motion in the House had its second from the husband of Cyriack Skinner's niece Bridget.[2] Yet an occasion for a panegyric to the poet seemed unlikely to occur. It did, of course, in the second edition of *Paradise Lost*. Before that, Marvell would again come to Milton's defense, though Milton had had nothing to do with the circumstance. *The Rehearsal Transpros'd* drew contumely not only on Marvell, but also on Milton. Marvell would then defend Milton in the second part of *The Rehearsal Transpros'd* against accusations from Parker's reply, *A Reproof*, and his follower Richard Leigh's *Transproser Rehearsed*. Parker and Leigh had assumed that Milton had been a party to *The Rehearsal Transpros'd*, thus their attacks on the aging, blind poet. Masson presents a number of these insults; those which follow are from Leigh:

"He has all the terms of that art [railing] which Smectymnuus, Marchamont Needham, J. Milton, or any others of the professors, ever thought of."

"Dark souls may be illuminated with bright and shining thoughts. As, to seek no farther for an instance, the blind author of *Paradise Lost* (the odds betwixt a Transproser and a Blank Verse poet is not great) begins his third Book thus, groping for a beam of light:—

> Hail, holy Light, offspring of Heaven first-born
> Or of the Eternal coeternal beam
> May I express thee unblamed . . . .
> . . . . Thee I revisit safe,
> And feel thy sovran vital lamp; but thou
> Revisit'st not these eyes, that roll in vain
> To find thy piercing ray, and find no dawn;
> So thick a drop serene hath quenched their orbs,
> Or dim suffusion veiled.

No doubt but the thoughts of this vital lamp lighted a Christmas candle in his brain. What dark meaning he may have in calling it this *thick drop serene* I am not able to say; but, for his *Eternal coeternal*, besides the absurdity of his inventive Divinity in making light contemporary with its Creator, that jingling in the middle of his verse is more notoriously ridiculous because the blind bard (as he tells us himself in his apology for writing in blank verse) studiously declined rhyme as a *jingling sound of like endings*. . . . Unluckily, among other calamities of late, there has happened a prodigious conjunction of a Latin Secretary and an English Schoolmaster, the appearance of which none of our astrologers foretold, nor no comet portended. . . .

> O marvellous fate! O fate full of marvel!
> That Noll's Latin pay two clerks should deserve all,
> Hiring a gelding, and Milton the stallion."

"If you will have it in *his* elegancy, I never saw a man in *so high a state of salivation*. If in Milton's (I know he will be proud to lick up *his* spittle), he has invested himself with all the rheum of the town, that he might have sufficient to bespawl the clergy."

Marvell assumed that Parker had written the above, and in the Second Part of the *Rehearsal Transpros'd*, he answers in a tone of restrained ire, as if he would moderate himself the better to defend Milton:

"You do three times at least in your *Reproof*, and in your *Transproser Rehearsed* well nigh half the book thorough, run upon an author J.M.; which does not a little offend me. For why should any other man's reputation suffer in a contest betwixt you and me? But it is because you resolved to suspect that he had an hand in my former book; wherein, whether you deceive yourself or no, you deceive others extremely. For by chance I had not seen him of two years before; but, after I undertook writing, I did more carefully avoid either visiting or sending to him, lest I should any way involve him in my consequences. And you might have understood, or I am sure your friend the author of the *Commonplaces* could have told you (he too had a slash at J.M. on my account) that, had he took you in hand, you would have had cause to repent the occasion, and not escaped so easily as you did under my *Transprosal*. . . . J.M. was, and is, a man of great learning and sharpness of wit as any man. It was his misfortune, living in a tumultuous time, to be tossed on the wrong side, and he writ, *flagrante bello*, certain dangerous treatises. His books of Divorce I know not whether you may have use of; but those upon which you take him at advantage were of no other nature than that which I mentioned to you, writ by your own father: only with this difference, that your father's, which I have by me, was written with the same design, but with much less wit or judgment; for which there was no remedy, unless you will supply his judgment with his High Court of Justice. [The allusion is to the fact that Parker's father, the Puritan and Republican lawyer, John Parker, had been one of the High Court of Justice that sentenced to death the three great Royalist peers, Lord Capel, the Earl of Holland, and the Duke of Hamilton, immediately after the execution of Charles I.] At his Majesty's happy return J.M. did partake, even as you yourself did for all your huffing, of his regal clemency, and has ever since expiated himself in a retired silence. It was after that, I well remember it, that, being one day at his house, I there first met you, and accidentally. Since that I have scarce four or five times in your company; but, whether it were my foresight or my good fortune, I have never contracted any friendship or confidence with you. But then it was, when you, as I told you, wandered up and down Moorfields, astrologizing upon the duration

of his Majesty's Government, that you frequented J.M. incessantly,
and haunted his house day by day. What discourse you there used
he is too generous to remember. But, he never having in the least
provoked you, for you to insult thus over his old age, to traduce him,
by your scaramuccios and in your own person, as a schoolmaster,
who was born and hath lived much more ingenuously and liberally
than yourself; to have done all this and lay at last my simple book
to his charge, without ever taking care to inform yourself better,
which you had so easy opportunity to do; nay, when you yourself
too have said, to my knowledge, that you saw no such great matter
in it but that I might be the author: it is inhumanly and inhospitably
done, and will, I hope, be a warning to all others, as it is to me, to
avoid—I will not say such a Judas, but—a man that creeps into all
companies to jeer, trepan, and betray them."[3]

Marvell effectively illustrates the mean-spiritedness of Parker
who fawned over Milton when he thought to gain advantage—
before Parker decided to be of the king's party, in the days when
he consulted the stars to discover how long Charles II's reign
would last—only to revile him, and wrongly too, when Parker
(actually, Leigh, of course) merely suspected Milton of having
written against him. No matter that Leigh had been even more
insulting to Milton than Parker, Marvell is accurate in his contempt for Parker as one who has injured a benefactor. Marvell
strikes a double blow in saying that he will not call him a Judas,
for in saying he will not, he does; yet that he "will not say such
a Judas," he puts Parker lower than Judas.

Marvell's indignant and obviously carefully phrased response
to Milton's attackers reflects profound veneration of Milton. His
next defense of Milton would be wittier, against a subject who
seemed to inspire wit in others, Dryden, though Marvell's prefatory poem to the 1674 edition of Paradise Lost is only peripher-
ally involved with Dryden.

The story Aubrey tells of Dryden's coming to Milton to ask if
he might turn Paradise Lost into a rhymed drama or opera might
be said to justify Buckingham's having portrayed Dryden as
Bayes in The Rehearsall (1671). "Impudent," Masson names Dryden's attitude, but explains that "with Dryden's ideas, it was the
highest compliment he could pay to Milton."[4] He had already
paid such a "high compliment" to Shakespeare in adapting with
Davenant The Tempest to Restoration tastes. Milton responded
graciously that Mr. Dryden might "tag" his lines, and then shared
the story with Marvell, whose knowledge of it "On Mr. Milton's
Paradise lost" reflects. Dryden's opera was finished within a

month and licensed on 17 April 1674, although its publication was delayed until 1677. Yet it seems to have been widely read and ridiculed from the time it was licensed; Masson thinks that Milton and Marvell read it early in 1674.[5] In summation of Marvell's devotion to Milton and his defense of him, Masson speaks of Marvell as bearding Bayes the poet-laureate for Milton "as fearlessly as he had bearded Bayes the archdeacon on a more general account."[6]

Milton dismissed Dryden as "a rhymist but no poet."[7] Masson comments that of contemporary poets, Milton "admired Cowley most,"[8] but Cowley had been dead for seven years when the second edition of *Paradise Lost* was to appear. Cowley's early success had undoubtedly impressed Milton, but I wonder if Cowley were still his most admired poet in 1674.

In the seven years since the first publication of *Paradise Lost*, Milton's image had changed. The fallen defender of the regicides seemed no longer threatening nor was there anything reprehensible in his magnificent work—and nothing to prevent Marvell's poem of praise as a preface to *Paradise Lost*. Marvell could expect Milton's recognition of his fortunate fall pattern.[9] Milton's own ascent—the writing of *Paradise Lost*—had been accomplished. Therefore, Marvell hypothesizes. He presents himself as fearing the "Poet blind, yet bold" (1) will fall. Milton would hardly have taken it amiss, since in the literal sense, Marvell had a share in his preservation. The account that Marvell gives of Milton's "vast Design" (2) is evidence that he knew *Paradise Lost* very well. But he will continue his fiction of "What if Milton falls?" His next fear is for its success, knowing that it is likely to be misunderstood: "I lik'd his Project, the success did fear; / Through that wide Field how he his way should find / O're which lame Faith leads Understanding blind" (12–14). The "wide Field" refers overtly to the immense scope of Milton's work. Marvell refers covertly to the vast ignorance of the people as an audience, for whom he had altered his own approach. He fears, too, others' corruption of Milton's work—popularization by Dryden as an obvious example—for that "wide Field" of blind understandings.

But Milton does not fall, and Marvell's "surmise" is "causeless, yet not impious" to the "*mighty poet*" (23–24). Marvell reverses the order of his suppositions as he explodes them. Significantly, rhyme occupies the last place. That he has been "transported by the *Mode*" (51) is likely more than simply Marvell's self-accusing paraphrase of Milton's own "carried away by custom," the phrase with which Milton explains to the reader rhyme's use by "some famous modern Poets."[10] It perhaps refers also to Marvell's "transportation" by Cromwell's death and the Restoration—the "Mode"—to satiric verse and a political position in the current regime. This kind of transportation Milton had refused, as he refused to compromise his great poem with rhyme. More obviously, Marvell also plays on Milton's use of *transport* in God's comment to the Son: "sees't thou what rage / Transports our adversary, whom no bounds / Prescrib'd ... can hold" (*PL* III 80–84). The dictates of the times have been involved, too, in Marvell's delayed praise of Milton; he has been forced to protect—"And while I meant to *Praise* thee, must Commend" (52). Perhaps Marvell expected Milton to read an apology for those times; certainly it is an elegant statement. But praise is what he wished all along to give him, for Milton's "sublime" verse meets perfectly—"In Number, Weight, and Measure"(53–4)—his sublime theme. Marvell never better presented devotion, awe, admiration. He incorporates every characteristic of his poetry—wit, allusion and echo, history, prophecy, multiple levels of meaning, and his love for his subject, plus an amazing "'finesse" of his fortunate fall pattern—into his final and most magnificent poem of praise for a worthy man.

Were Marvell's responses as enthusiastic to Milton's earlier poetry? Did he always perceive him as the "*mighty poet*"? We have seen him to be involved in the "number, weight, and measure" of his own poetry, evidence of his knowledge of poetic forms. Annabel Patterson has illustrated this, as well as having provided evidence that he echoes Milton's *Second Defense* in "The First Anniversary." Resemblances, however, between that poem and George Wither's poem to the occasion of the carriage accident are also remarkable. Since occasions often elicit similar responses according to societal levels, I should like to ignore occasion briefly to consider how Marvell, whom scholars have shown to have echoed or been influenced by almost everyone's poetry, incorporated temptation, the main poetic theme of his friend who was surely the finest poet within his acquaintance.

Marvell would hardly have reacted to *Comus* as twentieth-century literary critics have, but he too may have been bemused at Milton's allocation of lovely though ultimately illogical language and preposterous actions that would have assured Comus's failure even with a less determinedly virtuous Lady. I think it likely from the evidence of several poems that Marvell was interested in Comus's loss of the debate and in the debate itself on whether one enjoyed the boon of earthly love available only to the living or lived "like Nature's bastards, not her sons"—a "penurious" existence. This last may have been Marvell's lot anyway, so that he thought it the greatest logic to take the opposite position. We know that in "To his Coy Mistress" he countered that argument, creating his own debate equivalent of Comus's "List, lady, be not coy, and be not cozened / With that same vaunted name virginity. . . . If you let slip time, like a neglected rose / It withers on the stalk with languished head."[11]

The voice in Marvell's poem is that of the tempter. He addresses the "coy mistress" to tell her that coyness is a "crime," a crime against time and space. The time is that of an earthly lifetime; the space is the earth's entire surface in opposition to the relatively minuscule space after death. Among the spaces is one the lover is already attached to—the Humber at Hull—which he seems to see as quite adequate for him, though she might prefer a more romantic space. One river is about the same as another, but if she likes the Ganges, he has no objection. While there, she may look for rubies. Nothing prevents her. His love, in that richness of temporality, would have its birth "ten years before the Flood," and she might have a virtual forever to be coy. He could spend the time well in admiration of her—"An age at least to every part." That she deserves such worship is not in question. As Comus would have it, "Beauty is Nature's brag." Years spent in appreciation of that beauty would not be too dear were there time. It needs interjecting here that Marvell speaks of his own plea in "To his Coy Mistress" as his "ecchoing song" (27); in Comus, the Lady sings to "Echo" to discover where her saviors, her brothers, are.

The central accent of "To his Coy Mistress" does not look forward to the lover's triumph but rather to time's: "But at my back I alwaies hear / Times winged Charriot hurrying near" (21–22). Whatever they do or do not do, time's chariot rolls on, rapid, "winged," ever on the verge of overtaking one—"hurrying near" as it does. Death alone bestows eternity. Thus to live in the brief time that is allotted is no crime. The crime is the imposition of honor, that quaint concept that has dictated her "Long-preserved virginity," a preservation unto the forever when only "worms shall try" her. Time's power determines space. While they possess time (albeit limited), their space is ample. If she confines herself with her adherence to the world's moral dictates, she imposes a self-imprisonment. Once time has ended and the eternity of death begins, she loses her power over space and gains a guaranteed prison, her private and narrow grave.

In the final movement he would remind her, indirectly and thus gently, that death palls. Youth is the morning of one's life when "the youthful hue / Sits on thy skin like morning glew."[12] He would have them love so that they "time devour." Although time devours all lives, its power is subjective; that is, to a life empty of love, time becomes "slow-chapped" (40). To forbid physical love while life exists—the only time physical love can exist—is a crime. Thus coyness becomes a crime against Nature, and that virginity must be preserved is a 'cozening.' The temptation resisted continues the crime. For this crime, the punishment is to live imprisoned by purity. To free oneself from the prison of the "long-preserved virginity," one would break through "the iron gates of life" (44). Marvell's poem thus ends with the proposal that would free them from the imprisonment caused by her coyness and make them so free to move that they control their time, however brief it may be.

The Lady in Milton's *Comus*, however, responds to Comus: "Fool . . . / Thou canst not touch the freedom of my mind / . . . although this corporal rind / Thou has immanacled, while heaven sees good" (663–65). And Comus responds in the vein of Marvell's tempter in "To his Coy Mistress":

Why are you vexed, lady? Why do you frown?
Here dwells no frowns, nor anger, from these gates
Sorrow flies far. See, here be all the pleasures
That fancy can beget on youthful thoughts,
When the fresh blood grows lively, and returns
Brisk as the April buds in primrose-season.

(666–71)

Comus experiences "enchanting ravishment" at the sound of the Lady's voice floating on "Wings / Of silence" (249–50) and pronounces it "divine" (245); he is the charmed whose mind retains its freedom because her pure song brings "waking bliss." Milton makes a distinction between the nature of charms: he has Comus contrast the enchantment of the Lady's voice to the enslavement effected by his mother's voice—"Circe with the Sirens three . . . / Who as they sung, would take the prison'd soul / And lap it in Elysium" (253–7). Since his is no "prison'd soul," he is secure of that as well as that his senses will not be lulled into slumber and thence into "sweet madness" (261). She feels equally secure in her mind's freedom; despite this confidence, she will be fettered, and by bonds that are as invisible as the airy wreaths binding the tempted Marvell in "Fair Singer."

Thus Marvell's "To his Coy Mistress" may be said to refute *Comus* in the sense that it seems to argue that no human can resist temptation without a consequent loss of freedom. He will present an attitude in *An Account of the Growth of Popery* that is much closer to Milton. Clearly, he respected and responded to Milton's thinking. But there is as well the possibility that Milton sometimes found Marvell's arguments influential (this can be no more than a possibility until we know for certain the dates of Marvell's poems). For example, the exchange between Christ and Satan in *Paradise Regained* strongly resembles the debate carried on in "A Dialogue Between the Resolved Soul and Created Pleasure." And the dual nature of the characters of *Samson Agonistes* and the remarkable relevance of the imagery of "A Dialogue between the Soul and the Body" to Samson's situation warrants ascribing to the drama some influence of Marvell's poem. The tormented Samson as he appears in the drama's opening may be said to echo Soul's lament in the first stanza of "A Dialogue between the Soul and the Body"; Soul speaks:

> O who shall, from this Dungeon, raise
> A Soul inslav'd so many wayes?
> With bolts of Bones, that fetter'd stands
> In Feet; and manacled in Hands.
> Here blinded with an Eye; and there
> Deaf with the drumming of an Ear.
> A Soul hung up, as 'twere, in Chains
> Of Nerves, and Arteries, and Veins.
> Tortur'd, besides each other part,
> In a vain Head, and double Heart.
>
> (1–10)

Samson may be seen as personifying soul, "so many wayes" (2) enslaved, blinded by "vain Head, and double Heart" (10) of Body. Obviously, he is also like Body, bound to that trammeled soul and caused by it to stretch beyond his nature into the "upright" position to create his "own Precipice" from which he "falls." Samson's Nazarite status coupled with his animalistic, non-contemplative nature makes him the prime example of the body/soul dichotomy.

Samson's complaint that his pain involves the whole of him is reminiscent of the Body and Soul's argument about who suffers most. He mourns:

O that torment should not be confined
To the body's wounds and sores
With maladies innumerable
In heart, head, breast, and reins;
But must secret passage find
To th' inmost mind,
There exercise all his fierce accidents,
And on her purest spirits prey,
As on entrails, joints, and limbs,
With answerable pains, but more intense,
Though void of corporal sense.[13]

(606–16)

As Soul must "endure" (27) not just the sicknesses of the body,
"but, whats worse, the Cure" (28), "Shipwrackt into Health
again" (30), so Samson speaks of himself as "shipwrecked" by
Dalila (198–200), who will come asking that she may "fetch
[him] . . . / From forth this loathsome prison-house, to abide /
. . . where [her] . . . redoubled love and care / With nursing diligence . . . / May ever tend about [him] . . . to old age" (921–25).
The Chorus also refers to him as shipwrecked (1044–45). In response to Soul, Body retorts that the real "Maladies" arise in
Soul, including "the Pestilence of Love" (32–35), a phrase that
Samson endorses. Marvell's expression of the impossible combination's unceasing dynamic would seem directed to the conclusion that only through a dual resolution for death—or life—can
the balance be gained. One must act with the whole being for
one or the other. Early critics were not wrong in categorizing
Marvell as a cavalier poet, but obviously they were not right
either. His was an independent mind; forced as he was to live a
politic existence, his life owned in a sense by those whom he
cultivated, admired, or represented as he did Hull for the last
twenty years of his life, his spirit and imagination were yet his
own. One can hardly blame him that he chose to keep his flights
to himself.

A congruence remains in the lives of these two so great poets
whose twenty-year political careers met at opposite ends of their
poetic careers: Milton's reappearance in 1673 as a pamphleteer
after his silence of thirteen years and Marvell's appearance as
a nonsatiric pamphleteer. Milton's *Of True Religion*, possibly
published between 13 March and 6 May 1673,[14] responds in part
to the Declaration of Indulgence proposed by Charles II in March
of 1672 and defeated by Parliament in February of 1673. In
March of 1673, Parliament passed the Test Act, requiring all

those in public office to take the Oaths of Allegiance and Supremacy, to receive the eucharist in accordance with the Church of England, and to renounce transubstantiation as a doctrine. Ronald Hutton sees the Test Act as having been "a mine which almost blew away the foundations of the regime, for it forced the resignations not only of Clifford but of James, the heir apparent, who thus revealed himself to the nation as a follower of Rome. The shock produced by this rendered English politics unstable for the next two decades."[15] To the populace and to the Parliament, all of Charles's previous actions took on a different hue in the light of the knowledge of James's apostasy. Rather than supporting the Dutch War as they had been willing to do before James's Roman Catholicism became known—not to mention that of Clifford, Lord Treasurer and a chief adviser to the king—many in Parliament came to see in the war more and more evidence of a close, secret alliance of the king and the French. Because of Clifford, "most of Charles's ministers were suspected of being Papists and Catholic uprisings were feared from Yorkshire to Sussex."[16] Thus, the "No Popery" theme became major; pamphlets against it poured forth. It is difficult to assess how much danger existed for Milton in renewed political writing, but the examples that Marvell presents in *An Account of the Growth of Popery*, written some four years later, would indicate a deal. Milton obviously felt speaking out worth what consequences might follow. *Of True Religion* is a simple statement that contains nonetheless a perception troubling to the English, that Charles's long and close relationship with Louis XIV, whom Christopher Hill describes as "the personification of the union of popery with absolutism,"[17] had had a subversive and Papist purpose that revealed itself in the Declaration of Indulgence and would lead to absolute power for the king. If that purpose did not succeed in the present, the future now held the succession of a Roman Catholic in the Duke of York. Milton justifies refusing religious toleration to Roman Catholics and encourages all Protestant sects (except the Quakers, whom he doesn't mention) to extend their toleration to each other.

Milton devotes the second half of his pamphlet to Roman Catholicism's dangers to state and church:

> Popery is a double thing to deal with, and claims a twofold Power, Ecclesiastical, and Political, both usurpt, and the one supporting the other.
> . . . The Pope by this mixt faculty, pretends right to Kingdoms and

States, and especially to this of *England*, Thrones and Unthrones Kings, and absolves the people from their obedience to them; sometimes interdicts to whole Nations the Publick worship of God, shutting up their Churches: and was wont to dreign away greatest part of the wealth of this then miserable Land, as part of his Patrimony, to maintain the Pride and Luxury of his Court and Prelates: and now since, through the infinite mercy and favour of God, we have shaken off his *Babylonish* Yoke, hath not ceas'd by his Spyes and Agents, Bulls and Emissaries, once to destroy both King and Parliament; perpetually to seduce, corrupt, and pervert as many as they can of the People. Whether therefore it be fit or reasonable, to tolerate men thus principl'd in Religion towards the State, I submit it to the consideration of all Magistrates, who are best able to provide for their own and the publick safety. As for tolerating the exercise of their Religion, supposing their State activities not to be dangerous, I answer, that Toleration is either public or private; and the exercise of their Religion, as far as it is Idolatrous, can be tolerated neither way.[18]

Evidence existed in 1673 that Charles intended to create an absolute monarchy. Lauderdale, a favored and powerful minister, was rumored to have "declared Charles's will to be above the law and had made ready Scottish soldiers to intervene in English affairs."[19]

In early November of 1674, Milton died. All the "worthies" that Marvell had honored in his verse were gone now.[20] And by 1677, Parliament's demise seemed imminent, or as Marvell will comment near the end of his *An Account of the Growth of Popery, and Arbitrary Government in England*, "if neither one Prorogation, against all the Laws in being, nor three Vitious Adjournments, against all Presidents, can Dissolve them, this Parliament then is Immortal.[21] Milton's pamphlet's full title is *Of True Religion, Heresie, Schism, Toleration, and what best means may be used against the growth of Popery.* Marvell assumes not only a part of Milton's title, but also in part the thesis.[22] The rest of Marvell's title places the pamphlet in time: *More Particularly, from the Long Prorogation of November, 1675, Ending the 15th of February 1676, till the Last Meeting of Parliament, the 16th of July 1677.* Milton is clearly present in the piece. Annabel Patterson has pointed out two allusions prominent enough to justify saying that Marvell's *Account* at times "sounds like . . . the unabashedly heroic resonance of Milton's *Areopagitica: A Speech for the Liberty of Unlicensed Printing.*"[23] An echo of *Areopagitica* other than those Patterson mentions may be heard in Marvell's definition of England as the perfect republic, a resonance of Milton's praise of the English Parliament that precedes his association of licensing with the Roman Catholics. More than resounding Milton's portrayal of Parliament, Marvell's opening reminds the House of Commons in especial how far they have come from that visionary presentation. Milton had written:

> For this is not the liberty which we can hope, that no grievance ever should arise in the Commonwealth—that let no man in this world expect; but when complaints are freely heard, deeply considered, and speedily reformed, then is the utmost bound of civil liberty attained that wise men look for. To which, if I now manifest by the very sound of this which I shall utter, that we are already in good part arrived, and yet from such a steep disadvantage of tyranny and superstition grounded into our principles as was beyond the manhood of a Roman recovery [as opposed to Rome's inability to resist kings' and popes' power]; it will be attributed first, as if most due, to the strong assistance of God our deliverer, next, to your faithful guidance and undaunted wisdom, Lords and Commons of England.[24]

Marvell's opening presents the contemporary situation and its first cause—Popery and the "fall" of Charles II into "Malice and Ambition":[25] "There has now for diverse Years, a design been carried on, to change the Lawfull Government of England into an absolute Tyranny, and to convert the established Protestant Religion into down-right Popery: than both which, nothing can be more destructive to the Interest and Happinesse, to the Constitution and Being of the King and Kingdom."[26] His immediate continuation of this is the construction of the English myth, referred to above and to which I will return presently. Just beyond that segment, he illustrates, as Milton has in *Of True Religion*, that Popery is no religion, "nor is it to be mentioned with that civility which is otherwise decent to be used, in speaking of the differences of humane opinion about Divine Matters."[27] Since it frustrates Christ's design in forbidding "the use even of the ordinary languages," their sequestering the Bible "only into such hands as were intrusted in the cheat, they [have] the opportunity to vitiate, suppresse, or interpret to their own profit those Records by which the poor People hold their salvation."[28]

Milton illustrates early in his discussion that Popery is "false Religion or Heresie, . . . taken up and believ'd from the traditions of men and additions to the word of God,"[29] and thus to be shunned, not tolerated.

Marvell emphasizes the Pope's assumption of absolute power quite as much as Milton: "That he is the Ruler over Angels, Purgatory and Hell. . . . That all that God, he can do, *Clave non errant*, and what he does is as God and not as man. That he is . . . sole Interpreter of Scripture. . . . That he is still Monarch of this World, and that he can dispose of kingdoms and Empires as he pleases."[30] Marvell examines what seems inconceivable, that other princes allow his continuance, "a Power so pernicious, and Doctrine so destructive to all Government." His conclusion, "as farre as [he] can comprehend, [is] there is more of Sloth then Policy on the Princes side in this whole matter."[31] (Charles was known as slothful; his reputation still bears that taint to the extent that Hutton deems it necessary even now to defend him.) Historians have considered that between 1670 and 1673, the English government very nearly became an absolute monarchy.[32] There can be little doubt that the French king wished Charles to dispense with Parliament; failing that with Charles, by the time Marvell wrote *An Account of the Growth of Popery*, he had "distributed large sums of money amongst MPs hostile to the court to encourage their work: . . . [he] was spurring on the Commons to wreck [Parliament]."[33]

Marvell's rhetoric includes the assertion that few Englishmen would be pleased by conversion as a country to Roman Catholicism with the reversion of church lands that must accompany it, as well as by a return to the Roman Catholic multiple exactions in addition to the tithe. Yet "there are those men among us, who have undertaken, and do make it their businesse, under so Legal and perfect a Government, to introduce a French slavery, and instead of so pure a Religion, to establish the Roman Idolatry: both and either of which are Crimes of the Highest nature. For, as to matter of Government, if to murther the King be, as certainly it is, a Fact so, horred, how much more hainous is it to assassinate the Kingdome?"[34]

Annabel Patterson has illustrated that Marvell, the relator as he calls himself in *An Account*, fulfills the role that I have often spoken of his assuming, that of historian. But as he combined the role with that of poet, so I also perceive him as having assimilated his poetic into his historian role in this particular piece of prose. In other words, allegorical structure in *An Account* performs as it does in the poetry; because the circumstances are historical, Marvell's shaping of them is less noticeably evident. Nonetheless, the entirety functions as an allegorical representation of the fall, with echoes of *Paradise Lost*. If, in "Upon Appleton House," he wondered "What luckless Apple did we tast" (327), he knew the cause this time. And he would not have forgotten his so recent lines in his prefatory poem expressing his hypothetical fear that Milton "would ruine (for I saw him strong) / The sacred Truths to Fable and old Song, / (So *Sampson* groap'd the Temples Posts in spight) / The World o'rewhelming to revenge his Sight" (7–10). Nor his poetic answer to that fear: "That Majesty which through thy Work doth Reign / Draws the Devout, deterring the Profane. / And things divine thou treatst of in such state / As them preserves, and Thee inviolate" (31–34). Sustaining in a remarkable degree his studied objectivity as relator, Marvell cannot conceal his anger at the contempt with which the House of Commons has been treated, nor can he prevent his own contempt—and sorrow—that they have in part drawn this on themselves in their venality. In 1670, he had written to his nephew Popple of the king's having taken up attendance at the House of Lords' sessions, so that

> In this Session the Lords sent down to Us a Proviso for the King, that would have restored Him to all civil or eclesiastical Prerogatives which his Ancestors had enjoyed at any Time since the Conquest. There was never so compendious a Piece of absolute universal Tyranny. But the Commons made them ashamed of it, and retrenched it. The Parliament was never so embarassed, beyond Recovery. We are all venal Cowards, except some few.[35]

Annabel Patterson speculates that he counted himself among the venal; that is, "Marvell did not dissociate himself from the collapse of parliamentary integrity."[36] Yet it remains possible that he perceived his publishing of *An Account* as redemptive; it is as bold and declarative as any thing that Milton had written. Perhaps he even saw it as possessing that which he avowed of Milton: "That Majesty which through thy Work doth Reign / Draws the Devout, deterring the Profane. / And things divine thou treatst of in such state / As them preserves, and Thee inviolate" (31–34). Furthermore, he seems to take on the responsibility of illustrating the sin of those who will not resist temptation, for he presents the story of the Pope/Louis XIV's seduction of Charles II and Charles's seduction of the Parliament and their willingness to succumb with less than subtle hints that it is the Christian myth playing itself out once more.

He begins with the fiction of the perfect state, a long passage yet necessary to quote in full:

> For if first we consider the State, the Kings of *England* Rule not upon the same terms with those of our neighbour Nations, who, having by

force or by addresse usurped that due share which their People had in the Government, are now for some Ages in possession of an Arbitrary Power (which yet no prescription can make Legall) and exercise it over their persons and estates in a most Tyrannical manner. But here the Subjects retain their proportion in the Legislature; the very meanest Commoner of England is represented in Parliament, and is a party to those Laws by which the Prince is sworn to Govern himself and his people. No Mony is to be levied but by the common consent. No man is for Life, Limb, Goods, or Liberty at the Soveraigns discretion: but we have the same Right (modestly understood) in our Propriety that the Prince hath in his Regality; and in all Cases where the King is concerned, we have our just remedy as against any private person of the neighbourhood, in the Courts of Westminster Hall or in the High Court of Parliament. His very Prerogative is no more then what the Law has determined. His Broad Seal, which is the Legitimate stamp of his pleasure, yet is no longer currant, than upon the Trial it is found to be Legal. He cannot commit any person by his particular warrant. He cannot himself be witnesse in any cause: the Ballance of Publick Justice being so dellicate, that not only the hand only but even the breath of the Prince would turn the scale. Nothing is left to the Kings will, but all is subjected to his Authority: by which means it follows that he can do no wrong, nor can he receive wrong; and a King of *England*, keeping to these measures, may without arrogance be said to remain the onely Intelligent Ruler over a Rational People. In recompense therefore and acknowledgment of so good a Government under his influence, his person is most sacred and inviolable; and whatsoever excesses are committed against so high a trust, nothing of them is imputed to him, as being free from the necessity or temptation, but his Ministers only are accountable for all and must answer it at their perills. He hath a vast Revenue constantly arising from the Hearth of the Housholder, the Sweat of the Laboures, the Rent of the Farmer, the Industry of the Merchant, and consequently out of the Estate of the Gentleman: a larg competence to defray the ordinary expense of the Crown, and maintain its lustre. And if any extraordinary occasion happen, or be but with any probable decency pretended, the whole Land at whatsoever season of the year does yield him a plentifull Harvest, So forward are his Peoples affections to give even to superfluity, that a Forainer (or English man that hath not been long abroad) would think they could neither will nor chuse, but that the asking of a supply, were a meer formality, it is so readily granted. He is the Fountain of all Honours, and has moreover the distribution of so many profitable Offices of the Houshold, of the Revenue, of State, of Law, of Religion, of the Navy (and, since his present Majesties time, of the Army) that it seems as if the Nation could scarce furnish honest men enow to supply all those imployments. So that the Kings of *England* are in nothing inferiour to other Princes, have in being more abridged from injuring their own subjects: But have as large a field as any of external felicity, wherein to exercise their own Virtue and so reward and incourage it in others. In short, there is nothing that comes nearer in Government to the Divine Perfection.[37]

Despite this "divine perfection" in government, there are conspirators as there were in Heaven, those who would change all. Marvell assures us that the conspirators are not the "honest old Cavaliers," but "these Conspirators are such as have not one drop of *Cavalier Blood*."[38] The conspirator is Charles. Marvell makes this evident in excluding James and those who responded to the Test Act as "the more honest, the less dangerous," in spite of their having "so long appeared the most zealous Sons of our Church."[39] Marvell praises Charles's Triple Alliance of 1668, created in little more than five days; however, his journey to Dover in 1670 had changed all. The consequences of that meeting, Marvell interprets as mysterious—the death of Charles's youngest sister, which occurred immediately afterward (apparently with no connection, though Marvell implies that there is) and the "invisible League, in prejudice of the Triple one, struck up with *France*, to all the height of dearnesse and affection. As if upon dissecting the Princess there had some state Philtre been found in her bowells, or the reconciliation with *France* were not to be celebrated with a lesse sacrifice then of the Blood Royall of *England*." Designating the "invisible" treaty a "work of Darknesse," he maintains that it could show itself only through its effects and those effects could not appear until "Parliament should after the old wont be gulled to the giving of mony."[40] Thus the fall of Charles occurs; money is the temptation, not religion; motivated by "the most sacred tyes of Malice and Ambition to advance the ruine of the King and Kingdome," the conspirators "are such as ly under no temptation of Religion." Only the king of France is "so abounding in wealth" that he may "go to the price of their wickednesse."[41] Gulling of the parliament to give money is initially quite easy because of the Triple League, "a thing of so good a report and so generally acceptable to the Nation," that they "gave with both hands .... *Tripple-Supply*."[42] Charles, responding to his "invisible" treaty, no longer either invites or accepts any other nations into the Treaty of *Aix la Chapelle*, turning them "off with blind Reason, and most frivolous Excuses." The purposely created quarrel with the Dutch was planned to yield "the conspirators" great plunder from a "great and rich Fleet"; "with this Treasure they imagined themselves in stock for all the wickednesse of which they were capable, and that they should never, after this addition, stand in need again or fear of a Parliament."[43] Marvell thus makes obvious that "the conspirators" are one conspirator, Charles, since none other would fear or need a Parliament. In the conspirators' onward movement, the next step is religion, thus the Declaration of Indulgence. Marvell sees it as Milton has earlier, as an intended precedent "to abrogate and at last inact what they pleased, till there should be no further use for the Consent of the *People in Parliament*."[44] Then the conspirators declare the war with the Dutch after they have begun it, an action directly opposed to the Triple League, yet in the declaration they maintain that they are still observing the Treaty of Aix la Chapelle. The only faith observed was that with France, "though on all other sides broken."[45] Marvell observes that "what is here declared, if it were reconcileable to Truth, yet could not consist with Possibility (which two do seldom break company) unless by one only Expedient, that the English, who by this new League with France, were to be the Infractors and Aggressors of the Peace of *Aix la Chapelle* (and with Holland) should to fulfill their Obligations to both Parties, have sheathed the Sword in our own Bowels."[46]

In the "gulling" of Parliament for money, Charles seduces the Commons to their fall, which Marvell has occupy the center of the pamphlet and which concerns the meeting of Parliament designated in the title. Having experienced the long prorogation, the Parliament sitting was no longer legal since they had been prorogued for thirteen months. At the opening of the session, however, the Commons immediately began their debate not on whether they were dissolved because of the long prorogation, but "Whether this *Prorogation* were *not an Adjournment*." In the House of Lords, the Duke of Buckingham "argued by all the Laws of Parliament, and with great Strength of Reason, that this Prorogation was Null and this Parliament consequently Dissolved."[47] Buckingham and the others—Shaftsbury, Salisbury, and Wharton—who defended this point were as their consequence imprisoned, and Marvell writes "Thus a *Prorogation* without President, was to be warranted by an Imprisonment without Example." He comments further on the "sad" incident: "For nothing but Parliament can destroy Parliament."[48] And so with the opposition out of the way, Parliament went on, satisfied with having taken away its own "liberty of speech." Yet very soon after, Commons' members object to the many who are among them illegally by virtue

of their being "outlaws" or Papists or "*Bribed, or Pensioners.*"
Adding this to the earlier matter of the long prorogation, they
have every reason to dissolve themselves that they may be replaced by a body legal in those respects in which they are so
flagrantly illegal. Instead, they further compound their sin by
continuing to sit in violation of the requirement of English law
and constitution that Parliament meet frequently and change itself with regularity. They have taken the liberty of supposing
"that the Question Concerning this *Prorogation*, were by the Custom of *Parliaments* to be justified, (which hath not been done
hitherto)." Marvell comments that "who that desires to main-
taine the reputation of an honest man, would not have layed hold
upon so plausible an occasion, to breake company when it was
grown so Scandalous."[49]

Categorizing them by their characters, Marvell divides them
into thirds. Speaking to the notoriety of the circumstance as well
as the ignominy, he describes the first third as those who "have
beneficiall Offices under his Majesty, in the Privy Council, the
Army, the Navy, the Law, the Houshold, the Revenue both in
England and *Ireland*, or in attendance on his Majesties person."[50]
Because there are so many of them, they effect a dominance for
their views by their number rather than providing a balance of
opinion. Their view is "necessarily" biased in favor of the king's
interests since they owe their gratitude to him for their "honors."
Drawing an analogy between the House of Peers who represent
the English people, Marvell maintains this third of the House of
Commons represents the king since the preservation of their self-
interest depends on their preservation of their obligation to him.
They have positioned themselves where "much may be gained
by betraying"[51] the people. Not only this, but they consider themselves justified by their own circumstances, necessitated, in voting against the country's interests, though "their hearts indeed
are, they say, with the Country, and one of them had the boldness
to tell his Majesty, That he was come from Voting in the House
Against his Conscience."[52]

Despite their opportunistic behavior, these members of Commons seem "less dangerous" to the public than "those that are
hungry and out of Office, who may by probably computation,
make another Third part of this House of Commons. Those are
such as having observed by what steps, or rather leaps and
strides, others of their House have ascended into the highest
Places of the Kingdom, do upon measuring their own Birth, Estates, Parts, and Merit, think themselves as well and better quali-

fied in all respects as their former Companions. They are generally men, who by speaking against the *French*, inveighing against the Debauches of Court, talking of the ill management of the Revenue, and such Popular flourishes, have cheated the Countrys into Electing them. . . . they are all of them to be bought and sold, only their Number makes them cheaper."[53] Constituting the third part are those who are "either the worst, or the best of Men; The first are most profligate persons, that have neither Estates, Consciences, nor good Manners . . . ; The charges of their Elections are defraied. . . . Tables are kept for them at *White Hall*, and through *Westminster*, that they may be ready at hand, within Call of a Question: All of them are received into Pension, and know their Pay-day, which they never faile of."[54] All of these are satisfied with the "long and frequent Adjournments." But none of them wants a dissolution. Constituting the other part of the last third are the men of Light, the "hanfull of *Salt*, a sparkle of *Soul*, that hath hitherto preserved this grosse Body from Putrefaction;"[55] so few are they as scarcely to form a quorum. He sees no hope for this few among the stone and lumber heads:

> Insomuch that it is lesse difficult to conceive, how Fire was first brought to light in the World then how any good thing could ever be produced out of an House of Commons so constituted, unless as that is imagined to have come from the rushing of Trees, or battering of Rocks together, by accident, so these by their clashing of Rocks together, by accident, so these by their clashing with one another, have struck out, an usefull effect from so unlikely causes.[56]

Through the viciousness of their habits, "the House hath lost all the antient weight and authority, and being conscious of their own guilt and weakness, dare not adventure, as heretofore, the Impeaching of any man before the Lords, for the most hainous Crimes of State, and the most Publick Misdemeanours. . . . and if the House has Emancipated itself beyond Instructions, then by Chastizing them with *Prorogations*, frighting them with *Dissolution*, comforting them with long, frequent, and seasonable *Adjournments*, now by suspending, or diminishing their pensions, then again by increasing them, sometimes by a scorn, and otherwhiles by a favour, there hath a way been found to reduce them again under discipline."[57]

Since the imprisonment of the four lords, the House of Lords had been under the virtual rule of the Lords Frechwell and Arundel of Trerise, whose manipulation of the group Marvell presents as if to invite a comparison to Satan and Beelzebub in Books I and II of *Paradise Lost:* "all things fell out as they could have wished, if under their own direction. For most of them . . . sate mute in the House, whether, as is probable out of reverence to their two Persons, and confidence in their wisdom, they left all to their Conduct, and gave them a general Proxy." As consequence of this moral erosion of the Parliament, justice ceases. Marvell cites the case of Dr. Cary whom the Lords fined a thousand pounds and imprisoned in the Tower for carrying to the printer a book concerning the illegality of the prorogation. Justice failed totally, for no one in Commons could bear to bring before that house his petition. The second case of the House of Lords' injustice involved Mr. Harrington whom they imprisoned because he asked to be excused from answering "improper" questions during his voluntary report of French impressment of Scottish soldiers. He managed to give a sheet of paper with his name "that a Petition might be written above it, to be presented to the House of Commons."[58] Brought before the House, they so supported the previous treatment despite Harrington's modest demeanor that he not only "found no redresse, but might thank God that he escaped again into Close Prison."[59] To "hedg in, and purchase their own continuance," the House of Commons voted the king "double the summe that in the former Sessions they had thought necessary towards the Fleet."[60] To be very sure to purchase *their* continuance, they voted a three-year continuance of an excise tax on beer and ale, originally instituted for the Triple League. Marvell dryly observes that it "might, considering their present want of Legality, have been properly intituled, *An Act for the Extraordinary Occasion of the House of Commons.*"[61] The Lords passed quickly and sent on to the Commons the bill for educating the royal children in the Protestant faith and another for the prosecution of Roman Catholic recusants (which Marvell calls "two Cockatrice Eggs"),[62] plus a rigorous licensing act that amplified L'Estrange's power to search. Marvell makes clear that the bills' easy passage through the Lords had entirely to do with the "great unanimity among them, after the committing of the four Lords, and to the Power of those two noble Peers, their Adversaries, which was now so established, that their sense being once declared, the rest seemed to yeild them an Implicite Faith and Obedience."[63] Again, and with such finesse that it seems clear that he did not wish to risk compromising the historicity of his account, Marvell has reminded us of resemblances between their fallen behavior and that of the fallen angels in Hell

and their obedient response to Satan and his chief minister
Beelzebub.

Despite this, the House's suspicion had finally to have its say
in the light of the king's evident favor toward the French; thus,
in this session, they also requested that the king "strengthen"
alliances that might assist him in preserving the Spanish Nether-
lands. Seeing no consequence of their first message, they sent to
him some three weeks later, again urging alliances and promising
all aid should he find it necessary to go to war against the French
"in pursuance of such Alliances."[64] The king stalled until the
French won Valenciennes and St. Omar and defeated the Prince
of Orange before he inspecifically responded that his will was
that he should be sufficiently provided with funds that he might
protect the kingdom. He also suggested that they adjourn for
Easter. They did not rise to the bait with their previous alacrity,
but assured him that they had provided "a security" for him on
which he might raise £200,000 should he have need during their
adjournment. This time, he responded with haste, informing
them that he must have the £600,000 or he could not "speak or
act those things which should answer the ends of their severall
Addresses,"[65] to create the alliances. Most of the Commons having gone home for Easter, the few remaining returned the answer
that they did not think it "Parliamentary in their absence to take
upon [themselves] the granting of money."[66]

The king had, however, a great French conference about to
convene: "at the same moment of their rising, a Grand *French*
Ambassador was coming over. For all things betwixt *France* and
England moved with that punctual Regularity, that it was like
the Harmony of the Spheres, so consonant with themselves, although we cannot hear the musick."[67] Commenting that the
French, with "a Traine of three or four hundred persons of all
Qualities, . . . with so many of their Commons, meeting the King
at Newmarket, it looked like another Parliament, And that the
English had been Adjourned, in order to their better Recep-
tion,"[68] Marvell lists the topics "in discourse":

> An Act for continuing his Majesties subjects in the service of France.
> An Act of abolition of all Claymes and demandes from the subjects
> of France, on Account of all Prizes made of the English at Sea, since
> the year 1674 till that day, and for the future.
> An Act for marring the Children of the Royal Family to Protestants
> Princes.
> An Act for a further supply of French mony.

Whereas the English Commons had been shut out from privy information concerning "War, Peace, and Alliance, as Improper for their Intermedling, & Presumptuous. Yet with these 3 Estates of France all these things were Negotiated and transacted in the Greatest confidence."[69]

The Commons' resumption was accompanied by Charles's message to hurry their business, for he planned a recess soon. The promised alliances had not advanced in the five weeks of the adjournment. Since they had met with the expectation of alliances, they were willing to be adjourned until they were drawn. The king's advisors objected that they had not had sufficient time for so difficult a task; even if they were concluded, the moment was not right for the king to move on them and that he could not do so without the money. Without the £600,000, "his Majesty could not so much as speak out."[70] Commons pointed out that ten weeks had actually passed since they first requested the alliances and that the Triple League, which represented far more difficult alliances, was accomplished in five days. Examining the notion that the king must not speak without the money, they dismissed it since all were aware that the French had knowledge of his purpose. Thus exploding his rationalization, they reasonably wondered why it was apparently only they, his Parliament, to whom he could not "speak."[71]

Realizing that his "gulling" the Parliament of money had been too apparent, the king then addressed them in person to assure them that he had not called them together "only to get money ... for other uses than you would have it imployed." He assured them that he had "not lost one day since [their] last meeting, in doing all [he] could for [their] defence."[72]

In the debate following, those speaking for the king presented the case as merely the Commons and the king's fulfilling their functions: they could not have alliances without him; he could not have money without them. They included, however, the thinly veiled threat that if the money were not forthcoming, the "nakednesse and weaknesse" of the Commons would "be exposed."[73] Others, who spoke "somewhat different," and who established straightway that all messages from the king that erred were to be considered messages from his counselors "*For the King can do no wrong*," said that "certainly the treating and concluding of Alliances, requirs, not a previous summe of mony, however the kings Counsel may misinform."[74] These "somewhat different" voices debated heatedly, contending that "the debate of this day it is as great and weighty as ever was any in *England* it concerns our very being, and includes our Religion, Liberty and Property; *The doore towards France must be shut and Garded, for so long as it is open our Treasure and Trade will creep out and their Religon creep in at it.*" Evidence existed that falsified the contentions about the forward movement of the alliances, for "Their have continually almost to this hour gone out of *England* succours to *France*, of *Men*, Powder, Ammunition, Ordnance, &c. Not to rake into the matter, how far the Ministers have been active or passive in this, nor to mention any other particulars, we must say that unless the Ministers, or their minds are altred, we have no reason to trust money in their hands."[75] Concluding their deliberations, the House again sent their request that the king make alliances against "*the growth and power of the French King, and for the preservation of the Spanish Net'er-lands;*"[76] they assured him that when the alliances were made, they would supply him with the funds necessary to support and maintain those alliances.

The king's excoriating response accused Commons of meddling, entrenching "upon so undoubted a Right of the Crown," "dangerously" invading "the Prerogative of making Peace and War."[77] Shocked into silence, when they *would* speak, the Speaker adjourned them, officiously assuming what had been the prerogative of the House—to adjourn itself. The king had sanctimoniously concluded his address with the avowal that he would 'apply' himself "to let the World see [his] concern both for the Security and Satisfaction of [his] People, although it may not be with those Advantages to them, which by [Commons'] Assistances [he] might have procured,"[78] which drew sympathy from those who read it in the news books of the following day, and marked the Commons "out to their own, and all other Nations, as refractory disobedient Persons, that had lost all respect to his Majesty. Thus were they well rewarded for their *Itch of Perpetual Sitting*, and of *Acting; the Parliament* being grown to that height of Contempt, as to be *Gazetted* among Run-away Servants, Lost Doggs, Strayed Horses, and High-way Robbers."[79] Marvell could hardly fail to remember and compare Cromwell's dissolving of Parliament in 1653, a Parliament that was determined to hold their places against their word to him.

Despite their descent, so that they may be called the "Barn of Commons," rather than the House of Commons, Marvell points out that they have at least stymied Popery through rejecting two bills, the act for educating the Royal children and the act for the prosecution of Popish recusants.[80]

They experienced two more adjournments by the Speaker; insulted, yet "they were kickt from Adjournment [sic] to Adjournment, against all President, as from one stair down to another, and when they were at the bottom kickt up again, having no mind yet to *Go out of Doors*."[81] The fall that began with their ambition for place that was not rightly theirs ended with total loss of autonomy; even the semblance of that privilege was taken from them and given to a "Menial servant."[82]

Marvell has incorporated the allegorical structure into a historical account that ends in no triumph but rather ignominy for Parliament in their countrymen's eyes. Sad conclusion. Except that Marvell rose from the circumstance to probably the bravest deed of his life, thus deserving a place among the "worthies"[83] that he had celebrated. He published the *Account*, knowing that he would be identified and arraigned. His last letter to William Popple refers to it with insouciance *and* pride, I think:

There came out, about Christmass last, here a large Book concerning *the Growth of Popery and Arbitrary Government*. There have been great Rewards offered in private, and considerable in the Gazette, to any who could inform of the Author or Printer, but not yet discovered. Three or four printed Books since have described, as near as it was proper to go, the Man being a Member of Parliament, Mr. Marvell to have been the Author; but if he had, surely he should not have escaped being questioned in Parliament, or some other Place. My good Wishes attend you.[84]

Notes

INTRODUCTION

1. "John Aubrey's comments," in *Andrew Marvell The Critical Heritage,* ed. Elizabeth Story Donno (London: Routledge & Kegan Paul, 1978), 101.

2. John Shawcross, *Intentionality and the New Traditionalism: Some Liminal Means to Literary Revisionism* (University Park: Pennsylvania State University Press, 1991), 180–84.

3. Philip Larkin, "The Changing Face of Andrew Marvell," *English Literary Renaissance* 9 (Winter 1979): 155.

4. "Tom May's Death," *The Poems and Letters of Andrew Marvell,* ed. H. M. Margoliouth, 3rd ed., rev. Pierre Legouis with E. E. Duncan Jones (Oxford: Clarendon Press, 1971), 2:2. All poetry quotations from Marvell are from volume 1 of this edition.

CHAPTER 1. "OUR TIMES ARE MUCH DEGENERATE": MARVELL'S EARLY LIFE, HIS FRIENDSHIP WITH LOVELACE, AND HIS ALLEGIANCES

1. Carlos Cipolla, *Clocks and Culture: 1300—1700* (New York: Walker, 1967), 43.

2. Philippe Aries, *The Hour of Our Death,* trans. Helen Weaver (New York: Knopf, 1981), 62.

3. Aries, *The Hour of Our Death,* 62–63.

4. *The Poems and Letters of Andrew Marvell,* ed. H. M. Margoliouth, 3d ed., rev. Pierre Legouis with E. E. Duncan-Jones (Oxford: Clarendon Press, 1971), 2:2.

5. Kevin Sharpe, *The Personal Rule of Charles I* (New Haven: Yale University Press, 1992), 540–45.

6. Christopher Hill, *The Century of Revolution 1603–1714* (New York: W. W. Norton, 1961), 76–77.

7. Pierre Legouis, *Andrew Marvell: Poet, Puritan, Patriot* (Oxford: Clarendon Press, 1965), 2.

8. Caroline Robbins, "Absolute Liberty: the Life and Thought of William Popple, 1638–1708," *William and Mary Quarterly* 24 (April 1967): 196.

9. Eleanor Withington, "Mildmay Fane's Political Satire," *Harvard Library Bulletin* 11 (1957): 40–64.

10. David Morse, *England's Time of Crisis: From Shakespeare to Milton* (New York: St. Martin's Press, 1989), 30.

11. Charles Carlton, *Archbishop William Laud* (London: Routledge and Kegan Paul, 1987), 122.

12. *Andrew Marvell, The Rehearsal Transpros'd and The Rehearsal Trans-*

pros'd, *The Second Part*, ed. D. I. B. Smith (Oxford University Press, 1971), 203–4.

13. *Andrew Marvell Poet and Politician 1621–78: An exhibition to commemorate the tercentenary of his death*, catalogue (London: British Museum Publications Ltd., 1978), 16.

14. Carlton, 102.

15. Sharpe, *The Personal Rule*, 620–24.

16. Edward Gillett and Kenneth A. Macmahon, *A History of Hull* (Oxford: Published for the University of Hull by Oxford University Press, 1980), 158.

17. Legouis, *Andrew Marvell*, 6.

18. Carl E. Bain, "The Latin Poetry of Andrew Marvell," *Philological Quarterly* 38 (October 1959), 436–37.

19. Sharpe, *The Personal Rule*, 899–900.

20. *DNB*, 1302–5. Both Hothams were later to be convicted of treason against the parliament. The Earl of Newcastle induced Sir John Hotham to resume royalist support, but he was discovered before he could actually allow the king's troops into Hull. His son Captain Hotham permitted his parliamentary soldiers to plunder indiscriminately, and personally refused any constraint; Cromwell had him arrested and charged with "misconduct and desertion in battle"; after appealing to Parliament on the basis of his service, he wrote to the queen for help; he escaped and was arrested again in Hull. He was executed on 1 January 1645, and Sir John Hotham on 2 January 1645. *DNB*, 1304–5.

21. G. P. Gooch and H. J. Laski, *English Democratic Ideas in the Seventeenth Century*, 2d ed. (Cambridge: University Press, 1927), 91.

22. Hill, *Century*, 89.

23. Michael Craze, *The Life and Lyrics of Andrew Marvell* (New York: Barnes and Noble, 1979), 28, n. 3.

24. John Dixon Hunt, *Andrew Marvell: His Life and Writings* (Ithaca: Cornell University Press, 1978), 25.

25. "Natural Magic and Populism in Marvell's Poetry," in *Andrew Marvell: Essays on the tercentenary of his death*, ed. R. L. Brett (Oxford: Published for the University of Hull by the Oxford University Press, 1979), 37–38.

26. *Andrew Marvell: Poet and Politician, 1621–78, an exhibition to commemorate the tercentenary of his death*, 32.

27. Margoliouth estimates, on the basis of lines 21–32, that the poem was written "not much more than half way through the interval between *Fleckno* (1645) and *Upon the death of the Lord Hastings* (1649) (*Poems I*, 216). Michael Craze says that "It can be confidently dated in, or very soon after, December 1647" (*The Life and Lyrics*, 9).

28. Manfred Weidhorn, *Richard Lovelace* (New York: Twayne Publishers, Inc., 1970), 23.

29. Craze cites J. P. Cutts's *Times Literary Supplement* letter of 8 August 1952 in which he unfolds his discovery of "A Dialogue between Thyrsis and Dorinda, "In the British Museum in the writing of William Lawes, set to his music but with no poet's name" (*The Life and Lyrics of Andrew Marvell*, 9 and n. 11, 28).

30. Leah Marcus, *The Politics of Mirth Jonson, Herrick, Milton, Marvell, and the Defense of Old Holiday Pastimes* (Chicago: University of Chicago Press, 1986), 214–17.

31. Marcus, *The Politics of Mirth*, 215–17.

32. Manfred Weidhorn (*Richard Lovelace*) and L. N. Wall (*N&Q* [April 1957], 170–73) have assembled Marvell's Lovelacian echoes.

33. The protective insulation advocated by Lovelace for himself, his friends, and fellow Royalists, curiously resembles the compelling image of "green ice" from his poem "The Grasse-hopper." Marcus illustrates that "The Grasse-hopper" since it is the single one of Lovelace's "elusive political hieroglyphs" in the *Lucasta* of 1649 (though there are a number in the posthumous poems) presents the elements of royalist doctrine that Marvell will "rewrite" into realism in the Mower poems (229–33).

34. R. I. V. Hodge, *Foreshortened Time Andrew Marvell and Seventeenth Century Revolutions* (Cambridge: D. S. Brewer, 1978), 151–54.

35. Christine Rees, "'Tom May's Death' and Ben Jonson's Ghost: A Study of Marvell's Satiric Method," *MLR* LXXI (July 1976): 486.

36. Weidhorn, *Richard Lovelace*, 157.

37. Noted in Margoliouth, *Poems*, 258.

38. "The Civil War saw a rebirth of the enigmatic poetry of the Renaissance, in which emblems, parallelism, beast fable, pastoral, parable, or allegory—'darke' conceits of various kinds—were employed to carry a hidden meaning for those who shared knowledge and assumptions with the author but not for others. In the middle decades of the seventeenth century, the enigmatic mode was commonly employed to support the Royalist cause (the parliamentary victors could speak more plainly) and also by men like Marvell with divided feelings. Lovelace's poem 'The Grassehopper' is a notable instance of this kind, and it is highly likely that another poem by him, 'The Falcon,' possesses a similar significance. In such poems the styles of various poets in the first half of the century are blended into semi-opaque dark conceits dealing with events of the realm." "The Death of Innocence in Marvell's 'Nymph Complaining for the death of her Faun,'" in *Marvell: Modern Judgments*, ed. Michael Wilding (Nashville, Tenn.: Aurora Publishers, 1970), 282. I do not agree with Miner that Marvell's feelings were "divided" in this way, but his statement seems quite correct otherwise.

39. Lois Potter, *Secret rites and secret writing Royalist Literature, 1641–1660*, (Cambridge University Press, 1989), 51–52, also 1–2.

40. Thomas Clayton, "'It is Marvel he outdwells his hour': Some Perspectives on Marvell's Medium," *Tercentenary Essays in Honor of Andrew Marvell*, ed. Kenneth Friedenreich (Hamden, Conn.: Archon Books, 1977), 58–60.

41. Ibid., 71–73.

42. Ibid., 59.

43. Donald Friedman observes of this passage: "That Nature should give lessons in coyness is Marvell's generalization about womankind, since the laws of courtly love were admittedly highly artificial." *Marvell's Pastoral Art* (Berkeley: University of California Press, 1970), 115. This statement is hard to understand.

44. Elsie Duncan-Jones has observed that Marvell's poetry often has a "surprisingly literal element." "A Reading of Marvell's *The Unfortunate Lover*, in *I. A. Richards Essays in his Honor*, ed. R. Brower, Helen Vendler, and John Hollander (New York: Oxford University Press, 1973), 225.

45. Lois Potter writes that "the royalist journals show a notable slackening of enthusiasm in the latter part of 1648, and their appearance is more sporadic [in the newsbooks]. Their coverage of the king's trial and execution is particularly disappointing. *Elencticus* and *Melancholicus* did not appear at all in the

last part of January, presumably because their printers were being too closely watched. The tone of their numbers for early January suggests that they had no idea how close the king was to the death which they had so often, in their more sensational moments, predicted for him" (*Secret rites* 18).

46. Carlton, *Laud*, 208.

47. Potter, *Secret rites*, 58–60.

48. Introduction to *Reactions to the English Civil War 1642–1649* (New York: St. Martin's Press, 1983), 20.

49. Margoliouth, *The Poems and Letters of Andrew Marvell*, 1. 223, and Elizabeth Donno, ed., *Andrew Marvell The Complete Poems*, (New York: Penguin Books, 1978), 229, give this date on the basis of Marvell's use in lines 57–58 of Lovelace's lines 15–16 of *Dialogue—Lucasta, Alexis* (1649).

50. Annabel Patterson, *Marvell and the Civic Crown* (Princeton: Princeton University Press, 1978), 20–23.

51. Ibid., 23.

52. Ibid., 23, n. 12.

53. Ibid., 24–25, n. 16.

54. Margarita Stocker, *Apocalyptic Marvell The Second Coming in Seventeenth-Century Poetry* (Athens: Ohio University Press, 1986), 257. Stocker's exegesis of "The Unfortunate Lover" begins with a description of the poem as a "'masque,' of loyalty and criticism," with "the antimasque-masque pattern." This kind of masque opened "with an 'antimasque' of some unfortunate character, then proceeded to expel the antimasque—the main masque celebrating that expulsion. . . . The masque-form therefore implies that the tragedy of Charles is part of a larger "comedic" movement. Stocker also illustrates that Marvell, in "revealing his 'weakness' as a lover," reveals "also his weakness as a king. (In the terms of the masques, king and lover are the same.)" In addition to the "ironic adaptation of the ideal 'heroic' Charles of *Love's Triumph*, and of comparable masques," Marvell draws on Davenant and Inigo Jones's masque *Salmacida Spolia* (1640) as an analogue for Charles as "'Philogenes,' 'lover of his people.' This, the very last of the Caroline masques, anticipates the posthumous hagiography of Charles by portraying him as a king patient of his subjects' fury; it is full of ironic premonitions of his fate in the Civil War." Rather than the "heroic lover" of *Love's Triumph*, however, Stocker says that Philogenes's "pre-eminent qualities . . . are patience and endurance, a victim's rather than a victor's virtues. As such they presage posthumous portraits of Charles, such as that in *Eikon Basilike* of Charles the Martyr." In the masque, the "rebellious political passions . . . [are] curbed by Philogenes' order-inspiring love. . . . With hindsight, Marvell's Philogenes becomes the 'Unfortunate' lover of his people. The 'frustrated love' of Marvell's protagonist is that of Charles as Philogenes, repudiated by his people" (261–66).

55. Ibid., 269.

56. Stocker interprets this oppositely, that "A monarchical love makes more enduring meteoric 'impressions' because it participates in the general destiny." Ibid., 268.

57. Ibid., 273.

58. Morrill, *Reactions to the English Civil War*, 2.

59. Potter, *Secret rites*, 20.

60. Maren-Sofie Rostvig, *The Happy Man: Studies in the Metamorphosis of a Classical Ideal, 1600–1700*, 2 vols. (Oslo, 1962), 249.

61. Carlton, *Laud*, 192–96.

62. Ibid., 196–98.

63. Ibid., 205.

64. Ibid., 207.

65. Ibid., 82–83.

66. Philip A. Knachel, introduction to *Eikon Basilike The Portraiture of His Sacred Majesty in His Solitudes and Sufferings* (pub. for Folger Shakespeare Library by Cornell University Press, 1966), xiii.

67. *Eikon Basilike*, 179.

68. Elsie Duncan-Jones has commented on these lines: "The lover covered with his own blood as a garment, he says, is what is most enjoyed, gives most delight. There is an implication too that he fully realizes the cruelty of the convention." Duncan-Jones makes a connection between the meaning of these lines in the sense of dressing the lover as if he were a dish "to gratify a palate," and the mention of cannibalism in "Daphnis and Chloe." "A Reading of Marvell's *The Unfortunate Lover*," 220–21.

CHAPTER 2. "I HAVE A GARDEN OF MY OWN":
MARVELL'S POETIC DIRECTION

1. Alastair Fowler, *Triumphal Forms: Structural Patterns in Elizabethan Poetry* (Cambridge: University Press, 1970), 13.

2. Fowler explains the general trend that Marvell follows in the use of the sovereign position. "The growth of absolutist monarchy in the sixteenth and seventeenth centuries brought a specially heavy emphasis on the sovereign centre" (26). "The spatial tendency of renaissance thought facilitated direct control of formal organization by ideas; and conventions of centralized symmetry naturally carried over from political protocol into poetry, as they did into architecture. Poets developed the habit of distributing matter through the metrical structure with careful regard to the centre's sovereignty. Almost as a regular practice, they would devote the central place to some principal figure or event, or make it coincide with a structural division of the poem" (Ibid., 62).

3. Marvell consistently extols a selfless attitude; his own self-effacement reflects an internalization of the value. Donald Friedman (*Marvell's Pastoral Art*, Berkeley and Los Angeles: University of California Press, 1970) observes that for Marvell "selflessness is the surest way to greatness, a thought that dominates Marvell's poems on Cromwell and on Fairfax, although the two men chose different ways to achieve the control of self" (282).

4. Fowler, *Triumphal Forms*, 79.

5. "An Apology for Poetry," in *Criticism: The Major Texts*, ed. Walter Jackson Bate (New York: Harcourt, Brace & World, Inc., 1952), 83.

6. John Coolidge, "Marvell and Horace," in *Andrew Marvell: A Collection of Critical Essays*, ed. George de F. Lord (Englewood Cliffs, N.J.: Prentice Hall, Inc., 1968), 88.

7. I see little justification for assuming that the Mower of "The Mower Against Gardens" is also Damon.

8. Critics have frequently assumed that Marvell's position is the Mower's. Nicholas A. Salerno ("Andrew Marvell and the *Furor Hortensis*," *Studies in English Literature 1500–1900* 8 [Winter 1968]: 103–20), however, perceives, as I have, the Mower's comments as "directly opposed to Marvell's" (103).

9. The intense heat in "Damon the Mower" comes not from the sun nor

the Dogstar, but "from an higher Beauty" (19), Juliana. Maria, "to higher Beauties rais'd" (705), passes and "by her *flames*, in *Heaven* try'd, / *Nature* is wholly *vitrifi'd*" (687–88).

10. Donald Friedman does not consider that a "discernible narrative structure" exists. *Marvell's Pastoral Art*, 119.

11. Robert Graves, *The Greek Myths*, vol. 1 (New York: Penguin), 5b.

12. I once thought that Juliana represented the destructive effect of the war-changed atmosphere and ravaged landscape on the poet, and in the light of that, and because Damon wounds himself in the leg as priests of Bellona were said to do, supposed that she might be a descendant of that goddess of war and Julius Caesar.

13. In his excellent essay, "'The Nymph Complaining for the Death of Her Fawn': A Brief Allegory," Geoffrey H. Hartman perceives the nymph as a "Muse in little, a figure created by the poet to mourn his own loss of power or perhaps that of poetry" (115). Hartman's view (with which I consider my own thesis basically in concurrence) is that history has so intruded into the pastoral world that poetry and the poet's existence have been 'fatally' set upon (125). He concludes that "the movement of history seems to doom the 'ancient Rights' of poetry as well as those of a time-honoured regime" (135).

14. Warren Chernaik, *The Poetry of Limitation: A Study of Edmund Waller* (New Haven: Yale University Press, 1968), 85–86.

15. William Empson, *Some Versions of Pastoral* (New York: New Directions, 1968), 132.

16. John Carey discusses naming in Marvell: "Little T. C. names, but tames, the wild flowers. To know a thing, you must name it; but once you have named it, it is no longer the thing you were trying to know." "Reversals transposed: An aspect of Marvell's imagination," in *Approaches to Marvell The York Tercentenary Lectures*, ed. C. A. Patrides (London: Routledge & Kegan Paul, 1978), 139.

17. Friedman continues with the observation that "Another reason for believing that 'The Coronet' is best understood within this genre is the fact that the poem is constructed almost entirely of symbols and allusions drawn from conventional religious and pastoral poetry" (83). *Marvell's Pastoral Art*.

18. Margaret Carpenter, "From Herbert to Marvell: Poetics in 'A Wreath' and 'The Coronet.'" *JEGP* 69 (January 1970): 50–62.

CHAPTER 3. "'TWAS NO *RELIGIOUS HOUSE* TILL NOW":
MARVELL AND THE RETIRED LIFE WITH FAIRFAX

1. For example, while Rosalie L. Colie sees the section as thematically "important and integrated," she considers it "an incident interesting in itself but weighing heavily on the poem." *"My Ecchoing Song": Andrew Marvell's Poetry of Criticism* (Princeton: Princeton University Press, 1970), 265. Donald M. Friedman expresses uncertainty that "there is a completely satisfactory answer" to "why so much effort has been spent on what should be an incidental allusion in the body of the poem." *Marvell's Pastoral Art*, 220. My theory supplements and is essentially in harmony with several readings, including those of Annabel M. Patterson, *Marvell and the Civic Crown*, 103; Maren-Sofie Rostvig, "'Upon Appleton House' and the Universal History of Man," *ES* 42 (1961): 342; M. J. K. O'Loughlin, "This Sober Frame: A Reading of 'Upon Apple-

ton House,'" in *Andrew Marvell: A Collection of Critical Essays*, ed. George de F. Lord (Englewood Cliffs: Prentice Hall, 1968), 127; Kitty W. Scoular, *Natural Magic* (Oxford: Clarendon Press, 1965), 168; and Isabel G. Maccaffrey, "The Scope of Imagination in *Upon Appleton House*," in *Tercentenary Essays in Honor of Andrew Marvel*, ed. Kenneth Friedenreich (Hamden, Conn.: Archon Books, 1977), 229.

2. Although Fairfax accepted a place in the newly formed Council of State in 1649, he refused to sign the declaration expressing agreement with the abolition of monarchy and of the House of Lords. When he resigned in 1650, he made a statement that suggests an explanation for his earlier refusal to participate in the regicide: "What my conscience yields unto as just and lawful, . . . I shall follow; and what seems to me to be otherwise I will not do. My conscience is not satisfied, and therefore I must desire to be excused." In Clements R. Markham, *A Life of the Great Lord Fairfax* (London: Macmillan, 1870), 360.

3. Williams, the last archbishop of York until Accepted Frewen's appointment after the Restoration, died in Wales on 25 March 1650, and was buried there. Although the date of his death might be helpful in establishing a more exact date for the poem, probably Fairfax and Marvell were not aware that he was dead. At any rate, the reference allows also a general interpretation. For Williams, Cawood Castle had proved no sanctuary; within a few months of his arrival, he was sent fleeing by a Yorkshire troop (*DNB*).

4. John Newman, "Marvell's Appleton House," *TLS* (January 1972):99. See also A. A. Tait, "Marvell's Appleton House," *TLS* (11 February 1972): 157, and James Turner, "Marvell," *TLS* (31 March 1972): 367. John Dixon Hunt also presents an argument that supports its having been the older house. *Andrew Marvell*, 80–86. When they were first married, General Fairfax and Ann Vere lived at Denton, the family's main residence, with Sir Thomas, the general's grandfather. Sir Thomas seems to have quickly grown uncomfortable with this arrangement and assigned to them his house at Nunappleton. It may have been intended as an interim dwelling, a place for the young couple to live for a few years; Fairfax, however, ever preferred it. Markham, *A Life of the Great Lord Fairfix*, 22.

5. Keith Thomas, *Religion and the Decline of Magic* (New York: Scribner's, 1971), 96–102.

6. Sir Henry Spelman, *The History and Fate of Sacrilege*, ed. Samuel J. Eales (London, 1888), 136–58.

7. As the third Lord Fairfax, he was also the possessor of Bilborough and Bolton Percy, both formerly belonging to the Church. He returned these properties' tithes to the clergy, assigning those of Bilborough to the clergyman, Mr. Topham, for his lifetime, and in his will, to the "preaching minister of Bilbrough for ever." Markham, *A Life of the Great Lord Fairfax*, 397. When Parliament rewarded him with the seignory of the Isle of Man, he directed the entire proceeds from the sequestrated bishopric as supplement to the incomes of the lower clergy and for establishment of grammar schools in the surrounding area. Markham, *A Life of the Great Lord Fairfax*, 365.

8. Almost certainly Marvell would have known this paraphrase, as would many others, for since Queen Elizabeth's time, the law had required the placement in churches of a volume of the *Paraphrases* in English so that it was accessible to all parishioners. William L. Edgerton, "Shakespeare and the 'Needle's Eye,'" *MLN* 66 (December 1951): 549–50.

9. Stephen Greenblatt's concept of "the alien constructed as a distorted

image of the authority," in *Renaissance Self-Fashioning from More to Shake-speare* (Chicago: University of Chicago Press, 1980), 9, prompted my awareness of the correspondences between the nun and the narrator, as well as the nuns' gardens and behavior as a parody of Fairfax's garden and the bees and flow-ers' actions.

10. Spelman includes the story of Edward Paston in his accounting of the families who had suffered because of the possession of monastic lands. He makes particular note that Paston is the third generation. When Paston tried to clear the property for his "mansion-house upon or near the priory, ... a piece of wall fell upon a workman and slew him: perplexed with this accident in the beginning of this business, he gave it wholly over, and ... built his mansion-house, a very fair one, at Appleton" (143). Though no connection seems to have been made between the Pastons and the Fairfaxes, Appleton property was part of the Fairfaxes' holdings, and tiny Appleton is only about two miles from Nunappleton. This section of Spelman's treatise was probably written in the late 1620s, so the incident is possibly within the time of General Fairfax. The story is the sort that might often be repeated, and perhaps Fairfax had heard it.

One cannot be sure that the Fairfaxes knew the Paston tale, but one can be fairly sure that they were superstitious. The general's grandfather, Sir Thomas, wrote to his brother Henry Fairfax in 1613 that he had heard the devil could "be seen upon the sea, and this morning I heard it credibly spoken that the devil was upon the Thames in a sculler." *The Fairfax Correspondence. Memoirs of the Reign of Charles the First*, ed. George W. Johnson, 2 vols. (London: Rich-ard Bentley, 1848), 1: xxix. Edward Fairfax, the translator of Tasso's *Gerusa-lemme Liberata*, wrote an account of his two bewitched daughters entitled "A Discourse of Witchcraft. As it was acted in the Family of Mr. Edward Fairfax of Fuystone in the County of York, in the year 1621" (*DNB*).

11. Friedman, *Marvell's Pastoral Art*, 224–25. Rupert Taylor observes that "Noblemen, if they belonged to the great political houses, collected prophecies relating to the fortunes of their families or kept books containing prophecies concerning the history of the realm." *The Political Prophecy in England* (New York: Columbia University Press, 1911), 85. Horses were an interest grown into tradition with the Fairfaxes; the general wrote a treatise on horse breeding. His poem about the horse that Charles II rode in his coronation parade is a sad testimony to the hopeful prophecy that Marvell presents in the poem:

> Hence then Dispaire my hopes why should itt bury
> Sence this braue Steed Bredd first was in my Query
> Now thus aduanc't with highest honors loden
> Whilst his that bredd him on by most Mens troden
> But t'is noe matter Seing tho' has gott th' Aduance
> Then please the Royal Rider with thy Prance
> Soe may thy Fame much rayse thy Prayses higher
> Then Chessnut that begott the or Brid-la-dore his Sire.

The Poems of Thomas Third Lord Fairfax, ed. Edward Bliss Reed (New Haven: Yale University Press, 1909), 284.

12. Perhaps there were other prophecies particular to the Fairfaxes. The "Northern Star" of "Upon the Hill and Grove at Bill-borow" may be a reference to a prophecy.

13. The implementation of the ordinance was slow. John Morrill describes it:

In early 1643, the two Houses approved a *bill* abolishing the existing frame (archbishops, bishops, deans, chapters and so on), and this bill was sent to the King as part of Parliament's terms for a settlement, but the bill was not converted into an ordinance. It had no legal force. Fourteen of the twenty-six bishops had their temporal possessions sequestered by an ordinance of March 1643, but the remaining twelve were left free to enjoy their properties and powers; six of them were indeed invited (under their episcopal titles . . .) to be members of Westminster Assembly; . . . The most important effect of this failure to proceed to abolition was that the bishops retained sole right to ordain men to the ministry for most of the war, and those ordained up to October 1646 (in theory) and up to mid-1654 (in practice) were deemed qualified to hold a living in the national Church. "The Church in England," in *Reactions to the English Civil War 1642–1649* (New York: St. Martin's Press, 1982), 92–93.

Commons decreed in 1646 that all cathedral lands were to be sold. Christopher Hill, *The Century of Revolution: 1603–1714* (New York: W. W. Norton, 1961), 163.

14. Colie, "*My Ecchoing Song*," 211–13.

15. Joseph Summers, Introduction to *Marvell*, Laurel Poetry Series (New York: Dell, 1961), 19.

16. Colie, "*My Ecchoing Song*," 206–7.

17. Marcus, *The Politics of Mirth*, 220.

18. Richard Baxter, *Reliquiae Baxterianae I* (London, 1696), 48.

19. Patterson, *Marvell and the Civic Crown*, 97.

20. Bulstrode Whitelocke, *Memorials of English Affairs*, Oxford, 1853, ii., 20.

21. Interestingly enough, Lucy Hutchinson quotes Fairfax as saying that God had laid him aside. *Memoirs of the Life of Colonel Hutchinson*, ed. James Sutherland (London: Oxford University Press, 1973), 195.

22. Margoliouth dates "An Horatian Ode" as possibly "early in the summer of 1650." He adds that "It has been suggested that it represents the attitude of Fairfax; but evidence is lacking that the poet's acquaintance with Fairfax had begun at the time of the General's retirement." *Poems and Letters*, 236.

23. "An Horatian Ode," 12.

Chapter 4. "Mine own Precipice I go": Marvell and the Active Life

1. David Masson, *The Life of John Milton Narrated in Connexion with the Political, Ecclesiastical, and Literary History of His Time Vol. IV* (New York: Peter Smith, 1946), 150–51, 156, 226.

2. J. G. A. Pocock, in Introduction to *The Political Works of James Harrington*, ed. (Cambridge: Cambridge University Press, 1977), 37.

3. Masson, *Life of John Milton*, IV, 325–27.

4. E. E. Duncan-Jones, "The Erect Sword of Marvell's *Horatian Ode*," *Etudes Anglaises*, XV (1962): 172–74.

5. Blair Worden, "Marvell, Cromwell, and the *Horatian Ode*," in *Politics of Discourse The Literature and History of Seventeenth-Century England*, ed. Kevin Sharpe and Steven N. Zwicker (Berkeley: University of California Press, 1987), 159–62.

6. Either in a sense are tenable since evidence now exists that Marvell's poetry did circulate more than was supposed. *Andrew Marvell Poet and Politician 1621–78: An exhibition to commemorate the tercentenary of his death*, catalogue compiled by Hilton Kelliher, 43–44.

7. *The Latin Poems of Andrew Marvell*, trans. William A. McQueen and Kiffin A. Rockwell (Chapel Hill: University of North Carolina Press, 1964), 42–43.

Nec sterilem te crede; licet, mulieribus exul,
Falcem virginae nequeas immitere messi,
Et nostro peccare modo. Tibi Fama perenne
Proegnabit; rapiesque novem de monte Sorores;
Et pariet modulos *Echo* repetita Nepotes.

8. C. V. Wedgwood, *Poetry and Politics under the Stuarts* (Cambridge: University Press, 1960), 101–2.

9. C. V. Wedgwood, *The King's War, 1641–1647* (New York: Macmillan, 1959), 402. John Beresford, *Gossip of the Seventeenth and Eighteenth Centuries* (London: Richard Cobden-Sanderson, 1923), 43.

10. Richard Baxter, *Autobiography*, ed. N. H. Keeble, abridged by J. M. Lloyd Thomas (London: Dent, 1974), 66.

11. John Wallace has noted that the London newspapers presented the Irish attitude as one of acquiescence, yet Cromwell's own notions about what he had accomplished in Ireland are also to the point here. *Destiny His Choice: The Loyalism of Andrew Marvell* (Cambridge: Cambridge University Press, 1968), 85–88.

12. Quoted in Charles Firth, *Oliver Cromwell* (London: Putnam, 1923), 268.

13. Quoted in Christopher Hill, *God's Englishman: Oliver Cromwell and the English Revolution* (New York: Dial Press, 1970), 122.

14. Worden, "Marvell, Cromwell, and the *Horatian Ode*," 174–75.

15. Michael Wilding, "Marvell's 'An Horatian Ode Upon Cromwell's Return from Ireland,' the Levellers, and the Junta," *MLR* (January 1981), 3.

16. Ibid., 3–4.

17. Ibid., 6.

18. Ibid., 5.

19. From *The Levellers (Falsely so called) Vindicated* in Wilding, "Marvell's 'An Horatian Ode upon Cromwell's Return from Ireland', the Levellers, and the Junta," 6.

20. Maurice Ashley, *Oliver Cromwell and his world* (New York: G. P. Putnam's Sons, 1972), 54.

21. Henry C. Wilkinson, *The Adventurers of Bermuda*, 2d ed. (London: Oxford University Press, 1958), 250.

22. Gooch and Laski, *English Democratic Ideas in the Seventeenth Century*, 115.

23. Worden, "Marvell, Cromwell, and the *Horatian Ode*, 176.

24. Wilding, "Marvell's 'An Horatian Ode,'" 14.

25. Pocock, *Political Works*, 25–26.

26. Quoted in Pocock, *Political Works*, 33.

27. John Milton, *Complete Prose Works of John Milton*, Vol. IV, 1650–55, Part II, ed. Don M. Wolfe (New Haven: Yale University Press, 1966), 859.

28. As well, Blair Worden presents evidence that Marvell knew Oxenbridge first at Hull. "Marvell, Cromwell, and the *Horatian Ode*," p. 330, n. 19.

29. Hunt, *Andrew Marvell*, 116.

30. Craze, *The Life and Lyrics of Andrew Marvell*, 143.

31. Ibid., 180.

32. Ibid., 266.

33. Marvell's use of Petrarchan military metaphor prompts one to weigh the possibility that he intended an artificial atmosphere to prevail, or at the least, that he was encouraging his audience to enjoy his wit.

34. James Heath, *Flagellum* (London, 1663), 166–67.

35. Quoted in Firth, *Oliver Cromwell*, 456.

36. Jonathan Goldberg, "The Typology of 'Musicks Empire,'" *Texas Studies in Language and Literature* 13 (Fall 1971): 421–30. Goldberg asserts that "Only in the last stanza is true harmony achieved, the harmony of earth and heaven, and only in the last stanza is the pattern of foreshadowment relieved by the self-contained 'gentler Conqueror.'" In his discussion of the pun on "organ" (8), Goldberg sees organ with its multiple meanings as an "image . . . used for its political implications," and thus sees the poem as Hollander reads it, as honoring Cromwell. Goldberg goes on to make an interesting point:

> if Cromwell is the "gentler Conqueror," the poem then operates in much the same way as the *First Anniversary of the Government* under O.C. Typology, music, and politics are there combined in such a way that Cromwell is assured of a place in Christian history. The distinction that must be made in reading "Musicks Empire" is that if the poem is meant as an oblique compliment to Cromwell, it makes its point by suggesting that Cromwell is Christlike. Thus, within the frame of the poem, the primary meaning of the reference is to Christ, and the possibility of the poem as political panegyric occurs because typology is a means of praise. (427–30)

CHAPTER 5. *"CROMWELL* ALONE": MARVELL AS CROMWELL'S POET

1. *A Full and Perfect Relation of the Great Plot and Terrible Conspiracy* (London, 1654, Thomason Tracts).

2. *Weekly Intelligencer*, August 8–15 (1654 Thomason Tracts).

3. *Every dayes Intelligence*, January 17–20 (1653/4 Thomason Tracts).

4. *The Faithful Scout*, February 3–10 (1654 Thomason Tracts).

5. Barbara Taft, "The Humble Petition of Several Colonels of the Army: Causes, Character, and Results of Military Opposition to Cromwell's Protectorate," *Huntington Library Quarterly* 42 (1978–79): 15–16.

6. Ibid., 16–20.

7. Caroline Robbins, "Absolute Liberty: the Life and Thought of William Popple, 1638–1708" *William and Mary Quarterly* 24 (April 1967), 196.

8. Taft, "The Humble Petition," 19–20.

9. Ibid., 21.

10. Baxter, *Autobiography*, 24.

11. Taft, "The Humble Petition," 31.

12. Ibid., 33.

13. Ibid., 15.

14. Ibid., 34.

15. Ibid., 38.

16. Ibid., 39.

17. Blair Worden, *The Rump Parliament 1648–1653* (London: Cambridge University Press, 1974), 79.

18. Ibid., 12.

19. Ibid., 89.

20. Ibid., 92.

21. Ibid., 139.

22. Ibid., 330–31.

23. Ibid., 334.

24. Taft, *The Humble Petition*, 16.

25. Raymond Klibansky, Erwin Panofsky, Fritz Saxl, *Saturn and Melancholy: Studies in the History of Natural Philosophy, Religion and Art* (London: Nelson, 1964), 177.

26. Annabel Patterson "Against Polarization: Literature and Politics in Marvell's Cromwell Poems," *English Literary Renaissance* 5 (Spring 1975): 258.

27. Carlton, *Archbishop William Laud*, 94–95.

28. Ibid., 99.

29. Patterson, "Against Polarization," 259.

30. Firth, *Oliver Cromwell*, 478–79.

31. Hill, *God's Englishman*, 193–94.

32. John Wallace has observed that "The Amphion myth offered further advantages; it allowed him to glide over the troubles of that anxious year, and indeed to pretend that the quarrels and disappointments of the republicans were a concordant discord, not a real threat to the state; it afforded an excellent illustration of that speed of action that so often caused Cromwell to be compared with Caesar (a comparison conspicuously missing in the poem); and it permitted him to allude to the military operations, of which the Western design was the chief, and to the controversial new ecclesiastical settlement as elements of Cromwell's success." *Destiny His Choice*, 118.

33. Hill, *God's Englishman*, 145.

34. Firth, *Cromwell*, 479–81.

35. Worden, *Rump*, 92.

36. Ibid., 140.

37. Firth, *Oliver Cromwell*, 419.

Chapter 6. "Angelique *Cromwell* . . . *Angel* of our Commonweal": The Raised Leader and the Fallen Populace

1. W. C. Abbott writes of what may be called Cromwell's obsession:

Even had the Protector's intelligences informed him of the real position of the Papacy at this moment—its declining political prestige, its decaying revenues, its administrative difficulties, the opposition which it faced within the church establishment—it may be doubted whether that would have prevailed against the deep impression made in his youth. Between Cromwellians and the Church of Rome was a quarrel to the death.

The Writings and Speeches of Oliver Cromwell, vol. III (Cambridge: Harvard University Press, 1945), 160–61.

2. Abbott, *Writings*, 501.

3. Ibid., 504.

4. Ibid., 539.

5. Ibid., 533.

6. Ibid., 532.

7. Ibid., 538.

8. Hill, *God's Englishman*, 155.

10. Some confusion exists about Cromwell's actual words in this speech. Carlyle-Lomas (*The Letters and Speeches of Oliver Cromwell with Elucidations*, intro. C. H. Firth [London: Metheun and Co., 1904], 299) provide a variation in the text from another source, a pamphlet printed in 1654 (272). This variant reads, "'and this hath been set upon our hearts and upon all the faithful of the land; it may be that it is not our duty to deliver it over to any other people, and that Scripture may be fulfilling now to us; but I may be beyond my line. But I thank God I have my hopes exercised in these things and so I am persuaded are yours'"; Lomas observes that "This is probably the more correct version of the two." The fear that the millennium would not be for England was apparently prevalent: John Owen, preaching the day after the regicide, said that "'As the days approach for the delivery of the decree, so the shaking of Heaven and Earth, and all the powers of the World, to make way for the establishment of that kingdom which shall not be given to another people . . . must certainly grow!'" In Bernard Capp, *The Fifth Monarchy Men* (Totowa, N.J.: Rowman, 1972), 50.

11. John Milton, *Complete Poems and Major Prose*, ed. Merritt Y. Hughes (New York: Odyssey Press, 1957), 47–48.

12. The Fifth Monarchists themselves were largely responsible for the failure of the Barebone's Parliament. Louise Fargo Brown observes that they had discovered that Cromwell was not entirely in favor of the final plan "to summon an assembly of godly men," but "had decided to modify it by giving seats to such men as Fairfax, who had no connection with the gathered churches, [which] gave rise in some hearts to the feeling that perhaps the leading role in the new order was to be reserved for some one more enlightened regarding it. Naturally that other would be Harrison, the chief champion of the new plan in the Council of Officers." Louise Fargo Brown, *The Political Activities of the Baptists and Fifth Monarchy Men in England during the Interregnum* (London: Oxford University Press, 1912), 30–31.

13. Hill, *God's Englishman*, 183. Firth quotes Thurloe on the parliament's pushing Cromwell to take the crown: "'it's the office, which is known to the laws and to the people. They know their duty to a king and his to them. Whatever else there is will be wholly new, and upon the next occasion will be changed again. Besides they say the name Protector came in with the sword, and will never be the ground of any settlement, nor will there be a free Parliament so long as that continues, and as it savours of the sword now, so it will at last bring all things to military.'" *Oliver Cromwell*, 423.

14. Carlyle-Lomas, *Letters and Speeches*, 303.

15. John Wallace presents this somewhat differently. His summary is useful: "Time, for instance, is an obsessive theme, and most of the parts of the poem are related to it: obliterating, useful, and useless time in the first section; hoped-for millennial time in the third; destructive time (death) in the fourth, and restored time (the extended simile of the returning sun) in the seventh and last." *Destiny His Choice*, 109.

16. Anna Trapnel, *The Cry of a Stone* (London, 1654, *Thomason Tracts*), 12–13.

17. "It had become evident after five days of debate that any arrangement between the Parliamentarians and the Protectoral party was virtually out of the question. Had the result hinged on the issue of the debate, Cromwell might well have been overthrown." Abbott, *Writings*, 451. Cromwell resolved the situ-

ation for the time with his speech and the requirement of their signing the loyalty "test" to him.

18. In Capp, *The Fifth Monarchy Men*, 58.

19. James Heath, *Flagellum* (London, 1663), 127–28.

20. Margoliouth, *The Poems and Letters of Andrew Marvell, Vol II*, 306.

21. Quoted from Masson (p. 607) in Margoliouth, *The Poems and Letters, Vol. II*, 379.

22. Taft, "The Humble Petition," p. 37.

23. Capp, *The Fifth Monarchy Men*, 150–55.

24. Ibid., 82.

25. Ibid., 65. In the same context, Capp goes on to say that "Simpson's views were probably close to those of Feake."

26. Capp, *The Fifth Monarchy Men*, 67.

27. Ibid., 68–74.

28. Ibid., 68–69.

29. John Thurloe, *State Papers*, I, 621.

30. *The Grand Politique Post*, 7–15 February 1654 (*Thomason Tracts*).

31. Abbott, *Writings*, 545–46.

32. Ibid., 547. This is virtually identical to a part of his speech to the House on 12 September 1654: "'Every sect saith, Oh! Give me liberty. But give it him, and to his power he will not yield it to anybody else.'" Ibid., 459.

33. Ibid., 548.

34. Ibid., 549.

35. Ibid., 556.

36. J. N., a Mechanick, *Proh Tempora! Proh Mores!*, London, 1654 (*Thomason Tracts*).

37. Capp, *The Fifth Monarchy Men*, 100.

38. John Wallace writes, "When Marvell cursed them as the locusts from the bottomless pit (311–12) he was only turning their own imagery against themselves and applying a text which had long been used to condemn heretics and schismatics." *Destiny His Choice*, 134. Wallace also cites in note 2 on the same page several titles containing the phrase, "Bottomless Pit."

39. Capp, *The Fifth Monarchy Men*, 74. The quote is from John Hall, *Confusion Confounded*, 1654, 7.

40. *The Portraiture of His Sacred Majesty in His Solitudes and Sufferings*, ed. Philip A. Knachel (Ithaca: Cornell University Press for The Folger Shakespeare Library, 1966), 92.

41. Knachel, *Eikon Basilike*, 86.

42. Ibid., 91.

43. Ibid., 93–94.

44. The navy had not been involved as the army had been in politics. Taft (35) writes that after the dismissal of the Rump, "the generals at sea had issued a bland declaration indicating that the navy considered itself a nonpolitical service." But even they had submitted a petition in November of 1654; their concerns were the vital ones that had been extant too long: "impressment, involuntary foreign service, arrears of pay to distressed families." One short passage alone indicated a certain unity with the army. Cromwell arranged for them to be paid, which settled the matter quickly.

45. Marvell may be prophetic here. A. J. N. Wilson speculates: "May it not be, then, that Marvell, either foreseeing the dissolution, or even perhaps privately informed of its certainty, here strikes a warning note: the Protector, with the

drastic step he plans of an early dissolution and with the terms in which he will dismiss the Parliament, is quite prepared to create anger against himself and among Englishmen, in order that good may come of his 'troubling of the waters.' 'Yearly' is, of course, crucial. The passage about 'sin' and the threat it constitutes to the Protector and his mission (ll. 153–74), though puzzlingly remote from the optimism of the Amphion/Cromwell allegory, does not associate drastic intervention by him with the completion of the year's cycle; this is just what this closing couplet does." "Andrew Marvell's 'The First Anniversary of the Government under Oliver Cromwell': The Poem and its Frame of Reference," *Modern Language Review* 69 (April 1974), 254–73.

CHAPTER 7. "SPECTATORS VAIN": THE DEATH OF CROMWELL

1. Joseph H. Summers, *The Heirs of Donne and Jonson* (New York: Oxford University Press, 1970), 175.

2. Annabel Patterson has identified this kind of poem as *soteria*, which defines "value by exploring its near loss." *Marvell and the Civic Crown*, 80.

3. Keith Thomas, *Religion and the Decline of Magic* (New York: Charles Scribner's Sons, 1971), 93. Providence was seen as such a leading cause of events that keeping a record of the mercies shown by God became, Thomas observes in the same context, a "religious duty for everyone" during the sixteenth and seventeenth centuries in England. One would record also in a journal the evidence of God's special care of others as heard or observed. These accounts began to be organized and published. They were avidly read and were an encouragement to the reader to keep an even closer watch on events; chance and coincidence turned into what Cromwell would call "dispensations" and the astrologers "accidents."

4. Ibid., 94–95.

5. *The Letters and Speeches of Oliver Cromwell*, 395 n.

6. Thomas Beard, *The Theatre of Gods Judgments* (London: 1597), p. 541.

7. Cromwell's letter of 30 October 1655 to Vice-Admiral Goodson, at Jamaica, in Carlyle, *Letters and Speeches*, vol 2, 469–72.

8. *Miscellaneous Works* (Spenser Society, 1872), n.p. Wither's philosophy concerning all the rulers of England under whose reigns he lived during his long life (1588–1667) was to do what he could for his ruler: "for, a Tyranny, / Is somewhat better than an Anarchy." His poem on the carriage accident was more generous than his true feeling, apparently, for he commented on it some years later: "their necks were both in hazard to be broken, by the Protectors usurping the Office of his Coach-man; and . . . they were both brought in so hurt, that their lives were in danger. Of that imprudent, if not disgraceful attempt mis-beseeming his person, I endeavoured to prevent as much of the dishonor, as I might, by a little Poem." In Abbott, *Writings and Speeches*, IV, 477. His annoyed tone was characteristic, particularly when he spoke of Cromwell who neglected his advice. But he directed that annoyance at his audience rather than at Cromwell in "A Rapture Occasioned by the late Miraculous Deliverance of his Highnesse the Lord Protector." Wither may have in mind that poem when he mentions a favor in *Salt Upon Salt*, written at Cromwell's death, that he did for Cromwell:

> For, 'tis at present, known, to more then One,
> Yet living, (and was known to him that's gone)

That, in the greatest hazzard he e'er had,
I, seas'nably, by Providence was made
An Instrument of Safety, when th'intention
Was almost rip'ned, beyond all Prevention.
Yea, to prevent them, who by his Disgrace,
Endeavour'd to destroy the publick Peace.

Miscellaneous Works of George Wither (Spenser Society, Manchester: Charles Simms and Co., 1875), 13–14.

9. Heath, *Flagellum*, 158.

10. *Rump: or an Exact Collection of the Choycest Poems and Songs Relating to the Late Times*, part I, London, 1662, 363.

11. *Cromwelliana, A Chronological detail of events in which Oliver Cromwell was engaged from the year 1642 to his death* (1810), 133.

12. Anna Trapnel, *A Legacy for Saints* (Thomason Tracts, London: 1654), 49.

13. Brown, *The Political Activities of the Baptists and Fifth Monarchy*, 49.

14. Among the visitors were members of Cromwell's council, high-ranking officers of the army, and participants in the last parliament. Christopher Feake came, as well as a "Mr. Berconhead," whom I suspect was Berkenhead, wit and alleged author of "Jolt." Trapnel, *Cry of a Stone* (January 1653/54), introduction, n.p.

15. Ibid., 6–7.

16. Ibid., 10.

17. Ibid., 13.

18. In Bernard Capp, "Extreme Millenarianism," in *Puritan Eschatology 1600 to 1660*, ed. Peter Toon (Greenwood, S.C.: Attic Press, 1972), 80.

19. Ibid., 82.

20. Wallace, *Destiny His Choice*, 128.

21. Hill, *God's Englishman*, 211–12.

22. Abbott, *Writings*, IV, 261.

23. Ibid., 273.

24. Ibid., 274.

25. Ibid., 278. The brackets are in the text.

26. Wallace, *Destiny His Choice*, 243.

27. This is Abbott's judgment of Giavarina (Vol. IV, 754). Unlike other reporters, such as Heath, his accounts are not marred by personal animus against Cromwell.

28. Abbott, *Writings*, Vol. IV, 744–45 (Giavarina to Doge, Feb. 12/22, *Cal.S.P.Ven.* (1657–59), 168).

29. "I must beg your pardon, that I do not right to you so oft ase I would doe; but in earnist, I have bin so extreme sickly of late, that it has made mee unfit for anything. . . . Truly the Lord has bin very gratius to us, in doeing for us abofe what we could exspekt; and now had shod him more extraordinary in delevering my father out of the hands of his enymise, which wee have all reson to be sensible of in a very pertikeller manner; for sertingly not ondly his famely would have bin ruined, but in all probabillyti the hol nation would have bin invold in blod. June 12 [1658]." John Thurloe, *State Papers*, vii, 171.

30. Abbott, *Writings*, Vol. IV, 820.

31. Ibid., 864.

32. Ibid., 784.

33. Ibid., 751.

34. Quoted in Maurice Ashley's foreword to Roy Sherwood, *The Court of Oliver Cromwell* (London: Croom Helm, 1977), n.p.

35. In Abbott, *Writings*, IV, 754 (Giavarina to Doge, March 5/15, *Cal.S.P.Ven.* (1657–59), 173–75).

36. In his memorial *Salt Upon Salt*, Wither, for example, observes early in the poem that the Protectorate, except by a miracle, will fall with the Protector:

> The main prop, of this *Government* is gone,
> The Stone, our *Master-builders* built upon
> Is now remov'd; and, either I mistake,
> Or, all that's built thereon begins to *shake*,
> And quite asunder too, will fall at length,
> Unless upheld, with more than *humane strength*.

Miscellaneous Works (Manchester: Charles Simms and Co., 1875), 3.

37. Edmund Ludlow, *Memoirs*, in F. J. Varley, *Oliver Cromwell's Latter End* (London: Chapman and Hall, Ltd., 1939), 17–18.

38. Varley, *Oliver Cromwell's Latter End*, 24.

39. Ibid., 53.

40. Marvell, *Letters*, 7.

41. Maurice Ashley, *Oliver Cromwell and his world* (New York: G. P. Putnam's Sons, 1972), 112.

42. Ashley, *Oliver Cromwell*, 111.

43. *The Diary of John Evelyn*, ed. E. S. deBeer, Vol. III, *Kalendarium, 1650–1672* (Oxford: Clarendon Press, 1955), 224.

44. *Cromwell*, ed. Maurice Ashley (Englewood Cliffs, N.J.: Prentice Hall, Inc., 1969), 109–11. David Underdown, "Cromwell and the Officers, February 1658," *English Historical Review*, LXXXIII (1982): 101–7.

45. *The Essayes of Montaigne*, trans. John Florio, intro. J. I. M. Stewart (New York: Modern Library, 1933), 46–48.

46. Lois Potter, in *Secret rites and secret writing*, cites Fanshawe's poem "On the Earle of *Straffords* Tryall" as an inspiration for "An Horatian Ode" in the "stage/scaffold analogy." She cites several lines that seem pertinent to "The Death of O.C." as well: "for his lifes *last* act, / *Times* shall admiring read it, and this age, / Though now it hisse, claps when he leaves the Stage" (14–16), 88–89.

47. Cromwell was comforted by this thought in his depressed and perplexed last days. Antonia Fraser gives an account of the often-repeated story of Cromwell, near death, turning "anxiously to a minister . . . : 'Tell me, is it possible to fall from Grace.'" *Cromwell The Lord Protector* (New York: Alfred A. Knopf, 1974), 675.

48. Sacvan Bercovitch, in *The Puritan Origins of the American Self*, comments that "Secular realism tells us what is different, unique, about the individual; Mather uses detail to convert *historia* into *allegoria*. He makes the particular events of Winthrop's life an index to the hero's universality." (New Haven: Yale University Press, 1975), 8.

49. Cromwell was explicit about this. In 1657, for example, in discussing his decision concerning the crown, he considered accepting it because it "would please the children and permit them to enjoy their rattle." Ludlow, ii, 14, in Abbott, *Writings*, Vol. IV, 509.

50. Waller in his elegy memorialized his cousin's death by making the hurricane simultaneous with it: "Heav'n his great soul does claim / In storms as

loud as his immortal fame"(1–2). In *The Later Renaissance in England*, ed. Hershel Baker (Boston: Houghton Mifflin Co., 1975).

51. Cromwell's love of horses was well known. The horses, brutes though they may be, mourn for him. Men die, as well, and fail to recognize the cause:

> The Race of warlike *Horses* at his Tomb
> Offer themselves in many an Hecatomb;
> With pensive head towards the ground they fall,
> And helpless languish at the tainted Stall.
> Numbers of *Men* decrease with pains unknown,
> And hasten not to see his Death their own. (123–28)

Wither also mentions the phenomenon of the recent death of horses:

> But, hear me further, and relate I shall
> Some things, which do not ev'ry year befall;
> Our ablest *Horse*, (ev'n those perhaps, wherein
> More *trust* reposed was, then should have bin)
> Die suddenly, and Ditches are bestrow'd
> With those *Bones*, whereupon our Gallants rode:
> Their *Stink*, (as once a *Prophet* said) ascends,
> Yet, still, his hand against us, GOD, extends.

Salt Upon Salt, 23.

52. And in historic fact, 1658 had been a year of "high mortality." Firth relates that beginning in April of 1658, many died of what was called "the new disease" that took its heaviest toll in London. There were days of public fasting and praying, then days of thanksgiving when it abated. Cromwell was attacked by the malignant fever when it made its August foray, so there were many dying at the time of his death. *The Last Years of the Protectorate 1656–58*, vol. 2 (London: Longmans, Green, and Co., 1909), 294–96.

53. The peacefulness of his death was commented on by Nedham who described it as "serene." Hyde, who was not there, no doubt based his description on hearsay: "Never monarch . . . died with more silence." Quoted in Godfrey Davies, *The Restoration of Charles II, 1658–1660* (San Marino, Calif: Huntington Library, 1955), 3, 8.

54. Hugh Peter preached on Joshua 1:2, "My servant Moses is dead," on the Sunday after Cromwell's 3 September death. Roy Sherwood writes that "Comparisons between Cromwell and Moses were not uncommon. In a work published in 1659 and dedicated to Protector Richard Cromwell the author, H. Dawbeny, describes Oliver as 'our second Moses' and goes on to draw what he calls thirty 'lively parallels' between Oliver and the first Moses." Sherwood, *The Court of Oliver Cromwell*, 109.

55. Many felt that Cromwell's earthly obsequies were so elaborate that no king had ever been "solemniz'd with so much state." In *Salt Upon Salt*, Wither speaks of its being patterned on that of Philip II of Spain; he calls it a "very costly Puppet-Play," and says that he hated it: "But, I abhor it, when I do behold / Walls clothed, and poor men expos'd to cold / And nakedness"(17–18). Waller's "Upon the Late Storm and Death" makes no mention of the funeral, though a hint of the less than mournful spirit of the populace may glimmer through his call for tears: "Ungrateful then, if we no tears allow / To Him, who gave us Peace, and Empire too"(25–26).

56. Varley adds to Evelyn's assessment of the troops' apparent indifference

to their leader's death during his funeral procession: "They were probably a discontented and undisciplined lot, and, as it was generally known that the Great Protector had been buried long ago the crowds behaved as they would do at an ordinary State Pageant." *Cromwell's Latter End* (London: Chapman and Hall, Ltd., 1939), 38.

57. In Hill, *God's Englishman*, 65.

58. In Hill, *God's Englishman*, 66.

59. Firth, *Last Years of the Protectorate*, 205.

60. In Hill, *God's Englishman*, 226–27. Cromwell's precedent was Calvin: "God crowns none but well-tried wrestlers." *Commentary on Genesis*, trans. J. King, 1965, I, 171.

61. Respect for Richard was negligible. Sir Henry Vane's blunt appraisal in a speech in the Upper House helped to shorten Richard's reign: "'The people of England are renowned all over the world for their great virtue; yet they suffer an idiot without courage, without sense, to have dominion in a country of liberty. One could bear a little with Oliver Cromwell, though he usurped the government, his merit was so extraordinary. But as for Richard, his son, who is he? Is he fit to get obedience from a mighty nation? For my part it shall never be said I made such a man my master.'" In Gooch and Laski, *English Democratic Ideas*, 240.

Chapter 8. "That Majesty which through thy Work doth Reign": Marvell and Milton

1. Christopher Hill, "Marvell and Milton," in *Approaches to Marvell The York Tercentenary Lectures*, ed. C. A. Patrides (London: Routledge and Kegan Paul, 1978), 8.

2. Ibid.

3. The above quotations from Leigh and Marvell are found in Masson, *The Life of John Milton: Vol. VI 1660–1674* (New York: Peter Smith, 1946), 705–8.

4. Ibid., 709.

5. Ibid., 710. Earl Miner ("Dryden's admired Acquaintance, Mr. Milton," *Milton Studies* XI [1978]: 8) perceives Marvell—in a "curious poem"—as "introducing a querulous note that had been absent in the known relations between Milton and Dryden."

6. Masson, *The Life of John Milton*, 716–17.

7. Ibid., 682.

8. Ibid.

9. As Alastair Fowler illustrates in *Triumphal Forms: Structural Patterns in Elizabethan Poetry* (Cambridge: Cambridge University Press, 1970) Milton was quite involved in numerological applications.

10. Christopher Hill, for one, discusses Milton's verse in *Samson Agonistes*, in which although he rhymes he avoids the ubiquitous and rigid end-stopped couplets of Restoration drama and thus 'totally liberates' rhyme. *Milton and the English Revolution* (New York: Viking, 1977), 483.

11. There is no reason to think that Marvell was long familiar with *Comus* when he wrote his poem on Lovelace; a more likely assumption is that he came to both in the years after he returned to England from his supposed sojourn on the continent and that he would not have read *Comus* before departing.

12. I agree with Michael Craze's observation that the glue/dew combination

of the Haward MS is "better than the Folio's 'hew-glew'" because the point seems to be that youth holds the human dust, and as time dissolves youth, to the 'dust' the substance returns. *Life and Lyrics*, 321.

13. *John Milton Complete Shorter Poems*, ed. John Carey (New York: Longman, 1990).

14. Keith W. F. Stavely, preface and notes to *Of True Religion, Heresie, Schism, Toleration*, in *Complete Prose Works of John Milton Vol. VIII* (New Haven: Yale University Press, 1982), 412.

15. Ronald Hutton, *Charles the Second King of England, Scotland, and Ireland* (New York: Oxford University Press, 1991), 301.

16. Ibid., 308.

17. Hill, *Milton and the English Revolution*, 219.

18. Milton, *Complete Prose Works*, 429–30.

19. Hutton, *Charles II*, 311.

20. Fairfax had died in 1671.

21. Marvell, *An Account of the Growth of Popery and Arbitrary Government in England, More Particularly, from the Long Prorogation of November, 1675, Ending the 15th of February 1676, till the Last Meeting of Parliament, the 16th of July 1677* (Amsterdam, 1677), with an Introduction by Gamini Salgado (Heppenheim/Bergstrasse, Western Germany: Gregg International Publishers Limited, 1971), 153.

22. Caroline Robbins has written that "in the eighteenth century . . . Marvell and Milton were not only linked by their pleas for liberty of conscience, they were also famous for their condemnation of popery. Over and over again the arguments which they used were reiterated in support of penal laws exempting Catholics from the privileges and duties of citizenship. Both men felt strongly that it was difficult to be a loyal subject and a sincere Catholic at one and the same time." *The Eighteenth-Century Commonwealthman* (New York: Atheneum, 1968), 52.

23. Patterson, *Marvell and the Civic Crown*, 241.

24. Milton, *John Milton Complete Poems and Major Prose*, ed. Merritt Y. Hughes (New York: Odyssey Press, 1957), 719.

25. Marvell, *Growth of Popery*, 16.

26. Ibid., 3.

27. Ibid., 5.

28. Ibid., 6. Marvell's wit is irrepressible: in condemning transubstantiation, he writes, "But above all their other devices, that Transubstantiall solacisme, whereby that glorified Body, which at the same time they allow to be in Heaven, is sold again and crucifyed daily upon all the Altars of their Communion. For God indeed may now and then do a Miracle, but a Romish Priest can, it seems, work in one moment a thousand impossibilities.

29. Milton, *Complete Prose*, 421.

30. Marvell, *Growth of Popery*, 8.

31. Ibid., 11.

32. See Maurice Lee, Jr., *The Cabal* (Urbana: University of Illinois Press, 1965).

33. Hutton, *Charles II*, 348.

34. Marvell, *Growth of Popery*, 14.

35. Marvell, *Letters II*, 317.

36. Patterson, *Marvell and the Civic Crown*, 246.

37. Marvell, *Growth of Popery*, 5.

38. Charles and James possessed only a thin strain of English blood, their English connection a matter of the early sixteenth century.

39. Marvell, *Growth of Popery*, 15.

40. Ibid., 19.

41. Ibid., 16.

42. Ibid., 27.

43. Ibid., 31.

44. Ibid., 35.

45. Ibid., 36.

46. Ibid., 37. Marvell echoes the beginning of Tom May's translation of Lucan's *Pharsalia*, which he parodied in "Tom May's Death."

47. Ibid., 71.

48. Ibid., 72.

49. Ibid., 73.

50. Ibid., 73–74.

51. Ibid., 75.

52. Ibid., 77.

53. Ibid.

54. Ibid., 78.

55. Ibid., 79.

56. Ibid.

57. Ibid., 81.

58. Ibid., 83.

59. Ibid., 84.

60. Ibid., 85.

61. Ibid., 86.

62. Ibid., 88.

63. Ibid., 87.

64. Ibid., 102.

65. Ibid., 117.

66. Ibid., 119.

67. Ibid., 120.

68. Ibid.

69. Ibid., 121.

70. Ibid., 123.

71. Ibid., 125.

72. Ibid., 126.

73. Ibid., 127.

74. Ibid. 127–28.

75. Ibid., 129.

76. Ibid., 134–37.

77. Ibid., 147–48.

78. Ibid., 148.

79. Ibid., 149.

80. Ibid.

81. Ibid., 153.

82. Ibid., 151.

83. The perspicuity of his revelations has been enduring; justly enough, I think, this pamphlet brought a fame to him that lasted until his poetry could be appreciated. Caroline Robbins has observed of him that "his own fame has never been clouded by the faintest suggestion of dishonesty in an age when

even a Sidney felt he could take money from the king of France. . . . In the heyday of parliamentary corruption, Marvell's example and Marvell's diatribes against his less upright colleagues were a rallying point for all critics of the unreformed Commons." *The Eighteenth-Century Commonwealthman*, 53.

84. Marvell, *Letters*, 357.

Bibliography

I. PRIMARY SOURCES

An Account of the Growth of Popery, and Arbitrary Government in England, More Particularly, from the Long Prorogation of November, 1675, Ending the 15th of February 1676, till the Last Meeting of Parliament, the 16th of July 1677. Introduction by Gamini Salgado. Heppenheim/Bergstrasse, West Germany: Gregg International Publishers Limited, 1971.

Andrew Marvell. The Complete Poems. Edited by Elizabeth Story Donno. Penguin English Poets. Reprint. New York: Penguin Books, 1978.

Andrew Marvell. The Rehearsal Transpros'd and The Rehearsal Transpros'd. The Second Part. Edited by D. I. B. Smith. Oxford: Clarendon Press, 1971.

The Complete Works of Andrew Marvell. Four volumes. Edited by A. B. Grosart. Privately printed, 1872–75.

The Latin Poems of Andrew Marvell. Translated by William A. McQueen and Kiffin A. Rockwell. Chapel Hill: University of North Carolina Press, 1964.

Marvell. Edited by Joseph H. Summers. The Laurel Poetry Series. New York: Dell Publishing Co., 1961.

The Poems and Letters of Andrew Marvell. Two volumes. Edited by H. M. Margoliouth. Third edition. Revised by Pierre Legouis with the collaboration of E. E. Duncan-Jones. Oxford: Clarendon Press, 1971.

II. SECONDARY SOURCES

"A Full and Perfect Relation of the Great Plot and Terrible Conspiracy." Thomason Tracts, London, 1654.

Aries, Philippe. The Hour of Our Death. Translated by Helen Weaver. New York: Knopf, 1981.

Ashley, Maurice. Oliver Cromwell and his world. New York: G. P. Putnam's Sons, 1972.

Aubrey, John. "John Aubrey's comments." In Andrew Marvell The Critical Heritage, edited by Elizabeth Story Donno. London: Routledge and Kegan Paul, 1978.

Bain, Carl E. "The Latin Poetry of Andrew Marvell." Philological Quarterly 38 (October 1959): 436–49.

Baker, Hershel, ed. The Later Renaissance in England. Boston: Houghton Mifflin Co., 1975.

Baxter, Richard. Autobiography. Edited by N. H. Keeble, abridged by J. M. Lloyd Thomas. London: Dent, 1974.

——. *Reliquiae Baxterianae I.* London, 1696.

Beard, Thomas. *The Theatre of Gods Judgment.* London, 1597.

Bercovitch, Sacvan. *The Puritan Origins of the American Self.* New Haven: Yale University Press, 1975.

Beresford, John. *Gossip of the Seventeenth and Eighteenth Centuries.* London: Richard Cobden-Sanderson, 1923.

Brown, Louise Fargo. *The Political Activities of the Baptists and Fifth Monarchy Men in England during the Interregnum.* London: Oxford University Press, 1912.

Capp, Bernard. "Extreme Millenarianism." In *Puritan Eschatology 1600 to 1660,* edited by Peter Toon. Greenwood, SC: Attic Press, 1972.

——. *The Fifth Monarchy Men.* Totowa, NJ: Rowman, 1972.

Carey, John. "Reversals transposed: An aspect of Marvell's imagination." In *Approaches to Marvell The York Tercentenary Lectures,* edited by C. A. Patrides. London: Routledge and Kegan Paul, 1978.

Carlton, Charles. *Archbishop William Laud.* London: Routledge and Kegan Paul, 1987.

Carpenter, Margaret. "From Herbert to Marvell: Poetics in 'A Wreath' and 'The Coronet.'" *JEGP* 69 (January 1970): 50–62.

Chernaik, Warren. *The Poetry of Limitation: A Study of Edmund Waller.* New Haven: Yale University Press, 1968.

Cipolla, Carlos. *Clocks and Culture: 1300–1700.* New York: Walker, 1967.

Clayton, Thomas. "'It is Marvel he outdwells his hour': Some Perspectives on Marvell's Medium." In *Tercentenary Essays in Honor of Andrew Marvell,* edited by Kenneth Friedenreich. Hamden, CT: Archon Books, 1977.

Colie, Rosalie L. *"My Ecchoing Song": Andrew Marvell's Poetry of Criticism.* Princeton: Princeton University Press, 1970.

Coolidge, John. "Marvell and Horace." In *Andrew Marvell: A Collection of Critical Essays,* edited by George de F. Lord. Englewood Cliffs, NJ: Prentice Hall, Inc., 1968.

Craze, Michael. *The Life and Lyrics of Andrew Marvell.* New York: Barnes and Noble, 1979.

Cromwell. Edited by Maurice Ashley. Englewood Cliffs, NJ: Prentice Hall, Inc., 1969.

Davies, Godfrey. *The Restoration of Charles II 1658–1660.* San Marino, CA: Huntington Library, 1955.

Duncan-Jones, Elsie E. "A Reading of Marvell's 'The Unfortunate Lover.'" In *I. A. Richards Essays in his Honor,* edited by R. Brower, Helen Vendler, and John Hollander. New York: Oxford University Press, 1973.

——. "The Erect Sword of Marvell's Horatian Ode," *Etudes Anglaises* XV (1962): 172–74.

Edgerton, William L. "Shakespeare and the 'Needle's Eye.'" *Modern Language Notes* 66 (December 1951): 549–50.

Eikon Basilike The Portraiture of His Sacred Majesty in His Solitudes and Sufferings. Edited by Philip A. Knachel. Ithaca: Cornell University Press for The Folger Shakespeare Library, 1966.

Empson, William. "Natural Magic and Populism in Marvell's Poetry." In *An-*

drew Marvell: Essays on the tercentenary of his death, edited by R. L. Brett. Oxford: Published for the University of Hull by the Oxford University Press, 1979, 36–61.

———. Some Versions of Pastoral. New York: New Directions, 1968.

"Every dayes Intelligence." Thomason Tracts, January 17–20 1653/4.

Fairfax, Thomas. The Poems of Thomas Third Lord Fairfax. Edited by Edward Bliss Reed. New Haven: Yale University Press, 1909.

Firth, Charles. "Cromwell's Views on Sports." Macmillan's Magazine No. 420 (October 1894), 401–9.

———. Oliver Cromwell. London: Putnam, 1923.

———. The Last Years of the Protectorate 1656–58, Vol. II. London: Longmans, Green, and Co., 1909.

Fowler, Alastair. Triumphal Forms: Structural Patterns in Elizabethan Poetry. Cambridge: Cambridge University Press, 1970.

Fraser, Antonia. Cromwell The Lord Protector. New York: Alfred A. Knopf, 1974.

Friedman, Donald M. Marvell's Pastoral Art. Berkeley: University of California Press, 1970.

Gillett, Edward, and Kenneth A. Macmahon. A History of Hull. Oxford: Published for the University of Hull by Oxford University Press, 1980.

Goldberg, Jonathan. "The Typology of 'Musicks Empire.'" Texas Studies in Language and Literature 13 (Fall 1971): 421–30.

Gooch, G. P., and H. J. Laski. English Democratic Ideas in the Seventeenth Century. Second edition. Cambridge: Cambridge University Press, 1927.

Graves, Robert. The Greek Myths, Vol. I. New York: Penguin, 1955.

Greenblatt, Stephen. Renaissance Self-Fashioning from More to Shakespeare. Chicago: University of Chicago Press, 1980.

Hartman, Geoffrey H. "'The Nymph Complaining for the Death of Her Fawn': A Brief Allegory." Essays in Criticism 18 (April 1968): 113–35.

Heath, James. Flagellum. London, 1663.

Hill, Christopher. God's Englishman: Oliver Cromwell and the English Revolution. New York: Dial Press, 1970.

———. "Marvell and Milton," In Approaches to Marvell The York Tercentenary Lectures, edited by C. A. Patrides. London: Routledge and Kegan Paul, 1978.

———. Milton and the English Revolution. New York: Viking, 1977.

———. The Century of Revolution 1603–1714. New York: W. W. Norton, 1961.

Hunt, John Dixon. Andrew Marvell: His Life and Writings. Ithaca: Cornell University Press, 1978.

Hutchinson, Lucy. Memoirs of the Life of Colonel Hutchinson. Edited by James Sutherland. London: Oxford University Press, 1973.

Hutton, Ronald. Charles the Second King of England, Scotland, and Ireland. New York: Oxford University Press, 1991.

J. N., a Mechanick. Proh Tempora! Proh Mores!. Thomason Tracts, London, 1654.

Kelliher, Hilton. Andrew Marvell Poet and Politician 1621–78: An exhibition to commemorate the tercentenary of his death, catalogue. London: British Museum Publications Ltd., 1978.

Knachel, Philip A. Introduction to *Eikon Basilike The Portraiture of His Sacred Majesty in His Solitudes and Sufferings*. Ithaca: Published for Folger Shakespeare Library by Cornell University Press, 1966.

Larkin, Philip. "The Changing Face of Andrew Marvell." *English Literary Renaissance* 9 (Winter 1979): 149–57.

Legouis, Pierre. *Andrew Marvell: Poet, Puritan, Patriot*. Oxford: Clarendon Press, 1965.

The Letters and Speeches of Oliver Cromwell Vol. 2. Elucidations by Thomas Carlyle. Edited by S. C. Lomas. Introduction by C. H. Firth. London: Methuen and Co., 1904.

Marcus, Leah. *The Politics of Mirth Jonson, Herrick, Milton, Marvell, and the Defense of Old Holiday Pastimes*. Chicago: University of Chicago Press, 1986.

Markham, Clements R. *A Life of the Great Lord Fairfax*. London: Macmillan, 1870.

Masson, David. *The Life of John Milton Narrated in Connexion with the Political, Ecclesiastical, and Literary History of His Time Vol. IV*. New York: Peter Smith, 1946.

Milton, John. *Complete Prose Works of John Milton, Vol. IV. 1650–55 Part II*. Edited by Don M. Wolfe. New Haven: Yale University Press, 1966.

———. *John Milton Complete Poems and Major Prose*. Edited by Merritt Y. Hughes. New York: Odyssey Press, 1957.

———. *John Milton Complete Shorter Poems*. Edited by John Carey. New York: Longman, 1990.

Miner, Earl. "Dryden's admired Acquaintance, Mr. Milton." *Milton Studies* XI (1978): 3–27.

———. "The Death of Innocence in Marvell's 'Nymph Complaining for the death of her Faun.'" *Marvell: Modern Judgments*. Edited by Michael Wilding. Nashville, TN: Aurora Publishers Incorporated, 1970.

Morrill, John. "The Church in England, 1642–9." In *Reactions to the English Civil War 1642–1649*, edited by John Morrill. New York: St. Martin's Press, 1983.

Morse, David. *England's Time of Crisis: From Shakespeare to Milton*. New York: St. Martin's Press, 1989.

Newman, John. "Marvell's Appleton House." *Times Literary Supplement*. 28 January 1972: 99.

Patterson, Annabel. "Against Polarization: Literature and Politics in Marvell's Cromwell Poems." *English Literary Renaissance* 5 (Spring 1975): 251–72.

———. *Marvell and the Civic Crown*. Princeton: Princeton University Press, 1978.

Pocock, J. G. A. Introduction to *The Political Works of James Harrington*. Edited by J. G. A. Pocock. Cambridge: Cambridge University Press, 1977.

Potter, Lois. *Secret rites and secret writing Royalist literature, 1641–1660*. Cambridge: Cambridge University Press, 1989.

Raymond Klibansky, Erwin Panofsky, Fritz Saxl. *Saturn and Melancholy: Studies in the History of Natural Philosophy, Religion and Art*. London: Nelson, 1964.

Robbins, Caroline. "Absolute Liberty: the Life and Thought of William Popple, 1638–1708." *William and Mary Quarterly* 24 (April 1967), 190–223.

————. *The Eighteenth-Century Commonwealthman*. New York: Atheneum, 1968.

Rostvig, Maren-Sofie. *The Happy Man: Studies in the Metamorphosis of a Classical Ideal 1600–1700*. 2 vols. Oslo, 1962.

Rump: or an Exact Collection of the Choycest Poems and Songs Relating to the Late Times, Part I. London, 1662.

Salerno, Nicholas A. "Andrew Marvell and the Furor Hortensis." *Studies in English Literature 1500–1900* 8 (Winter 1968): 103–20.

Sharpe, Kevin. *The Personal Rule of Charles I*. New Haven: Yale University Press, 1992.

Shawcross, John. *Intentionality and the New Traditionalism: Some Liminal Means to Literary Revisionism*. University Park: Pennsylvania State University Press, 1991.

Sherwood, Roy. *The Court of Oliver Cromwell*. London: Croom Helm, 1977.

Sidney, Sir Philip. "An Apology for Poetry." In *Criticism: The Major Texts*, edited by Walter Jackson Bate. New York: Harcourt, Brace & World, Inc., 1952.

Spelman, Sir Henry. *The History and Fate of Sacrilege*. Edited by Samuel J. Eales. London, 1888.

Stavely, Keith W. F. Preface and Notes to "Of True Religion, Heresie, Schism, Toleration." *Complete Prose Works of John Milton Vol. VIII*. New Haven: Yale University Press, 1982.

Stocker, Margarita. *Apocalyptic Marvell The Second Coming in Seventeenth Century Poetry*. Athens: Ohio University Press, 1986.

Summers, Joseph H. Introduction to *Marvell*. Laurel Poetry Series. New York: Dell, 1961.

————. *The Heirs of Donne and Jonson*. New York: Oxford University Press, 1970.

Taft, Barbara. "The Humble Petition of Several Colonels of the Army: Causes, Character, and Results of Military Opposition to Cromwell's Protectorate." *Huntington Library Quarterly* 42 (1978–79): 15–41.

Tait, A. A. "Marvell's Appleton House." *Times Literary Supplement*. 11 February 1972: 157.

Taylor, Rupert. *The Political Prophecy in England*. New York: Columbia University Press, 1911.

The Diary of John Evelyn, Vol. III, Kalendarium, 1650–1672. Edited by E. S. deBeer. Oxford: Clarendon Press, 1955.

The Essayes of Montaigne. Translated by John Florio, introduction by J. I. M. Stewart. New York: Modern Library, 1933.

The Fairfax Correspondence. Memoirs of the Reign of Charles the First. Edited by George W. Johnson, 2 vols. London: Richard Bentley, 1848.

The Grand Politique Post. Thomason Tracts, February 7–15, 1654.

The Letters and Speeches of Oliver Cromwell, with elucidations by Thomas Carlyle Vol. II. Edited by S. C. Lomas with introduction by C. H. Firth. London: Methuen and Co., 1904.

Thomas, Keith. *Religion and the Decline of Magic*. New York: Scribner's, 1971.

Thurloe, John. *State Papers, I and VII*.

Trapnel, Anna. *A Legacy for Saints*. Thomason Tracts, London; 1654.

————. *The Cry of a Stone*. *Thomason Tracts*, London, 1654.

Turner, James. "Marvell." *Times Literary Supplement*. 31 March 1972: 367.

Underdown, David. "Cromwell and the Officers, February 1658." *English Historical Review*, 83 (1982): 101–7.

Varley, F. J. *Oliver Cromwell's Latter End*. London: Chapman and Hall, Ltd., 1939.

Wall, L. N. "Some Notes on Marvell's Sources." *Notes and Queries* (April 1957): 170–73.

Wallace, John. *Destiny His Choice: The Loyalism of Andrew Marvell*. Cambridge: Cambridge University Press, 1968.

Wedgwood, C. V. *Poetry and Politics under the Stuarts*. Cambridge: Cambridge University Press, 1960.

————. *The King's War, 1641–1647*. New York: Macmillan, 1959.

Weidhorn, Maurice. *Richard Lovelace*. New York: Twayne Publishers, 1970.

Whitelocke, Bulstrode. *Memorials of English Affairs*. Oxford, 1853.

Wilding, Michael. "Marvell's 'An Horatian Ode upon Cromwell's Return from Ireland', the Levellers, and the Junta." *Modern Language Review* (January 1981): 1–14.

Wilkerson, Henry C. *The Adventurers of Bermuda*. 2d edition. London: Oxford University Press, 1958.

Wilson, A. J. N. "Andrew Marvell's 'The First Anniversary of the government under Oliver Cromwell': The Poem and its Frame of Reference." *Modern Language Review* 69 (April 1974): 254–73.

Wither, George. *Miscellaneous Works*. Manchester: Charles Simms and Co., 1875.

The Writings and Speeches of Oliver Cromwell, Vol. III. Edited W. C. Abbott. Cambridge: Harvard University Press, 1945.

Withington, Eleanor. "Mildmay Fane's Political Satire." *Harvard Library Bulletin* 11 (1957): 40–64.

Worden, Blair. "Marvell, Cromwell, and the *Horatian Ode*." In *Politics of Discourse the Literature and History of Seventeenth-Century England*, edited by Kevin Sharpe and Steven N. Zwicker. Berkeley: University of California Press, 1987.

————. *The Rump Parliament 1648–1653*. London: Cambridge University Press, 1974.

Index